Foreign Investment and Political Regimes

Political democratization and economic globalization have been two of the most important global trends of the past few decades. But, how are they connected? Do the domestic political institutions affect a country's attractiveness to foreign investors? Can countries that democratize attract relatively more foreign investments? Drawing on three in-depth case studies of oil-rich countries and statistical analyses of 132 countries over three decades, Oksan Bayulgen demonstrates that the link between democratization and FDI is nonlinear. Both authoritarian regimes and consolidated democracies have institutional capabilities that, though different, are attractive to foreign investors. Democracies can provide long-term stability, and authoritarian regimes can offer considerable flexibility. The regimes that have started on the road to democracy, but have not yet completed it, tend to have political institutions that provide neither flexibility nor stability. These hybrid regimes, then, also find it relatively more difficult to construct a policy environment that is attractive to foreign investments. These findings have deep implications for the link between democratization and globalization, but also for how globalization may affect political, social, and economic development.

Oksan Bayulgen is an assistant professor of political science at the University of Connecticut. Bayulgen has published numerous articles on foreign investment, oil politics, democratization, and microfinance. She has received research grants from the Ford Foundation, University of Texas at Austin, and University of Connecticut to conduct extensive field work in Azerbaijan, Russia, Norway, Kazakhstan, and Turkey.

Foreign Investment and Political Regimes

The Oil Sector in Azerbaijan, Russia, and Norway

OKSAN BAYULGEN

University of Connecticut

CAMBRIDGE UNIVERSITY PRESS
Cambridge, New York, Melbourne, Madrid, Cape Town, Singapore,
São Paulo, Delhi, Dubai, Tokyo

Cambridge University Press
32 Avenue of the Americas, New York, NY 10013-2473, USA

www.cambridge.org
Information on this title: www.cambridge.org/9780521425889

First published 2010

Printed in the United States of America

A catalog record for this publication is available from the British Library.

Library of Congress Cataloging in Publication data
Bayulgen, Oksan.
    Foreign investment and political regimes : the oil sector in Azerbaijan, Russia,
and Norway / Oksan Bayulgen.
        p.   cm.
    Includes bibliographical references and index.
    ISBN 978-0-521-42588-9
    1. Petroleum industry and trade – Azerbaijan.   2. Petroleum industry and
trade – Russia (Federation)   3. Petroleum industry and trade – Norway.
    4. Investments, Foreign – Azerbaijan.   5. Investments, Foreign – Russia (Federation)
    6. Investments, Foreign – Norway.   I. Title.
    HD9576.A982B39 2010
    338.2'72820947–dc22   2009042537

ISBN 978-0-521-42588-9 Hardback

To my parents, Dogudan and Umit Bayulgen

Contents

List of Figures and Tables

Acknowledgments

This book is a culmination of many years of work, more than I dare to admit. It could not have been what it is today if it was not for the assistance, enthusiasm, and friendship I received along the way from mentors, colleagues, friends, and family.

This research began as my dissertation, written at the University of Texas, Department of Government. My committee members Robert Moser, Catherine Boone, John Higley, Clement Henry, and Cynthia Buckley were the first to introduce me to academic life in the United States, and they set a high standard of scholarship toward which I continue to strive. John Higley and Robert Moser, in particular, spent countless hours listening to my ideas and problems related to this project, while also providing guidance and detailed feedback – Prof Higley with his famous red pen! I feel extremely privileged to have been under their tutelage and to have received their unwavering support. My fellow graduate students and now colleagues were by far the most "exposed" to the birth pains of this project. I am grateful to Rob Barr, Oya Dursun, Julie George, Darin Foster, Sunila Kale, Anna Law, Dennis Plane, Brent and Liesl Riddle, Jennifer Suchland, Frank Thames, and Sultan Tepe among many others for sharing the intellectual and trying experience of graduate school and for making my life in Austin, Texas, an unforgettable one.

Being an international scholar, I had very few funding opportunities for this research project. So, I am especially thankful for a Ford Foundation Area Studies research grant and multiple University of Texas research grants and fellowships that made my field work in Azerbaijan, Russia, and Norway possible over the course of three years. Anyone who has done field work knows that one of the biggest challenges facing the researcher is finding people who are willing to open their homes, provide a work space, connect you to the right people, and, most importantly, offer their friendship and support. I have been extremely lucky in all three of these countries to have found such individuals. I owe a particular debt to Trygve Gulbrandsen, Anton Steen, Knut and Berit Groholt, Kristan and Beaty Higley, Jamaal and Nihal Quadir, Alexander Levshov, Robin Matthews, the staff of the Moscow CERA office, Anisa Nagaria, Okan and Ozan Ozerdem, Betul Peksen, and Orhan Gurbuz. My home is theirs anytime they want to come and visit!

During the transformation of this work from a dissertation into a book, I have also been inspired and mentored by Pauline Jones Luong, Peter Rutland, Quan Li, and my colleagues at the University of Connecticut: Sam Best, Mark Boyer, Larry Bowman, Betty Hanson, Shareen Hertel, Richard Hiskes, Kristin Kelly, Peter Kingstone, Monika McDermott, Lyle Scruggs, Donna Lee Van Cott, and Ernie Zirakzadeh. They have read parts of the manuscript, given me valuable insights, or taught me a thing or two about navigating the publishing process. I am very grateful to all of them. I was able to complete the manuscript thanks to the generous faculty grants I received at UConn. I also feel extremely lucky to have had Eric Crahan as my editor. He has, since day one, shown genuine enthusiasm for this project and given me sage advice, as well as unwavering support and friendship during the final stages of the book preparation. I also greatly appreciate the deep reading and insightful comments offered by the anonymous reviewers.

Just like every long, multiyear project in life, no manuscript can be completed without an extensive support network of friends and family. Over the years, my life-long friends in Turkey as well as those that I acquired in the United States have given me a sense of balance, helped me focus on the most valuable things in life, and, perhaps more importantly, kept me "sane." I especially thank Hande Paker, Baran Uncu, Emre Temiz, Alper Onder, Kaan Aktolug, Bertan Gurkan, Carmen Wesson, Ben Liu, Monika McDermott, Dave Jones, Sam Best, Kristin Kelly, and Aysegul Budak for always being there for me. Their friendship has sustained me all these years and made my life more meaningful and fun.

Finally, I am also extremely lucky to have a wonderful family that has given me unconditional love and support throughout the writing of this manuscript – no matter how much that meant being away from them. I am deeply thankful to Carol Ladewig, Bruce Ladewig, and Renee, Shane, Griffin, and Oliver Lathrop for opening their homes and hearts to me and allowing me to become part of their family in Wisconsin. Who would have thought a Turkish girl could one day become a Packers fan? I will forever be grateful to my grandparents, Nemika and Kenan Dagdeviren, as well as ciciannem Sehvar Turel for giving me a beautiful childhood and for teaching me the value of learning. I also thank my brothers Ozan and Okan Bayulgen, and my nieces Beliz and now baby Istanbul for reminding me about the importance of family. But, my greatest debt and admiration go to my parents Dogudan and Umit Bayulgen, to whom this book is dedicated. They have done everything they could to make sure I had the best possible education. And, with their wisdom, honesty, and integrity, they set the best example for my academic and personal growth. If there is one thing that I regret about this journey, it is the years that I spent away from them.

Last but not the least, I could not have written this book if it was not for the intellectual contribution and enthusiasm of my best friend, colleague, and husband Jeff Ladewig. More than anyone else, he has gone through the ups and downs of this process and has shared the sacrifices as well as the accomplishments with me. During the writing of this manuscript, we also had two wonderful boys, Aidan Kaan and Leo Batu. Despite the many hours I spent away from them to be able to complete this manuscript, I hope one day they will realize that none of this would have meant the same without them. They are the best thing that has ever happened to me. And I am forever grateful for that.

I

Introduction

In today's global economy, Foreign Direct Investment (FDI) is an essential link among national economies as well as a catalyst for economic growth.[1] The benefits that FDI brings, such as capital, knowledge, technology, skills, management know-how, market access, and employment opportunities are important for development as complements to domestic resources in host countries.[2] As such, it is aggressively sought by many countries.[3] FDI does not, however, flow evenly to all. Particularly in the developing world, only a handful of countries are able to attract investments that are commensurate with their market potential. Even when the necessary firm-level incentives and host-country economic conditions are present, some countries fail to provide a welcoming investment environment in the form of policy incentives, guarantees, and stability. Why are some countries able to offer investor-friendly policies and some are not? Which political institutions produce the policies that prove beneficial

---

[1] FDI is an investment involving a lasting interest by a home-economy entity in an enterprise in a host economy. It is defined as involving an equity stake of 10 percent or more in a foreign enterprise. According to United Nations Conference on Trade and Development – UNCTAD (2005) – since 1993, FDI has consistently surpassed other private capital flows as well as flows of official development assistance to developing countries.

[2] According to UNCTAD (2001) empirical evidence suggests that for emerging economies a 1 percent point increase in FDI (measured as a proportion of GDP) leads, ceteris paribus, to an extra 0.8 percent increase in per capita income.

[3] UNCTAD (2005) reports that the number of countries that adopted measures intended to improve their investment climates almost tripled, from 35 in 1991 to 102 in 2004. Moreover, of the national regulatory changes that have been made to attract investment, changes that are favorable to FDI have been between 90 and 100 percent on average since 1991.

to multinational operations? Does democracy matter in attracting FDI? These are the central questions of this book.

There is an extensive literature on economic and policy determinants of FDI flows, yet much less attention has been devoted to the role of political institutions in producing a favorable investment environment to attract foreign capital.[4] Foreign companies undertake significant political risks when they invest in a host country. Conditional upon the ease with which they can withdraw their assets, they fear the risk of government interference, be it nationalization, shifting tax burdens, or new regulatory requirements. Before they invest in a country, they ascertain the nature of FDI policies and the likelihood that such policies will remain in place over the course of their involvement in the host market.

This is where political institutions come in. Investment policies are not created in a vacuum. Some groups clearly benefit from the infusion of foreign capital and the new business opportunities that are created, while others are disadvantaged by the competition and/or the various ways foreign-company operations affect taxation, job opportunities, environment, and the like in the host country. The potential losers and winners from foreign capital use the political institutions available to them to shape investment policies according to their particular interests. Political institutions not only become a platform to exert pressure on decision makers but also determine how the struggle between stakeholders plays out and how various interests are reconciled or outweighed.

Recently, scholars have started looking more systematically at the relationship between democracy and FDI.[5] Their findings, however, have been mixed and thus inconclusive about the relative merits of political regimes in attracting FDI. Some find a significant positive relationship between democracy and the ability to attract FDI, others argue that authoritarian regimes can provide better entry deals for foreign investors, and still others argue that there is no significant relationship between regime type and FDI.

I argue that the existing literature oversimplifies the relationship between FDI and regime type, and underappreciates the complexities of host country politics. The exclusive use of readily available numerical

---

[4] See Hymer 1960, Kindleberger 1969, Buckley and Casson 1976, Graham 1978, Rugman 1981, 1985, Schneider and Frey 1985, Crenshaw 1991, Brewer 1991, 1992, Dunning 1993, Markusen 1995.

[5] See O'Neal 1994, Henisz 2000, Harms and Ursprung 2002, Jensen 2003, 2006, Li and Resnick 2003, Busse 2003, Busse and Hefeker 2005, Li 2006, Jakobsen and De Soysa 2006.

indices and generic regime labels, oftentimes by itself, does not capture the intricacies of relations between investors and host governments. To overcome this problem, I make extensive use of both the qualitative method and the rich theoretical insights from comparative democratization literature. I analyze the decision-making process inside a number of countries to show that the institutional structure that defines and shapes the relationship between the opponents and proponents of FDI is much more complex and intriguing than previously thought.

This book contributes to the literature in two principal ways. First, I provide an in-depth analysis of a single sector of FDI – the oil sector – across a small number of cases to control for possible differences among foreign investors in terms of their sector-specific risk calculations and expectations. Of all the possible sectors, I focus on oil because it provides a hard case for the relationship between political regimes and FDI. It is generally assumed that oil investors do not have any regime preferences as long as some level of stability is attained and that the political risks they encounter depend on their relative market power and bargaining position vis-à-vis the host governments rather than the political institutions in place. According to one well-known theory (the obsolescing bargaining theory), in the early stages of the relationship between foreign oil companies and the host government, the former are in a dominant position and able to extract highly favorable terms from the latter.[6] This suggests that in the beginning oil companies face few, if any, political risks and can work with whomever is in power. As the industry matures and the host government becomes more competent, the relative bargaining power of the firm obsolesces, changing the terms of the initial agreement and increasing the degree of political risk. However, at this stage, given the large up-front expenditures they make and the strategic need for ongoing access to resources that generate high rents, investors have very few choices but to work with host governments regardless of the political regime in place. Hence, according to this logic in either stage of the relationship, political institutions do not seem to matter in investment decisions.

Similar systemic theories also assert that market fluctuations in the price of oil, more so than the intricacies of political institutions, affect the relative bargaining position of investors vis-à-vis the host governments. When the price of oil is high, potential returns from an investment

---

[6] See Vernon 1971, 1980, Smith and Wells 1975, Mikesell 1971, Moran 1974, Rothgeb 1990, 1991.

increase, making oil development projects more attractive. With increased competition among investors for access to oil resources, the bargaining position of the host government increases and that of the investor ebbs. Conversely, when the price of oil goes down, costs and risks of investment increase and investors gain the upper hand in setting the terms of the investment relationship. Therefore, given these persuasive theories, oil provides a hard case because if political institutions turn out to be significant for investors in this sector, it is most likely that they will have some influence on investors in other sectors as well.

Second, I refine the theoretical debate on the merits of political regimes by reclassifying them in terms of the amount of institutional constraints and competition they provide in policy making. This approach captures the political dynamics behind investment policies more systematically. Simply put, I argue that the level of executive constraints in the state as well as the degree of political competition in society determines the stability and/or flexibility of investment terms, and thus, the attractiveness of the investment environment. I operationalize and measure these two variables in terms of the strength of state-veto players and the number and organizational capacity of political parties and interest groups, respectively. I argue that the low, partial, and high levels of constraints and competition in an institutional setting produce different incentives and opportunities for the proponents and opponents of FDI as they design the terms of the relationship between investors and governments.

I discuss and empirically test the impact of these institutional variables on the ability to attract FDI into the oil sectors of three oil-rich countries: Azerbaijan, a post-communist authoritarian regime; Russia, a post-communist "hybrid" regime; and Norway, an industrialized mature democracy. Although all three countries have had similar needs and attractiveness for foreign capital, during the initial phase of their resource development Azerbaijan and Norway received significant amounts of FDI, whereas Russia received very little. The purpose of this book is to explain this empirical puzzle and formulate a broader theory in our understanding of the political conditions under which an investment environment is shaped and why investors flock to certain countries and not to others.

An in-depth comparative analysis of investment environments in these countries reveals an important rejoinder to the existing literature that finds foreign capital to be compatible with either democracy or authoritarianism. I argue that, in fact, both democracies and authoritarian regimes can be attractive to foreign investors. With high levels of executive constraints in the state and open and institutionalized competition in society, consolidated democracies tend to provide long-term policy credibility, transparency, and stability for foreign investors. On the other hand, in authoritarian regimes – assuming that the government has pro-investment preferences – a lack of institutional constraints and political competition tends to insulate decision makers from policy pressures and allows them the flexibility and adaptability to provide exceptional incentives to foreign investors in the form of tax reductions, grants, subsidized loans, market preferences, regulatory concessions, guarantees in arbitration, and the like. Given their specific institutional characteristics, both consolidated democracies and authoritarian regimes have comparative advantages in attracting FDI. The debate, then, should not be over whether FDI will favor democracy or authoritarian regimes but what the trade-offs will be for foreign companies as they invest in one as opposed to the other.

My second argument is that hybrid regimes that produce some but limited constraints and competition tend to put in place investment environments that are neither flexible nor credible but, instead, are unstable and chaotic. Compared to authoritarian regimes, hybrid regimes are characterized by increased levels of political mobilization and participation. Executives often cannot easily overcome the opposition of state veto players through exclusion and repression because the challenges tend to be both formally legal and widely perceived as legitimate. The greater access to state institutions ensured by democratization also limits the generosity of the fiscal and financial incentives host governments can offer to attract FDI. Compared to executives in consolidated democracies, on the other hand, executives in hybrid regimes have a hard time reaching policy outcomes that are acceptable to foreign investors as well as domestic groups. The conflicts of interest among state-veto players cannot be overcome because in hybrid regimes representative institutions such as political parties and interest groups tend to be weak and inchoate. Decision makers find it very difficult to build enduring coalitions and facilitate negotiation and bargaining among competing veto players. The real losers of FDI, therefore, tend to be neither consolidated democracies nor authoritarian regimes; they are the hybrid regimes.

The experiences of Azerbaijan, Russia, and Norway demonstrate that foreign investors tend to favor two polar opposites: consolidated democracies and authoritarian regimes but penalize the middle category, hybrid regimes. The in-depth case study of the oil sector that I present in this book offers a more nuanced analysis and helps to refine the existing debate in the literature. To test the generalizability of my arguments, I further provide a brief analysis of the investment environment in another oil producer, Kazakhstan, as well as a statistical time-series analysis of 132 countries over 34 years and for all types of FDI. These findings confirm the relationship observed in the three cases, that is the link between democracy and FDI is nonlinear. An increase in executive constraints and political competition, that is further democratization, may not always enhance a country's ability to attract FDI. Things may get worse before they get better.

Case Selection

The three oil-producing countries – Azerbaijan, Russia, and Norway – studied in this book demonstrate how different political institutions affect investment decisions and thus the levels of FDI in the oil sector. Undoubtedly, there are major differences among these three states in terms of their size, economic structure, and cultural and historical background, yet they also share several crucial characteristics. First of all, they are all major oil producers with significant oil resources. Azerbaijan, Russia, and Norway possess 0.6 percent, 6.2 percent, and 0.8 percent of the world's total proven oil reserves, respectively.[7] Their oil industries remain the focus of most foreign interest.

Second, these three countries faced similar challenges as they embarked on their energy development programs. Azerbaijan and Russia in the beginning of the 1990s and Norway in the 1970s needed significant amounts of foreign capital and expertise to extract their oil resources and generate economic development. In the case of Azerbaijan and Russia, the disintegration of the Soviet Union had led to a breakdown of the all-union Soviet market, which had negative repercussions for both countries' oil industries. Following the collapse of the Soviet Union, Russia's oil industry, which accounted for approximately 90 percent of the former Soviet Union's oil output, fell upon hard times due to decreased domestic industrial demand and a decline in drilling and domestic capital investments. From 1992 to 1998, the country's oil production plummeted 23 percent, from 7.86 million to 6.07 million barrels per day.[8] Similarly, Azerbaijan's oil production fell almost 30 percent between 1990 and 1996 as a result of continuing depletion of existing fields, poor maintenance due to lack of funds, and the limitations of outdated technology.[9]

---

[7] British Petroleum – BP Global 2006. Azerbaijan, Russia, and Norway are ranked as having the 18th, 7th, and 16th largest oil reserves in the world, respectively.
[8] United States Energy Information Administration – USEIA 2002.
[9] International Energy Agency 1998.

Neither Azerbaijan nor Russia, however, could domestically generate the necessary investment capital. Even though the privatized Russian oil industry could provide some of the capital, most of the Russian companies' investments were directed toward increasing production from existing fields rather than developing new fields that required extensive capital and technology. Hence, from the beginning both Azerbaijani and Russian leaders acknowledged that the long-term development of their natural resources from harsher and undeveloped oil regions in East Siberia, the Far East, and the Caspian depended on an infusion of significant amounts of FDI, especially during times of low oil prices.

Russian authorities, specifically President Boris Yeltsin himself, repeatedly emphasized the need for external capital, particularly in the form of FDI from international oil companies. In 1993, Yeltsin used a presidential decree to propose legislation to facilitate the flow of foreign capital into oil extraction and development projects. Similarly, the first democratically elected leader of Azerbaijan, Abulfez Elchibey, started in 1991 to actively promote foreign investment in the oil industry. Following his example, his successor, President Heidar Aliyev, made FDI promotion a priority for his regime and in 1994 signed the "contract of the century" with ten foreign companies.[10]

In Norway, nearly four decades ago, the need for foreign investment was also clear. Oil had come as a surprise to Norway at the end of the 1960s. With no prior experience and expertise, the domestic industry was in no position to develop these resources on its own. Considering the difficulties of drilling in the deep offshore waters of the North Sea, the Norwegian government was determined to use foreign oil companies to build national competence in oil and increase the welfare of the society. Having acknowledged the importance of foreign participation, the government passed the Royal Decree of 1965 that established the first comprehensive investment regime for exploring and producing oil from the North Sea.

Despite the importance of oil for these economies and their similar needs for FDI, these cases demonstrate a significant variation in their ability to attract foreign capital. While Azerbaijan and Norway created favorable conditions for investors to put sizable amounts of capital in their oil resources, Russia failed to establish an attractive legislative and regulatory investment framework and consequently received very little investment capital throughout the 1990s.

---

[10] The "contract of the century" entailed the development of three offshore fields – Chirag, Azeri, and Gunesli – with US$8 billion foreign investment over the course of 30 years.

TABLE 1.1. *FDI Statistics for Azerbaijan, Russia, and Norway*

	Total FDI[a]	World FDI Ranking[b]	FDI in Oil[c]	FDI per barrel of Oil Reserves[d]
Azerbaijan	4,488	8th	3,590	0.51
Russia	19,907	104th	3,782	0.05
Norway	22,901	60th	9,160	0.94

Notes:
[a] FDI figures are millions of US$ from 1995 to 2000. See UNCTAD (2001). Average amount of FDI per country for 1995–2000 is US$21,928. The average figure for Oil FDI per country cannot be calculated due to the unavailability of consistent sectoral data.
[b] Rankings are by FDI Performance Index, which is the ratio of a country's share in global FDI flows to its share in global GDP, from 1998 to 2000. A total of 140 countries are ranked. Available data from the early 1990s show a similar pattern: Azerbaijan 3rd (1994–96), Russia 108th (1992–94), Norway 59th (1988–90). See UNCTAD 2002a.
[c] Calculations are estimates of sector share of total FDI from 1995 to 2000 and are in millions of US$. The source for Azerbaijan is USEIA (2001a); for Russia it is UNCTAD (2003); for Norway it is United States Department of State Bureau of Economic and Business Affairs Country Commercial Guide: Norway (2001).
[d] Figures are calculated by dividing total FDI in oil from 1995 to 2000 by total proven oil reserves in that country and are in US$. Reserve figures are from BP (2006).

The overall and oil-related FDI figures clearly attest to this variation (see Table 1.1).[11] According to the FDI performance index created by the United Nations Conference on Trade and Development (UNCTAD), in terms of success in attracting FDI among 140 nations, Azerbaijan ranked the third highest during 1994–1996 and eighth highest during 1998–2000.[12] Russia, on the other hand, ranked the 108th and 104th highest among 140 nations during 1992–1994 and 1998–2000, respectively. With 6.2 percent of world's total proven oil reserves, almost ten times the

[11] It is important to note that systematic, long-term comparable data on FDI statistics, especially on sector-specific FDI statistics, is hard to locate and frequently missing. UNCTAD compiles the most systematic and comparable statistics on FDI. But, even their full dataset provides information for a limited number of countries and years. In its 2007 World Investment Report, UNCTAD discusses the complexities of accessing data on FDI in general and especially in extractive industries. It states that incomplete reporting as well as different definitions and methodologies used in data collection make it extremely difficult to interpret and compare data (UNCTAD 2007: 101).
[12] UNCTAD 2002a. UNCTAD ranking is based on the ratio of a country's share in global FDI flows to its share in global GDP. It is considered a more accurate measure than absolute values of FDI inflows because it assesses how successful a country is in attracting FDI relative to the size of its economy. Azerbaijan was ranked the highest in 2004 (UNCTAD 2006).

oil reserves of Azerbaijan, Russia received just one-tenth the FDI for each barrel of its oil reserves compared to Azerbaijan in the 1990s. Calculations based on FDI figures from UNCTAD also show that Norway received about 94 cents of foreign investment per barrel of its proven oil reserves during 1995–2000 and ranked the 59th and 60th in terms of its overall FDI levels during 1988–1990 and 1998–2000, respectively.[13]

This variation occurred despite the fact that Russia was considered one of the top potential destinations for FDI in the 1990s. For instance, it had a clear advantage over Azerbaijan in terms of more significant oil reserves, a larger domestic market, and an existing pipeline infrastructure in which to bring oil to world markets. Moreover, given the assumptions of the obsolescing bargaining theory, the initial stage of the relationship between the Russian government and foreign companies – especially during the low international oil prices of the 1990s – should have favored the latter in terms of tremendous leverage over taxation, regulatory policies, and institutional design. Yet, the Russian investment environment was significantly more challenging and hostile toward foreign investors than either the Azerbaijani investment environment throughout the 1990s or the Norwegian investment environment in the 1970s and 1980s.

Research Methodology

A comparison of these three cases is based on field work conducted in Azerbaijan in the summer of 1999, in Norway in January 2001, and in Russia in the summer of 2000 and the spring of 2001. To analyze oil-sector investment environments in these countries, I conducted a total of 75 in-depth interviews with various foreign investors, their lobbying organizations, government bureaucrats, legislators, journalists, scholars, and special analysts. In addition, I studied numerous government and private reports, documents, journal and newspaper articles, and scholarly works.

The interviews consisted of two parts. In the first part, I posed questions regarding the investment environment in each country especially during the initial interaction between foreign companies and host governments. Respondents were asked to assess the contracting or licensing

[13] These numbers certainly do not reflect the overall performance of Norway in terms of attracting FDI since the 1970s when its oil development began. The data for those decades are missing and UNCTAD reports start with late 1980 figures. The closest but imperfect figure for the years between 1971 and 1996 is a total of US$200 billion invested in exploration, construction, and operations on the Norwegian continental shelf (International Trade Administration 2001). This figure, however, most likely also includes domestic investments.

policies of each state in terms of the legal and fiscal guarantees provided for foreign investors. The technical aspects of each investment regime were studied in depth with the help of numerous documents provided by oil companies and government officials. Historical data on the evolution of investment regime in each country were also collected through an archival study of various journal and newspaper articles.

The second part of the interviews consisted of questions about the political institutions and the policymaking structure in each country as well as an assessment of political risk facing investors. Respondents were asked to discuss the different interests of societal and state actors regarding oil investment policies and then to evaluate the institutional mechanisms through which these actors interacted with each other and reached policy outcomes. Despite the methodological difficulties in comparing such a small number of cases, these three case studies made it possible to examine different models of oil agreements more closely and to expose more clearly the mechanisms that link political institutions to foreign investment. Given its increasing importance as an oil producer in Central Asia, I also included in this book a brief analysis of Kazakhstan. I relied on secondary sources of information to assess the relationship between its political regime and the investment environment.

Finally, in addition to in-depth case studies, I constructed and analyzed a time-series cross-sectional dataset to test the generalizability of my hypotheses. The data were drawn from the World Bank's World Development Indicators and POLITY IV.[14] The economic and political indicators in these datasets together provide relevant data on 132 countries from 1970 through 2004. I analyzed the dataset using both a random-effects and a fixed-effects general least squares regression with robust standard errors.

Significance and Implications

The role of political institutions in attracting FDI has been seriously understudied. This book fills the gap by mapping out the types of institutional arrangements most conducive to FDI in the oil industry and the trade-offs involved in choosing one institutional arrangement over another. It also draws attention to the analytical importance of hybrid regimes that have limited executive constraints and political competition. I stress that some countries are stuck in between authoritarian regimes

---

[14] World Bank 2006, Marshall and Jaggers 2004.

and consolidated democracies and that they need to be analyzed not as a residual category of weak democracies in transition to a full democracy but as a distinct regime type with important implications for economic performance. Overall, this book emphasizes the need to introduce a finer institutional distinction among regime types to understand the political determinants of FDI procurement.

The political analysis in this book has significant implications for FDI's role in development. Political regimes shape the terms of an investment environment and at the same time they influence the way oil revenues are used. In other words, an analysis of political regimes is useful not just for understanding which countries are more success-ful in attracting FDI but also for identifying which countries are bet-ter at managing these resources once foreign capital is invested in the economy.

The findings herein challenge both the neoliberal and dependency the-ories that posit either a positive or negative relationship between foreign capital and development. The former contends that foreign capital brings economic prosperity to countries and sows the seeds of democracy.[15] Its proponents argue that national differences in an increasingly interdepen-dent world become less important and that foreign investment flows have the same uniform positive effect on economic and political development across the board. On the other hand, the dependency theories point to the ways in which foreign investment retards economic development, gener-ates inequality, and contributes to a concentration of political power in the host country by enabling a cozy alliance between the investors and the host government at the expense of societal interests.[16] Arguably a variant of dependency theory, the rentier state literature, further draws attention to the "curse" of particular industries, such as oil, in slowing down economic growth, weakening governance, producing conflict, and distorting the prospects of democracy.[17] A corollary to this logic would

---

[15] See Schumpeter 1950, Lindblom 1982, Held 1992, Weitzman 1993, Lipset 1994, Bhagwati 1994, Muller 1995, Mahon 1995, Stallings 1995, Frieden and Rogowski 1996, Block 1996, Henry 1996, 1998, Winters 1996, Maxfield 1997, De Soysa 2003.

[16] See Cardoso 1973, O'Donnell 1973, Magdoff 1978, Rubinson 1977, Evans 1979, Bennett and Sharpe 1983, O'Donnell 1994, Haggard and Kaufman 1995, Muller 1995, Gill 1995, Cox 1996, Sassen 1996, Martin and Schumann 1997, Rodrik 1997, Cammack 1998, Diamond 1999.

[17] See Mahdavy 1970, Hughes 1975, Delacroix 1980, Gelb 1986, 1988, Auty 1993, 2001, Shafer 1994, Sachs and Warner 1999, Mikesell 1997, Chaudry 1997, Karl 1997, Leite and Weidemann 1999, Ross 1999, 2001, Collier and Hoeffler 1998, 2005, Wantchekon 1999, De Soysa 2000, Jensen and Wantchekon 2004, Auty and De Soysa 2006, Snyder 2006, Ulfelder 2007.

be that the foreign investment that helps to generate oil rents creates obstacles for development.

The evidence presented in this book demonstrates that analyzing the effects of foreign capital without paying attention to the different capacities of political regimes to attract it in the first place fails to recognize divergence in state responses to financial globalization. The developmental effects of foreign capital depend significantly on the preexisting political structures. For example, the Azeri case demonstrates how an authoritarian regime that makes it possible to create an attractive investment environment can also make it extremely difficult to escape the oil curse. Given an unlimited executive authority and restricted competition in society, the oil rents that were generated thanks to the infusion of foreign capital have made the Azeri economy more dependent on oil, increased inequality and corruption in society, and weakened the government's ability and willingness to introduce reforms and provide welfare for its citizens.

The Norwegian case, on the other hand, reveals that mature democracies are better at realizing the benefits of FDI. Despite a few mistakes throughout its history as an oil-rich country, Norway is widely cited as one of the best examples of resource management. Its strong democratic institutions are characterized by high levels of executive constraints and political competition and these institutions have been successful not only in guaranteeing foreign investment but also in providing a transparent, equitable, and far-sighted state apparatus to use and distribute the oil wealth.

The Azerbaijani and Norwegian cases further demonstrate that in both authoritarian regimes and consolidated democracies, foreign investment can have a "reinforcing effect" on the political regime, albeit with opposite results. The success in attracting a significant amount of foreign capital into the economy strengthens and consolidates the existing regime. Foreign capital not only provides additional resources to state coffers but also gives legitimacy to the ruling elite. For instance, in Azerbaijan, foreign capital contributed to further strengthening of the authoritarian regime. President Aliev designed international oil contracts in ways that gave him and his entourage ultimate control over the distribution of oil rents. In a mature democracy like Norway, on the other hand, economic success brought on by the inflow of foreign capital, increased the legitimacy of decision makers and strengthened the foundations of the democratic welfare state. In short, political regimes help determine whether there will be foreign investment in the first place and mediate the effects of foreign capital once invested.

Finally, the Russian case in this book provides an interesting analysis of the nexus between politics and the developmental effects of FDI. Its hybrid regime in the 1990s made it extremely difficult for the government to create a stable and attractive investment environment but it also ironically slowed down the negative potential effects of oil rents. Many analysts point out that in the 1990s, Russia – to a large extent – escaped the economic and institutional malaise that is commonly associated with foreign investment and dependence on oil rents. However, as Russia moved toward more authoritarianism in the 2000s, it started to receive more FDI, became much more dependent on oil and started showing signs of an oil curse. In recent years, inequality and corruption have slightly increased and the chances for further democratization have become significantly less likely. The Russian case demonstrates that hybrid regimes are not viable in a globalized world. In order to effectively compete for limited foreign investment, these regimes are faced with the choice of moving toward either more authoritarianism or more democracy. If they are doing the former, they are more likely to increase FDI but ironically less likely to develop an equitable, transparent and efficient economy around oil, and less likely to escape the pull of authoritarianism.

Organization of the Book

The remainder of the book is organized as follows. Chapter 2 presents the theoretical justifications for focusing particularly on oil investments to study the relationship between political institutions and FDI. It begins with a discussion of a traditional political risk model – the obsolescing bargaining model – in the literature and an analysis of why this theory is not sufficient by itself to explain the sources of political risks facing oil investors. I outline the historical evolution of the relationship between multinational oil corporations and host governments and summarize the nature of political risks that oil investors have historically faced in the oil business. Next, I briefly discuss and compare the investment environments in Azerbaijan, Russia, and Norway to demonstrate the variation among them, as well as to show how their experiences with foreign companies have at times diverged from the predictions of traditional models of political risk. This chapter also discusses the differences among modern oil agreements in terms of the stability and flexibility they provide for foreign investors. A discussion of these investment models provides a background for the empirical chapters in this book.

Chapter 3 situates my main argument in the recent literature on the relationship between democracy and FDI. After mapping the various arguments in the FDI literature and showing their inconclusive results, I propose to focus on the level of executive constraints and political competition to explain the qualitative differences in investment environments. I measure executive constraints in terms of the strength of veto players in the state and political competition in terms of the number and organizational capacity of political parties and interest groups. Then I present a continuum from low, to partial, to high levels of constraints and competition to distinguish among political regimes in their ability to create an attractive investment environment. In the second part of the chapter, I provide a thumbnail sketch of the political regimes in Azerbaijan, Russia, and Norway as they fit into my theoretical model.

In Chapter 4, I discuss the implications of the theoretical model for the relationship between foreign capital and development and more specifically for the way oil revenues are managed and used. Challenging the conventional paradigms, I emphasize the importance of prior political institutions in understanding whether FDI and oil rents can be used for purposes of socio-economic and political development. I briefly summarize the experiences of Azerbaijan, Norway, and Russia to illustrate the differences among political regimes in managing the oil wealth.

The next three chapters provide in-depth analyses of each country's experience with the oil investors and the implications of these experiences for economic and political development. Chapter 5 analyzes the political conditions under which Azerbaijan's attractive investment environment was created. I argue that an unlimited executive authority and restricted political competition insulated decision makers in Azerbaijan and made it possible for them to establish a very innovative investment framework that provided extensive guarantees and incentives for foreign investors. The Azerbaijani case demonstrates how some developing countries compensate for their lack of credible institutions by offering flexible and generous terms to foreign investors. The chapter concludes with a discussion on how foreign capital and oil rents have, over time, produced significant levels of inequality and corruption in the Azeri society and reinforced the authoritarian and repressive tendencies of the ruling elite.

Chapter 6 analyzes the efforts by the Russian government throughout the 1990s to create an attractive investment regime in the oil sector and the ways in which some of the new veto players blocked these efforts every step of the way. This chapter draws attention to the weakness of hybrid regimes, characterized by some executive constraints in the presence of weak political competition. Considering the significant changes that took place in Russia since the beginning of 2000s, a separate section is devoted to the evolving political regime as well as ownership structure in the Russian oil industry and what these portend for the future of relations between the oil investors and Russian government. The chapter ends with a discussion of whether or not Russia has so far been able to use the limited FDI that it has received and the oil rents that it accumulated for the benefit of the Russian society.

Chapter 7 looks at the oil investment environment in Norway and the capacity of the political regime to overcome opposition to investment policies by effectively bargaining among different interests and reaching compromises. The Norwegian case provides an example of how a consolidated democracy with high levels of executive constraints and political competition can reduce political risks for foreign investors by providing policy stability and credibility. This case also demonstrates the positive effects of foreign capital in the further consolidation of a welfare democracy as well as in the successful management of oil resources.

Chapter 8 sets out to test the applicability of the theory to cases beyond Azerbaijan, Russia, and Norway as well as to foreign investment beyond oil. It starts with a brief analysis of Kazakhstan; another oil producer in Central Asia that has been successful in attracting FDI, albeit with a much rougher start than Azerbaijan. This chapter also discusses the generalizability of the theory, first to other oil-producing countries and then to all countries in the world. The statistical tests confirm that the relationships observed in the case studies also apply to all countries and for all types of FDI.

The final chapter presents a summary of the empirical evidence as it fits into the theoretical model developed in the first chapter. It concludes with a call for a revision in our understanding of the relationship between FDI and democracy as well as between oil and democracy.

2

Political Risks in Oil Investments: A History of Antagonistic Interdependence Between Companies and Host-Governments

The oil industry has historically been one of the most globalized in the world. Oil is a key fuel in industrial production, as well as a vital ingredient in the manufacture of a wide range of products. It is the backbone of capital-intensive industrial production, as it is the energy source for transportation, industry, military, communications, mechanized agriculture, and countless other services. Not only in terms of trade, but also in terms of oil exploration and production, the oil sector has historically been highly internationalized, involving many governments and multinational oil corporations.

The reason I focus on oil investments in this book is because they provide a hard case to test the relationship between politics and the ability to attract Foreign Direct Investment (FDI). Generally, it is assumed that foreign oil companies do not have political preferences. Due to severe competition in the parceling out of scarce oil resources in the world as well as the high returns associated with oil investments, foreign investors seem indifferent to political regimes as long as they provide stability for their projects. This is not to say that oil companies do not face any political risks in their interactions with host governments. In fact, given the structure of the industry, political risks are arguably the highest facing any investor in the global economy. Even so, one of the most prominent international business theories posits that the degree of political risk is determined not by the domestic political structure but by the relative market power and bargaining positions of the host governments and the multinational corporations with respect to one another. According to this view, to the extent that politics comes into the mix, it is political stability that is essential for the foreign investors regardless of which political regime can provide it.

This chapter analyzes what is missing in this type of a systemic explanation. After discussing the main tenets of the obsolescing bargaining theory, I outline the historical evolution of the relationship between oil investors and governments and the varying degrees of political risks facing oil companies as predicted by this model. In the last section of the chapter, I show how the bargaining model, by itself, is not enough to explain the variation in the political risks facing investors in Azerbaijan, Russia, and Norway. I provide a brief description of the investment environment in each country and discuss how their experiences have diverged from the patterns predicted by the bargaining theory. I conclude that the degree of political risk is not only a result of the relative market positions of investors but in fact is also a function of the domestic politics in each country.

Obsolescing Bargain and Political Risk

In the oil business, neither governments nor multinational corporations can do without the other. Even when governments are the owners of the energy resources, they usually lack either the necessary expertise and technology or the risk capital that multinational oil companies can offer. Multinationals, on the other hand, need the host governments to get access to resources and/or to provide for them the necessary legal and administrative framework to conduct business and make a profit.

The alliance between companies and governments, however, also contains elements of conflict in that each set of actors has different objectives. Companies essentially want to maximize their return on capital and ensure the long-term stability of their projects. Due to the enormous profits involved, governments also want to maximize their share of the financial gains and management (and in some cases ownership) of the oil industry. The zero-sum calculations essentially make their interdependent relationship antagonistic. Governments can create risks by regulating the economic attractiveness of the resources through taxation and regulation in ways that contradict the market mechanisms. The escalation of these politically determined costs affects the stability and credibility of an investment environment and thus the ability of states to attract foreign capital.

According to the best-known model of relations between multinational companies and host country governments – the obsolescing bargaining theory – the degree of political risk is determined by the relative market power of the companies and host governments and their bargaining relations in terms of the natural product cycle.[1] This model links the power of the two parties to the stages of their relationship, focusing on the shift in power that occurs over time.[2] Accordingly, the initial bargain favors the foreign company because it can invest in different locations and has the capabilities and resources to extract resources that the host country does not have. This dominant position allows the company to exact highly favorable terms from host governments. As a result, companies face few, if any, political risks and can work with whomever is in power. As the industry matures, however, the company becomes more dispensable, while the state increasingly senses its ability to exercise influence over the company. Over time, with the company's investments fixed and immovable, the commercial viability of the project proven, and the host government's expertise improved, the relative bargaining power of the government increases while that of the firm fades. The result is greater ability on the part of the host government to impose changes on the investment regime. Consequently, the shift in bargaining power translates into new agreement terms and hence to increasing degrees of political risks. In other words, political risks are considered as inherent within these systemic-level economic changes.

In addition to the shifts in the product-cycle, the fluctuations in the price of the product also affect the relative bargaining positions of the governments vis-à-vis the companies. The rise in the price of the commodity increases both the attractiveness for and the competition among the investors. When prices are high, companies have a higher propensity for risk and consequently host governments have a huge advantage in setting the terms of the investment relationship. In periods of low pricing, the profitability of investment projects declines, reducing the bargaining position of a country to attract investment.

Applying this model to the international oil industry, we see that in the beginning of the twentieth century, multinational oil corporations with their technological expertise and huge sums of capital had unprecedented control over the development of natural resources around the world (see Table 2.1). They effectively set and controlled the crude oil prices. They faced very little political interference in their operations. Unable to challenge the multinationals, for many years the oil-producing countries could not translate their interests into action.

---

[1] See Vernon 1971, 1980, Smith and Wells 1975, Mikesell 1971, Moran 1974, Rothgeb 1990, 1991.
[2] Andersen and Arnestad 1990, 51.

TABLE 2.1. *Effects of Oil Price on Investment Environment*

Years	Crude Oil Prices	Balance of Power in Favor of	Investment Environment
1950–73	⟷	Multinational Corporations	Open (Major concessions)
1973–84	⇑	Governments	Restricted (Nationalizations/ Expropriations)
1985–99	⇓	Multinational Corporations	Open (Deregulation/ Privatization)
1999–2008	⇑	Governments	Restricted (Creeping Expropriations)

In the late 1960s and 1970s, however, governments started to exert their political control and sovereignty over their resources and restrict the operations of multinational corporations. Governments soon regarded oil as one of the most strategic economic sectors, as "the commanding heights,"[3] and saw the control of the industry as the key to economic development. Given its strategic role in the two World Wars, oil had also become an indispensable part of national security. As a result, host governments started to impose tough terms on investors and in some cases even took it to the extreme of nationalizing and expropriating foreign assets. With an increased market control by the Organization of the Petroleum Exporting Countries (OPEC), oil prices began to climb steeply from the first oil crisis in 1973–74, until the early 1980s.

By 1985, following the discovery of new reserves in non-OPEC countries such as Angola, Mexico, Norway, the Soviet Union, and the United Kingdom, crude oil prices began to decline in real terms. These new sources of supply reduced the market control of OPEC. Due to the depressed prices of the 1980s and 1990s, oil was no longer singled out as the exception in the world of resource production and delivery; rather, it was viewed as a more ordinary commodity in a globalized world market that trades more or less freely in commodities.[4] By this time, the abundance of oil reserves, the decline in oil prices, and the

[3] According to Yergin and Stanislaw (1998), this term goes back to 1922, when Lenin first used it during his speech at the Fourth Congress of the Communist International. Later it was adopted by Nehru and the Congress Party in India and spread to many parts of the world. It refers to the most strategic parts of the economy.
[4] Fossum 1997.

commoditization of oil have once again given companies an upper hand in their relations with host governments. The interventionist trend was largely reversed as a result of comprehensive programs of deregulation and privatization. The fierce competition among oil-producing countries to get a share of the international investment capital led to a relaxation of the restrictions on foreign investment and at times to the introduction of new incentives to entice foreign investors. The restrictive investment and oil legislation of the 1970s was modified and/or replaced by new laws that reemphasized investment guarantees and incentives. According to the bargaining model, this changing relationship significantly reduced the political risks investors faced in host countries. It was believed that the need to attract foreign investment eliminated the opportunities for host governments to impose politically determined costs on the investors.

In the 2000s, the rules of the oil game have once again changed. The bargaining power of oil exporting countries vis-à-vis the oil companies systematically grew as a result of higher oil prices. The turning point in oil prices came in 1999, when prices increased as a result of an agreement signed in 1998 between OPEC and some non-OPEC producers – Mexico, Norway, Oman, and Russia – to reduce supply.[5] This new price boom was largely driven by an increased demand coming from developing countries like China and India, coupled with supply constraints due to reduced investments in production and refining capacity during the period of low oil prices. The geopolitical instabilities in the Middle East since 2003 have also contributed to this steep rise in oil prices.

This recent boom in prices has had important consequences. First of all, it prompted a worldwide surge in oil FDI. To take advantage of the high commodity prices, companies have been eager to expand their production facilities as quickly as possible. Second, the profitability of resource extraction projects once again increased the bargaining position of host governments vis-à-vis the companies. Reflecting their improved negotiating position, several host governments have recently changed their policies with regard to oil companies. Even though the likelihood of nationalization had declined significantly since the 1980s, foreign oil companies today encounter considerable political risks in terms of expropriation of revenue streams, unpredictable and exorbitant taxes, contract repudiation, and ineffective rule of law among others.[6] This creeping

---

[5] UNCTAD 2007.
[6] Fossum 1997.

expropriation is a major factor shaping investment relations among oil producing states and foreign investors today.[7]

The investment relationships depicted in the three cases of this book only partly conform to the patterns predicted by the bargaining model. In the late 1970s, for instance, Norway imposed new demands on the multinationals in accordance with the changing market conditions, but it also provided them with legal, fiscal, and administrative guarantees to ensure their stay. Changes in the terms of the investment relationship were seen as causing economic but not political risks. After the mid-1980s, developments in Norway once again deviated from the international bargaining pattern. Even though Norwegian government gave some concessions to the investors in line with the liberalizing trend in the world, it still retained significant control over and management of the industry and continued to strike a balance between the interests of investors and domestic groups.

Azerbaijan and Russia provide two other tests for the bargaining model. Restructuring their oil industries in the 1990s, these two countries needed to attract foreign investment at a time when investors had the upper hand and the political risks they faced were significantly lower. Despite generally positive developments for investors around the world at the time, the two countries had almost opposite experiences with oil investors. While Azerbaijan was able to provide legal guarantees and investment incentives to foreign companies in a short amount of time, Russia could not produce a workable investment environment throughout the 1990s. The empirical puzzle of this book is to understand why Azerbaijan and Norway under different international market conditions were able to provide the guarantees and incentives that foreign investors found attractive while Russia could not during an advantageous time for investors.

The changing relationship between host governments and foreign oil companies and the political risks associated with policy changes are best reflected in oil agreements, which establish the terms of the investment relationship regarding taxation, ownership, regulation, use of resources, and dispute management among others. To capture the dynamics of the investment relationship in each country, one needs to understand the characteristics of different oil agreements and the degrees of political risk they produce.

---

[7] Another interesting development in the last decade is the increase in state-owned companies' share of the world oil reserves and production. In 2005, the top 10 oil-reserve holding firms of the world were all state-owned companies from the developing world, accounting for an estimated 77 percent of the total (UNCTAD 2007, 116).

An outline of the historical evolution of international oil agreements and the different contexts in which they are being used follows.

International Oil Agreements

Traditional Concessions

The first type of arrangement between the governments and companies in developing oil resources was the concession system. It had its origins at the beginning of the century with the grant in 1901 by the Persian government of an oil concession to W.K. D'Arcy. He received the rights to 500,000 square miles of Persia for the next 60 years in exchange for a US$100,000 bonus, US$100,000 in stock in his oil company, and a 16 percent royalty.[8] Saudi Arabia, Kuwait, Bahrain, and Iraq followed suit and invited major international oil-producing companies – the majors – to explore and produce their natural resources.[9] In 1933, the king of Saudi Arabia granted a concession to the Standard Oil Company of California for a 60-year term that covered almost as much territory as the D'Arcy concession. The 1939 concession that Abu Dhabi granted to five major oil companies covered its entire territory for 75 years. The Kuwait concession was also a 75-year agreement that similarly covered the entire country.[10] Even though the early concessions were made on an ad hoc basis, over time a more systematic way of dealing with foreign companies emerged: some countries continued the practice of negotiated concessions, while others adapted petroleum laws and established clear-cut rights and responsibilities.

Compared to modern oil agreements, these traditional concessions were very simple and general in scope. They often covered very large geographic areas – even to the extent of including the whole territory of the host country. Moreover, their duration was very long, often extending beyond a half-century. The companies were not required to drill on any of the lands granted or to turn back territory if exploration and drilling did not take place after a certain period. There were very few or no limitations on the operations of the companies.

The main financial incentive for the host governments in this scheme was the payment of a royalty.[11] Typically, royalty was calculated as a flat

---

[8] Andersen 1984.
[9] The majors were British Petroleum; Standard Oil of New Jersey; Gulf; Mobil; Royal Dutch Shell; Standard Oil of California; Texaco; and Compaigne Francais des Petroles.
[10] Smith and Dzienkowski 1989.
[11] Cattan 1967.

rate per ton of oil rather than as a percentage of the value of the sale price.[12] In addition, the host governments received periodic rental payments and a signatory bonus payment. But overall, their control was limited to these financial returns; they had no say in the exploration and the production activities of the foreign companies. The companies controlled transportation, refining, and marketing functions and hence determined the pace of the development programs and production schedules.

As the name also implies, the "concessions" that the host governments granted to foreign companies were an outcome of the weak bargaining position of the host governments. Natural resources, for them, meant perhaps the only instrument for economic development and they had neither the capital nor the expertise to undertake this risky business by themselves.[13] Considering that at this time the sizeable reserves around the world had not been yet discovered and that the demand for oil was only beginning to be recognized, it was not surprising that the host governments conceded so much control to foreign companies.[14]

The Middle Eastern concessions were strikingly very similar to the oil and gas leases granted in the United States in the first decades of the twentieth century.[15] Faced with costly drilling and a greater need for more reserves to meet the expanding market demands, the U.S. government started leasing large tracts of land for very long periods of time. By the 1930s, however, a standard approach to oil and gas leases emerged in the United States that differed significantly from the Middle Eastern counterparts of the same period.[16] Leases covering large properties were still very common but the terms became limited to five to ten years and unless production and drilling had occurred by the end of the primary term, the lease was terminated. Under this scheme, the landowner was assured that land would not be tied up indefinitely by the payment of a small annual rent. The landowner was protected not only by the lease format but also by the courts. The courts started to redress imbalances in contractual rights between the oil companies and the landowners. The "lessee" in the United States had an implied duty to produce from a profitable well, a position that gave the landowners significant legal advantages not available to their Middle Eastern counterparts. In the Middle East, the companies, in expectation for larger demand at a higher price

[12] Smith and Dzienkowski 1989.
[13] Vernon 1966.
[14] Blinn 1978.
[15] Smith and Dzienkowski 1989, 18.
[16] Ibid., 19.

in this fashion had little incentive to drill new wells and develop certain fields after the initial drilling. The Middle Eastern states were deprived of the income from those wells until the company holding the concession chose to begin production.[17]

The Middle Eastern model was also used in other parts of the developing world. For instance, in Mexico, the oil companies, basing their claims on the mining laws enacted in the late nineteenth century during the regime of Porfirio Diaz, claimed huge areas of Mexican land with "irrevocable and perpetual" interest in the oil and gas in place. The 1901 oil law authorized concessions, gave the companies significant advantages such as tax exemptions, the right to import machinery, equipment and material and other special privileges including the right to expropriate land necessary for their oil operations.[18] These generous provisions took away from the sovereign rights of the states to control and manage the development of their natural resources.

"The Awakening"

The major change in natural resource extractive arrangements came at the end of World War II. Dissatisfaction of the host governments with the traditional concession system became a critical issue. The rising wave of independence enabled host governments to change the format of their relationship with foreign companies in line with their nationalistic political agenda. Other factors also helped their bargaining position to increase relative to the companies. By this time, substantial oil reserves had been discovered in the Middle East and demand for oil as an energy source by the industrialized countries of Europe and the United States greatly increased. Moreover, the entrance of newcomers (known as independents or new internationals) heightened the competition among the producing companies, thereby further enhancing the relative power of the host governments.[19] Host governments found themselves seeking "a greater share of oil profits, more restricted areas with expedited exploration schedules, provisions for periodic surrender of portions of the granted area, and commitments to train personnel in the related skills and technology."[20]

---

[17] Ibid., 21.

[18] Ibid., 26.

[19] According to Yergin (1991:531–32), in 1946, nine oil companies operated in the Middle East; by 1956, 19; and by 1970 the number had reached 81. By one estimate, between 1953 and 1972, more than 350 companies either entered the foreign oil industry or significantly expanded their participation in it.

[20] Blinn 1978, 310.

The greater assertiveness of host governments has forced multinational corporations to recognize escalating political risks surrounding their investment decisions.

The process by which these changes occurred differed greatly from one country to another. The United States, as mentioned above, had the option to turn to the courts and agencies to balance the rights of landowners and companies. The judicial decisions had produced a series of implied covenants that imposed a duty upon the companies to explore the fields for the mutual benefit of both parties. However, this option was not available to many of the other sovereign states; they instead turned to the option of expropriation or renegotiation. Some countries, notably the Middle Eastern countries, chose to pressure the oil companies to renegotiate the original concessions; others, like Mexico, turned to nationalization as a means of regaining control over their natural resources.

The unbalanced concentration of Mexico's natural resources in the hands of foreign companies was in fact one of the precipitating causes of the Mexican revolution and the expropriation of oil companies' assets in 1938. When the long reign of Porfirio Diaz had come to an end in 1911 with the Mexican revolution, the policies that had encouraged and attracted foreign investment were reversed. During the 20 years that followed the adoption of the 1917 Constitution, the dispute between the government and the oil companies intensified as the government imposed new taxes and demanded higher wages and better working conditions. In 1937, when the oil companies refused to give in to these demands, the oil workers went on a strike and on March 18, 1938, President Lazaro Cardenas announced the expropriation of the industry.[21]

Events in Mexico demonstrated that a sovereign nation could effectively take control over its resources from the powerful international corporations and that it could develop these resources itself. Petroleos Mexicanos (Pemex) was one of the first national oil companies to undertake the development of a national oil industry. For many host governments, national ownership had a symbolic political and emotional value that justified financial costs. National ownership was also seen as a rallying ground to unite the country. The satisfaction and the internal political benefits deriving from national control hence often seemed to outweigh technocratic and purely financial considerations.

---

[21] Smith and Dzienkowski 1989, 29.

In much of the Middle East, the original concessions were renegotiated and more equitable arrangements started to appear. One of the first examples was the agreement in 1950 between the Saudi government and Aramco to establish a 50–50 profit-sharing principle by imposing a 50 percent income tax on the company's profits. Saudi Arabia thereby quadrupled its petroleum revenues. Even though the major administrative and organizational functions remained with the company, the Saudi government and after it, many others, secured a better share of oil revenues and gradually tilted the balance of power in their favor.

Eventually, the Organization for Petroleum Exporting Countries (OPEC) was established by the oil-producing countries to present a unified and collective bargaining front to the major companies. During the 1960s, OPEC secured prices above the world petroleum market prices and further enhanced the revenue base of its members. Soon OPEC became a powerful instrument in delineating relations between the oil-producing countries and major oil companies. It changed the balance of bargaining power in favor of the producing countries.

Even though the attempts in the 1950s and 1960s were important, the major restructuring of the original arrangements occurred mostly in the 1970s. One principal turning point took place in September 1970. Having secured the will of the "independents" to increase the posted price of petroleum, Libya started to threaten the majors by announcing for the first time the possibility of nationalization. The demand was taken up by other host countries and in the same month, Iran sought the same terms that Libya had obtained from an independent, Occidental, in the Tehran agreement of 1971. This agreement resulted in a significant increase in the government take by raising the prices and establishing a 55 percent tax rate.[22]

Further attempts to gain more recognition of sovereign power changed the terms of the agreements to the benefit of the host countries. In 1971, Saudi Arabia introduced the concept of "participation agreements" by securing government participation to commence at an initial 25 percent level and scale up in annual increments beginning in 1978 until a majority of 51 percent would be held in 1982.[23] Even though at this point host governments still had not gained full control over the exploration and development operations, their influence over the utilization of their natural resources as an active partner had increased tremendously.

---

[22] Blinn 1978, 312.
[23] Ibid.

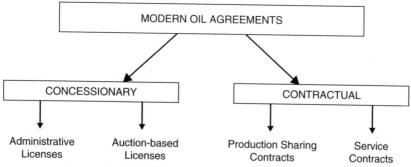

FIGURE 2.1. Types of Modern Oil Agreements.

The participation agreements as a new conceptual relationship between the host government and the foreign companies paved the way for new institutional arrangements.

Modern Oil Agreements

Since the 1970s, arrangements for developing oil resources have manifested a different orientation and maturation of national goals due to changes in the international oil industry. In this phase of the relationship, the government is no longer only the revenue collector but also the partner in oil operations as the sovereign over the management of its natural resources. As partners, governments and companies negotiate their interests mainly in two types of oil agreements: concessionary or contractual agreements. The fundamental differences between these modern agreements originate in different attitudes toward the ownership and control of mineral resources by the parties.[24] Concessionary agreements are divided into administrative licensing and auction-based licensing; the contractual agreements are divided into service contracts and production sharing agreements (PSAs) (Figure 2.1). Despite their specific characteristics, these arrangements are not mutually exclusive. Each borrows elements from the other, rendering the precise categorization

---

[24] The degree and methods of exercising sovereign control vary by country. Control may be exercised directly through a government agency, indirectly through a state oil company, or through both. In the United States, the arrangements for developing oil and gas have changed very little since the beginning. Landowners, including the federal government, still rely exclusively on private companies for the development of oil and gas reserves. The lease remains the only commonly used type of arrangement between the parties. In many other countries, however, the situation is much different; many still have state-owned companies. For more details, see Smith and Dzienkowski 1989, 35.

problematic. A brief description of each type of modern oil agreement and the potential political risks it may create for investors follows next.

Concessionary Agreements. A modern concessionary agreement grants exclusive rights to a foreign oil company to explore, search, drill for, produce, store, transport, and sell petroleum within the concession acreage for a specified number of years. The specified period in these current agreements is much shorter than the period of earlier concessions. And unlike traditional concessions, it contains clauses that impose a scheme of development based upon a monetary commitment for each year of the term and a work program that specifies when and how the acreage will be returned to the owner after completion of the project. The company finances the exploration, development, and production operations and has control over total production. In return, the country receives a bonus payment at the beginning of the concessions, and another payment later upon attaining certain levels of production. In addition, the concession provides for annual rental payments and a royalty based on levels of production. The government has the option to receive all or part of the oil royalty in kind rather than in cash. Furthermore, the company is required to pay the host country a specified amount of tax on the income earned in the country.[25]

The concessionary model exists in two versions. In the auction-based version, governments have less control over the distribution of licenses and the terms of the oil development projects. The legal and fiscal regulation is done through the general laws and courts. The United States, for instance, grants concessions based on auctions. The administrative licensing, on the other hand, retains more control for the government over the terms of the relationship by allocating licenses based on specific criteria that do not necessarily always reflect economic considerations. This type of licensing was first used by Norway and the United Kingdom (U.K.) in the 1970s and is known as the North Sea Model. With strong state traditions and equally strong needs for foreign investments, these countries elaborated this model of oil resource management to accommodate company interests under public control. The advantage was access to the experience and technology of foreign partners without totally giving in to their demands. To offset the domination of foreign companies, these governments created a set of legal and financial regulations in order to capture a given part of the rent and influence the behavior of foreign companies.[26]

[25] Smith and Dzienkowski 1989, 37.
[26] Noreng 1980, 34.

Such active state participation in this type of oil agreement makes investors vulnerable to political risks due to the fact that their rights are granted by administrative law and are subject to unilateral change. I argue that the reason countries like Norway and the U.K. can attract significant amounts of investment despite this potentially risky arrangement is because their political regimes respect property rights, provide legal stability and offer transparency. Conversely, investors demand contractual agreements based on civil law from developing countries to prevent any arbitrary and unilateral changes to the terms of their agreements. In a contractual relationship any changes made to the terms of the agreement have to be agreed by both sides to the agreement.

Contractual Agreements. Under contractual systems, the government retains ownership of minerals. As stated earlier, in the late 1960s and early 1970s, many countries abandoned the traditional concessionary agreements, which were historically linked to foreign dominance and gave host governments insufficient control over the resources. The control of the national oil industry was seen as an important step in establishing national independence. Centralization of the decision-making process gave corresponding opportunities for long-term planning of operations and coordination of the various state activities.

Generally there are two contractual agreements. In a service contract, the company receives a fee or share of production in exchange for providing the country and its state oil company with services and information to help the country develop its own resources. In case of discovery, production reverts to the country and the contractor recovers its costs, investment, and a fee for the risk incurred from part of the value of production according to a formula. It is less preferred by big multinational oil companies because it provides no right to production and gives fewer rights to the company in the acreage that is explored.[27]

Even more so than service contracts, the PSAs have become very popular among oil producing countries since the mid 1960s. They were first introduced in Indonesia in 1966. At the time of decolonization, the Indonesian government became acutely aware of the inequities inherent in the traditional oil concessions and refused to grant new concessionary agreements to foreign oil companies. However, in order to revive the

---

[27] There are also different types of service contracts, such as the pure service contract, the technical assistance agreement and the risk service contract. For details, see Smith and Dzienkowski (1989).

stagnant oil industry, the government had to come up with an arrangement that would be welcoming to the investors at the same time that it
protected the interests of the government. The issue was finally resolved
with the introduction of PSAs. These contracts were favored primarily
because they meant that the government would retain national ownership of resources and that it would have a direct managerial role in
setting the terms of the relationship with the investors. The principal
idea behind the PSA framework was the element of control and it was
consistent with growing national aspirations.

Initially, not all foreign investors were equally impressed with the PSA
model.[28] The major oil companies, in particular, hesitated to invest in
projects that they could not own or manage. They were also reluctant
about setting a precedent for their operations elsewhere. As a result, the
first foreign companies to enter into PSAs were the independent oil companies like IIAPCO in 1966 and Phillips Petroleum Co. in 1968.[29] PSAs
allowed opportunities for such companies to break the dominance of the
big companies and gain access to resources that were not available to
them before. The resulting competitive situation eventually tied the hands
of the big companies and forced them to take oil development projects
under PSAs. After the experience of Indonesia, PSAs spread globally to
many oil-producing regions.

A PSA is based on specific rights of ownership of production, loss of
some degree of governmental control, and particular methods of compensation. The most basic PSA concept is that the contractor is granted
the exclusive right to conduct petroleum operations in a contract area but
does not obtain any rights with respect to the underlying mineral rights.
Therefore, the contractor does not have an ownership interest in the oil
that is produced. The oil still belongs to the mineral rights owner, that
is, the host government, and the contractor obtains only title to its share
of the oil at the lifting point (production). Moreover, the contractor has
the contractual right to recover its costs out of the portion of the production that is devoted to cost recovery, in the event there are commercial
discoveries.

---

[28] It is interesting and ironic that in some places in the world today PSAs are vilified as a
capitalist tool but history shows that in fact PSAs originated as part of an anticolonialist
struggle. This paradox is partly a result of the historical ignorance of today's critics and
partly a reflection of the fact that the nature of PSAs varies from one context to another,
sometimes favoring foreign companies over host governments. I thank one of the reviewers for bringing this paradox to my attention.

[29] For more details on the history of PSAs, see Bindemann (1999).

Another characteristic of a PSA is that the contractor is usually exempt from the taxes and other duties that would otherwise be paid to the host government. The underlying logic for tax exemption is that the host government will have ample opportunity to retain a sufficient share of the production splits through the negotiation of the terms of the PSA. This provision is especially useful in countries where tax regime is complex and arbitrary.

The applicable terms for cost-recovery oil and profit splits are, however, subject to negotiations and change from one country to another, depending on the degree of state-oil company participation and the location of the operations: onshore frontier or in deep-water offshore areas. In Egypt, for example, because the national oil company (EGPC) does not participate in the PSAs, only 40 percent of the production is allowed to be devoted to cost-recovery oil. On the other hand, in Vietnam, the state oil company PetroVietnam has been known to allow a 50 percent cost-recovery ceiling and to provide profit splits in favor of the contractor because its wholly owned affiliate holds a significant participating interest under the PSA. The Indonesian PSA sets the profit oil splits (highly in favor of state oil company Pertamina) based on the production rate, instead of setting an upper limit for cost recovery. The Indonesian government's unique mechanism, First Tranche Petroleum, acts as a quasi royalty taken off the top of total revenues from sales of petroleum and shared by Pertamina and the contractor according to their respective profit oil shares.[30] This provides revenue to Pertamina in case the amount of costs to be recovered would exceed or be equal to the revenues for a given quarter.

In addition to the cost-recovery and profit-oil splits, there are a number of other commercial matters to be negotiated between the host governments and oil companies. The most important of these are the minimum work and financial obligations for exploration programs and the amount of signing bonus, commercial discovery, and production bonuses. The outcome of the negotiations on these issues has a major impact on the economics of any PSA project. Over the years many host governments have attempted to enhance their revenues and exert additional control by changing the basic mechanisms of the PSA. Therefore, today around the world, there are a variety of PSA models with different degrees of revenue sharing.

Even though the terms vary from one country to another, there are several principles on which international oil companies have traditionally

[30] Smith and Dzienkowski 1989, 38.

insisted when entering into a PSA. To attract significant amounts of investment, the host country is expected to include in a PSA the following incentives for investors: (1) the unfettered right to export its share of the production and retain proceeds from sales from abroad; (2) the ability to exert some degree of control over operational and managerial matters; (3) the stabilization of contractual rights; and (4) the settlement of disputes by third-party arbitration.[31]

First, the right to export has been deemed a minimum requirement due to its fundamental relation to the economic feasibility of any investment project. By exporting oil, the contractor gains access to the international crude oil trading market and is not constrained by the peculiarities of the domestic market of the host country. The exports provide convertible currency earnings for both the contractor and the host government. The right to export also gives the contractor the option to transport its share of the exported production to its own refineries, which may add considerably to the economic feasibility of undertaking a particular development project.

Once the export sale is consummated, it is important that its proceeds remain under the control of the contractor. The establishment of a foreign bank account is an intrinsic part of the right to export and is used both for the deposit of the contractor's convertible currency revenues and for the payment of obligations to the host government. This system also allows the contractor to avoid sending surplus convertible currency into the host country, where it might be subject to foreign currency conversion regulations and withholding taxes, if repatriated. This right to export can be diminished by conflicting legislation (as in the Russian PSA) or by the insertion of a domestic supply requirement that goes beyond the normal requirements in the case of a national emergency.

Second, some degree of operational control is viewed by the foreign investor as the natural corollary to its accepting the sole risk and expense for the project. Under such circumstances, the foreign investor wants to be free to use its technical and managerial expertise in accordance with sound and internationally accepted business and commercial principles and to be subject to only the usual environmental and operational regulations.

Third, the stabilization of contractual rights under a PSA is a principle upon which international oil companies depend when making long-term investments, especially when such investments are made in an otherwise

---

[31] Skelton 1997.

unstable political environment that could lead to nationalization or expropriation. In the first instance, the main objective of the contractor is to maintain the stability of its rights under the PSA in such a way that subsequent legislation will not affect them adversely. One method of ensuring such stability is the inclusion of a stabilization clause in the PSA that limits the applicability of laws to those that are in effect at the time the PSA is signed. An alternative approach is to provide that the PSA is governed by accepted principles of international law, an approach no longer acceptable to most sovereign governments. In Egypt, Azerbaijan, and Turkmenistan for instance, the PSA is submitted to the parliament, which approves it by making the agreement a law unto itself. This provides the foreign investor with some additional reason to believe the arrangement is stable.

Finally, the guarantee of third-party international arbitration at a neutral location, using a neutral governing law for the resolution of disputes is an extremely important aspect of the negotiation of every PSA. If mutual agreement on this fundamental issue is not reached, however, the contractor will be faced with the prospect of the resolution of disputes in the courts of the host country, where, depending on the development of the legal system and the independence of the judiciary, arbitrary and capricious decisions may be made to its detriment.

Overall, the most important aspect of a PSA framework is the fiscal and legal stabilization that it provides for the investors operating in an unpredictable environment. Oil and gas explorations require huge capital investments in projects that may produce profits only after five or more years. Because the assets cannot be moved and are located entirely in another country, foreign oil companies will simply not risk investing unless they have a reasonable level of comfort that the rules of the game and their projected profits will not change unexpectedly. By curtailing possible arbitrary intervention by the host government, a PSA provides a fiscal and contractual stability and incentives for the investors throughout the life of the contract. In a PSA setting, therefore, the investor has more control over the terms of the engagement than it would under a license. In exchange for giving up some control over the terms, however, the host government retains managerial and operational control by obligating the investor to submit a work proposal that would be regularly monitored. In this way the state maintains control over the manner in which the work is performed. Further, the PSA framework ensures that the host country increases its revenue base and thus its control over the economy by inviting the risk capital to develop and produce from oil fields. Hence, this institutional mechanism is more suitable for developing countries in managing their natural resources than for developed countries. It is no wonder that today PSAs are being used in more than 30 developing countries such as Indonesia, Nigeria, Angola, Peru, China, Egypt, Philippines, Libya, Malaysia, Turkmenistan, and Kazakhstan. As of June 2007, PSAs were the most frequently used contractual form, accounting for more than 50 percent of all contracts involving foreign companies.[32]

I now turn to a comparison of the investment environments in Azerbaijan, Russia, and Norway. These countries have exhibited significant variation in their ability to create a favorable investment environment. Albeit under different types of oil agreements, Norway and Azerbaijan were able to provide legal, administrative, and fiscal guarantees and incentives for foreign investors, while Russia drove eager foreign investors away in the 1990s with its arbitrary, unstable, and unrewarding investment rules. The experiences of these countries with foreign oil companies challenge the patterns of political risk predicted by the obsolescing bargaining model.

A Comparison of Investment Environments in Azerbaijan, Russia, and Norway

Azerbaijan signed the "contract of the century" in 1994, when ten foreign oil companies committed US$8 billion in oil investment over the course of the next three decades. Soon thereafter, the president of newly independent Azerbaijan embarked on an ambitious strategy to attract as many diverse foreign oil companies as possible to the Azeri oil industry. He pledged that as a result of this oil strategy, Azerbaijan in the next decades would experience "a new dawn."[33] And to the amazement and awe of analysts and policymakers alike, Azerbaijan, with a gross domestic product of only US$4 billion, attracted a US$3 billion investments in its oil industry over the next seven years.[34] Even though it is not the former Soviet republic with the largest oil reserves, Azerbaijan had the most FDI per capita of any state in the region by 2000. According to the FDI performance index created by UNCTAD, in terms of success in attracting FDI among 140 nations, Azerbaijan ranked the third highest during 1994–1996 and eighth highest during 1998–2000.[35] As such, not only

[32] UNCTAD 2007, 104.
[33] Wagstyl and Stern 2000.
[34] USEIA 2001a.
[35] UNCTAD 2002a.

did it become the "showcase for the art of doing business" in the former Soviet Union, but it was also depicted by foreign investors as the "frontier of global capitalism."[36]

Azerbaijan owes these acclaims to the PSA framework that it adopted as early as 1994. The government used PSAs, which by this time were proven to be instruments of stability for investors in the developing countries. It also created an investment regime in which each PSA acquired the force of law of the Azerbaijani Republic and prevailed over any other existing or future law and decree whose provisions differed from or were in conflict with it. In addition, the PSAs provided mechanisms for foreign energy companies to recoup their investments. For instance, the only tax levied on the contractor has been the profits tax payable at a fixed rate of 25 or 32 percent for each PSA, depending on when the agreement was signed. The investors have been exempt from all other existing or future taxes, duties, excise taxes, including export and import duties or taxes. These incentives and the contractual guarantees provided by the PSA framework resulted in 21 PSA contracts by the beginning of 2000 that committed an estimated total investment of US$60 billion throughout the course of these projects.[37]

Not too far from Baku, in Moscow, the capital of the biggest successor state to the Soviet Union, however, not much investment activity was taking place. Given the country's large endowment of natural resources and its educated labor force, as well as its potentially large domestic market, attracting foreign investment should not have been too difficult for Russia in the 1990s. Moreover, given the assumptions of the bargaining model, one would have expected the initial stage of the relationship between the Russian host government and foreign companies – especially during the low international price of oil in the 1990s – to favor the latter in terms of leverage over taxation, regulatory policies, and institutional design.

Yet, the record was discouraging. Despite explicit efforts by the government to attract foreign capital to reform its oil industry and bring production levels up, Russia received far less foreign investment than it could have both relative to the size of its economy and in comparison with other emerging markets. For the period 1990 to 1998, Russia ranked 21st among 25 countries of Central and Eastern Europe and Commonwealth of Independent States (CIS) in terms of per capita FDI.[38] According to the

[36] Goldberg 1998, 57.
[37] USEIA 2001a.
[38] Ernst and Young 1999, 7.

UNCTAD FDI performance index, Russia ranked the 108th and 104th highest among 140 nations during 1992–1994 and 1998–2000, respectively.[39] Between 1995 and 2000, Russia received about US$19.9 billion in total FDI, of which US$3.7 billion went into the oil sector.[40] The initial euphoria of investing in Russia turned into a nightmare for most investors as the first decade of transition came to an end. After so many years of Soviet isolation, the doors to the Russian "prize" were wide open but eager investors could not step in.

The disappointing FDI levels throughout the 1990s were mostly due to the weak investment environment created by the Russian political landscape. The initial legal system governing oil activities was fraught with complexity and ambiguity. For a very long time in the 1990s, the only regulated form of investment in the Russian oil sector was joint ventures in which a license to carry out oil development had to be obtained from administrative bodies. However, the licensing regime did not provide sufficient stability and incentives for foreign investors. Licenses were subject to state legislative action that resulted in unilateral changes and modifications, without granting foreign investors any ability to prevent or influence this process. Rules for the length, operation, or termination of licenses in many of the laws were contradictory and vague. Exporters struggled with cumbersome and restrictive quotas and licensing requirements. Moreover, the legal hierarchy established under the Constitution of 1993 was not very clear as to the distribution of authority between the federation and its components in which oil reserves were actually located. In addition, the tax burden was severe and it changed frequently and unpredictably. Finally, the turbulent ownership struggles and the fierce turf wars within the Russian oil industry created a lot of instability and made Russian oil companies reluctant and at worst hostile counterparts to foreign companies. All of these obstacles paralyzed the operations of foreign investors.

Given these problems with the Russian legal and fiscal framework, foreign companies preferred the PSA as the safest type of investment agreement in the oil sector. Russia in the 1990s provided an appropriate setting for the use of PSAs. It had rich, untapped energy resources and the domestic oil companies had neither the technical expertise nor the risk capital to invest in new, technically challenging fields. Moreover, as discussed earlier, Russia's tax and legal regimes have been too unpredictable

[39] UNCTAD 2002a.
[40] UNCTAD 2001.

and burdensome to attract large-scale, long-term investments in other forms. The PSA law would have immediately attracted large-scale oil and gas investment by establishing a special legal regime for oil agreements in an attempt to insulate investors from these risks. Despite the immediate need for and continuing insistence of foreign investors on PSAs, however, the adoption of the PSA law and the necessary regulations for its implementation was not completed by the end of the decade.

In the 1990s, while the two former Soviet republics were competing with each other to attract foreign investment, another major oil producer, Norway, was being commended in policy and academic circles as the example of a successful oil-producing state.[41] Starting its oil development in the 1970s, during a tough period for the oil industry around the world, Norway was able to attract significant amounts of FDI in its oil industry and then use these resources to build national competence in oil and meet the welfare demands of Norwegian society. Although systematic oil FDI figures are missing, according to one account from 1971 to 1996, a total of US$200 billion was invested in exploration, construction, and operations on the Norwegian continental shelf.[42] In recent years, Norway has been sharing its experience of oil development with other oil-producing countries, especially Russia and Azerbaijan. Norwegian delegations of oilmen have been frequenting Baku and Moscow, giving advice to governments and oilmen about how to successfully operate partnerships with foreign companies and how best to use oil revenues.

Norway started the development of its oil resources at the end of the 1960s. Having no geologists, petroleum economists, or lawyers specializing in petroleum, Norway needed foreign expertise and risk capital to share the burdens and costs of developing oil from the North Sea. In 1965, the government issued a Royal Decree that formulated a concessionary oil agreement model with administrative allocation of licenses. By means of this "North Sea model," instead of signing a civil contract with investors, as in a PSA, the state entered into negotiations with oil companies for exploration programs, and for commitments attached to licenses. The licenses were granted by an administrative procedure, in which the state chose companies according to specific criteria. General standards of treatment, such as dispute settlement mechanisms, expropriation, repatriation of funds, and work programs were embedded within these licenses.

---

[41] See, for instance, Karl (1997).
[42] International Trade Administration 2001.

In line with unprecedented growth in the bargaining power of host governments during the 1970s, the Norwegian state retained full control over the development of oil resources, and at times imposed relatively less favorable terms upon foreign investors. The state's bargaining power peaked in the early 1980s, reflected by a toughening of some of the fiscal and regulatory terms in licenses. By the mid 1980s, when oil prices collapsed and competition for investment intensified, the Norwegian government adjusted the economic terms of the agreements with the foreign companies. For instance, in 1986, the state initiated a tax reform by which the government take was reduced considerably. At the same time that it was being responsive to the interests of foreign companies – deviating from the expectations of the bargaining theory – the state also continued to pursue such goals as geographical and social distribution of offshore activities, and prevention of major accidents or negative side effects, among them harm to fishing grounds. Hence, the state was able to strike a balance between the interests of the foreign investors and domestic groups.

Some of the policy changes during these years reduced the profitability of some oil projects. Nevertheless, foreign investors continued to invest in Norway due to three main characteristics of the investment environment. First, the state offered the investors enough predictability to stay in Norway. For instance, the changes in the oil taxation were in line with the fluctuations in oil prices and were thus expected and accepted by the investors. The government was also able to provide some incentives to lessen the tax burden of the companies. Second, the clarity, consistency, and stability of the administrative and regulatory environment gave investors reasons to stay. The stated principles of the legal and administrative framework of the oil industry that were initially established remained intact, and there were no uncertainties regarding the rules of the game. No major changes were made in the principles, rights, and obligations of state institutions and the oil companies. Finally, the transparency of the oil administration also gave investors many access points and allowed them to have a level playing field on issues concerning their operations.

Conclusion

This chapter makes a case for why the oil industry provides an appropriate starting point to study the relationship between political regimes and FDI. Oftentimes investors cite the existence or absence of political risks in explaining their decisions to invest in particular countries. However, they refrain from referring to political regimes as the source of the political risks they encounter in different settings. They oftentimes speak of the degree of political risk as a function of the changes in the structure of the international oil industry. As the historical evolution of oil agreements in this chapter demonstrates, there is no doubt that the relative market and bargaining positions of host governments and multinational corporations determine the range of political risk possibilities. Given the structural differences and conflicts of interest between host governments and companies, especially in the oil business, the changing market position of these actors makes political risks more or less likely. Yet, as the cases in this book demonstrate, political risks do not always correspond to shifts in the balance of power in the oil market. In fact, sometimes political risks for investors are heightened even when the bargaining position of the host government is weak. The next chapter makes the argument that political institutions act as an intervening variable that can affect the bargaining power of host governments and thus the probability of political risks.

One interesting observation of this chapter is that policy stability for investors takes different forms. The use of different types of oil agreements around the world demonstrates that governments and investors have various tools at their disposal to manage political risks. In developing countries, where investors do not have full confidence in the general laws and administrative regulations, special contracts, such as PSAs, are preferred by investors to guarantee the future of their projects and by governments to signal stability and predictability in the investment environment – even when it means less control and revenue base for them.[43] In more advanced countries, on the other hand, investors do not object to working through the licensing system since they have more trust and confidence in the general legislative and administrative framework of these countries. Concessions as opposed to contracts are preferred by host governments who want to retain relatively more control and revenue for themselves.

Whether in the form of a contract or license, the guarantees, incentives, and stability that oil agreements provide for investors are crucial in understanding why some countries are more successful than others in attracting FDI. Globalization, in the form of competition for investment capital, increasingly gives incentives for states to reduce political risks by

---

[43] From a purely technical point of view, the amount of total financial benefit for government is far greater in a concessionary agreement than a contractual one like a PSA.

reversing their previous restrictive policies and by actively seeking out foreign investors that can offer capital, technology, managerial capacity, and access to markets. Given that worldwide oil consumption is growing at about 2 percent a year and that worldwide oil production from existing fields is declining at 4 to 5 percent a year, the resulting gap between production and consumption (which is growing at about 7 percent a year) translates into a need for additional 80 million barrels of oil per day of production in a decade. According to some estimates, this will cost about US$1 trillion over the next decade, with around US$100 billion annually compared with only about US$60 billion in 2000.[44] The resulting picture is one of immense challenge facing the worldwide oil industry and the countries that are trying to attract a share of that annual US$100 billion. How much FDI each country attracts will depend on its success in creating an investment environment with few or no political risks.

In the next chapter, I introduce a finer institutional distinction among political regimes to capture how politics matter in investment decisions. It may be true that oil investors do not openly favor one regime over another, but their expectations from host governments and experience in various investment environments depict a certain pattern of political institutions that are more successful in attracting FDI than others. The stability in the investment environment, which almost everyone acknowledges and cites as one of the most essential ingredients in investment decisions, can be conceived as a function of the political regime in place. Just because the simple dichotomy between authoritarianism and democracy does not capture the institutional nuance between success and failure in the global economy, we cannot conclude that political regimes do not matter in FDI decisions. In fact, distinguishing regimes in terms of the level of institutional constraints and competition provides us with a systematic framework by which to assess the success or failure of political institutions in attracting FDI.

---

[44] These figures are taken from a speech by H.J. Longwell, ExxonMobil's senior vice president for upstream, who addressed the outlook for worldwide exploration and production at the Cambridge Energy Research Associates (CERA) conference in Houston in February 2001.

3

With or Without Democracy? The Political Economy of Foreign Direct Investments

In the extensive business and economics literature, the determinants of FDI are generally explained from the perspective of firms. Generally, foreign companies are motivated to invest abroad by an interaction of company- and host-country-specific factors, also known as the push and pull factors (see Figure 3.1). Explanations that deal with company-specific advantages include the *product cycle model*, which regards FDI as a way that firms capture remaining profits by expanding overseas to protected markets in search of lower production costs.[1] Another company-specific explanation, the *industrial organization theory*, is that FDI is the natural outcome of size, management, engineering, and organizational skills, and international oligopolistic rivalry of multinational corporations.[2] Finally, *trade theories* emphasize FDI as emanating from differentials in the endowments of capital and labor among countries.[3]

Locational or country-specific advantages, on the other hand, refer to both the economic characteristics of host markets and the policy environment that the host governments produce. Economic factors include market size, access to raw materials (reserve levels), availability and cost of labor, size and growth of GDP, and infrastructure development.[4] The policy framework, on the other hand, determines the rules of entry,

---

[1] Vernon 1974.
[2] See Hymer 1960, Kindleberger 1969, Buckley and Casson 1976, Graham 1978, Rugman 1981, 1985, Dunning 1993.
[3] Markusen 1995.
[4] See Schneider and Frey 1985, Crenshaw 1991, Brewer 1991, 1992, Dunning 1993.

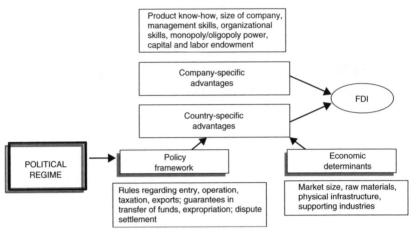

FIGURE 3.1. Determinants of FDI.

operation, taxation, exports, profit repatriation, transfer of funds, anti-trust regulation, expropriation, and dispute settlement.

Increasingly, business surveys depict the quality of the policy framework as an important component of success in attracting FDI.[5] Even when the economic endowments of a host country are attractive, foreign firms prefer to do business in places where the investment environment is conducive to their success. This is because policy environment has the potential to pose great risks for foreign investors at different stages of their projects. Host governments can attempt to design or modify investment policies, laws, and regulations in ways that can hurt foreign direct investors. At an extreme, governments can nationalize or expropriate foreign assets. At a minimum, they can renegotiate tax and tariff rates, impose new licensing requirements, increase the number of permits required, impose capital controls and the like.

What makes foreign direct investors particularly vulnerable to host government policies compared to other types of investors (i.e., portfolio investors) is the difficulty of withdrawing assets from a country in response to hostile, unfavorable policies. Foreign direct investors generally have limited influence on the investment environment *ex post* because sunk costs associated with start-up and the location of physical assets shift the bargaining position to the host government.[6] As also

---

[5] For example, the importance of host-government policies and institutional environment as locational determinants of FDI was confirmed in a survey of 39 mining transnational companies. Out of the 20 highest ranked factors influencing investment decisions, 18 were in one way or another related to government policies (Otto 1992).

[6] Vernon 1971, 1980.

discussed in Chapter 2, this "obsolescing" bargaining power of the foreign firm vis-à-vis the host government over time captures some of the risks considered by foreign investors at the initial stage of their investments. Governments that can lower these risks for multinationals tend to attract higher levels of FDI.

Essentially, what makes an investment environment attractive depends on the provision of three things by the host-government: *policy guarantees* against expropriation, seizures of assets, contract repudiation, ineffective rule of law, government corruption (i.e., sound property rights protection); *policy incentives* such as tax holidays, exemptions from import duties, investment grants, subsidized loans, donations of land or site facilities; and finally *policy stability* that makes policy commitments credible and lasting. The importance of these characteristics is widely acknowledged, yet very little attention has been given to the conditions under which they are provided in the first place. Considering the competition in the global economy among developing countries for access to foreign capital, the reasons for why some countries can come up with these guarantees and incentives more successfully than others have huge theoretical and practical implications.

An often-overlooked causal factor in this regard is politics. The connection between politics and FDI inflows that I discuss in this book hinges on the interaction between host governments and foreign companies with respect to the creation of such an attractive investment environment. One aspect of politics that has already received some attention in the FDI literature is political instability, manifested in the form of civil unrest, ethnic conflict, assassinations, strikes, riots, wars, and frequent government changes.[7] These factors may have the effect of disrupting or delaying foreign company operations in volatile regions, but it is also generally argued that companies learn to adjust and adapt fairly quickly to the conditions on the ground and hedge their entries into risky environments.[8] Moreover, foreign companies also occasionally encounter this type of instability in otherwise mature, stable political systems without significantly disrupting their operations.[9] The concern for foreign investors, then, is not so much political instability but is political risk. Different

---

[7] See Bennett and Green 1972, Levis 1979, Schneider and Frey 1985, Crenshaw 1991, Jun and Singh 1996.

[8] For instance, Frynas (1998) shows that Shell Oil Corporation adapted to political instability in Nigeria, thanks to its dominant market position and high profit margins. Li and Resnick (2003) also find that political instability is not statistically significant in explaining FDI inflows.

[9] Li and Resnick 2003.

from political instability, political risk captures the probability of government policies negatively affecting the ownership and management of foreign companies.[10] In sum, one can imagine a country with high levels of political instability but low levels of political risk and vice versa.[11] Changes in the ownership structure (nationalizations and expropriation) or in the policy environment regulating operations of foreign companies (creeping expropriation) constitute major political risks for foreign companies. I argue that political structure in the host country shapes the policy-making process and consequently the degree of political risk facing foreign companies.

I make two basic assumptions regarding the role of politics in FDI decisions. First, investment policies that protect the interests of foreign investors and provide them with investment incentives are not created in a vacuum. The investment environment is the product of a political process resulting from the interaction of various domestic groups. Because the investment guarantees and incentives for foreign companies may have distributional consequences – meaning that they may represent a transfer of benefits away from some domestic actors to foreign companies – the political struggle takes place between the supporters and opponents of FDI in the domestic political realm.

Second, the political struggle over investment environment takes place within an institutional context. Interests are essential in understanding policy success or failure but without a consideration of the institutional context within which they interact, they cannot tell us the whole story. Pluralist approaches explain policy willingness and design, but they do not adequately explain policy outcomes. Domestic political institutions define the investment environment by shaping the distribution of power among the supporters and opponents of FDI. They enable various groups to overcome dilemmas of collective action, or gain access to centers of decision-making and exercise influence. The institutions of the state not only affect the range of policy instruments available for domestic actors as they compete for influence over policies, but they also tend to favor certain types of conflicts and outcomes while actively discouraging or preventing others. A comparative study of institutions is therefore critical to understanding why some states are more successful than others in attracting foreign capital. The important question then becomes, under

---

[10] Jensen 2006, 46.

[11] In fact, Kobrin (1979, 1982) and Frynas (1998) both argue that political instability may actually reduce the probability of political risk for certain investors.

which institutional conditions can host governments attract foreign investment?

Democracy and FDI

In recent years, there have been a few cross-country studies that examine the relationship between democracy and FDI flows. Regime type is a logical place to start because it provides a basic way to look at the nature of all political institutions that influence policy making as a whole. It is a convenient starting point as well because there is a substantial amount of literature on the relationship between regime type and economic growth that scholars tap into to analyze the possible connections between democracy and FDI. Not surprisingly, the new debate over the effects of democracy on FDI very closely resembles this larger and earlier debate.[12]

In general, three competing hypotheses emanate from this literature. First, there are those who find no significant relationship between regime type and FDI.[13] According to this view, business opportunities rather than political factors shape FDI patterns. Investors are willing to assume a certain degree of political risk based on the expected returns on their investment. In addition to the findings of some cross-national studies, anecdotal evidence from interviews with foreign company officials in some studies also show that investors do not make investment decisions based on a comparison of regime types. For instance, Youngs (2004:136) argues that only a few multinational firms even have the vocabulary to engage in debates over the pros and cons of different forms of overarching political systems. Based on his interviews, he observes that "democracy is a word to avoid" among foreign investors.

Second, there are those who find a significant positive relationship between democracy and the ability to attract FDI.[14] They emphasize the importance of democratic institutions in providing credibility and stability for foreign investors. The argument is that democracies, by providing wide political participation and institutional checks and balances, reduce the ability of leaders to pursue predatory rent seeking and to

---

[12] See Huntington 1968, Przeworski 1990, Sirowy and Inkeles 1990, Przeworski and Limongi 1993, Olson 1993, 2000, Helliwell 1994, Barro 1996, Przeworski et al. 2000.

[13] See Schneider and Frey 1985, O'Neal 1994.

[14] See Rodrik 1996, Henisz 2000, Harms and Ursprung 2002, Jensen 2003, 2006, Li and Resnick 2003, Busse 2003, Busse and Hefeker 2005, Li 2006, Jakobsen and De Soysa 2006. Jensen (2003), for instance, finds that democratic governments attract as much as 70 percent more FDI as a percentage of GDP than do their authoritarian counterparts.

enact sweeping policy changes that would harm foreign companies. The potential for an electoral loss in case they renege on initial contracts with investors constrain democratic leaders in the first place in setting the terms for investment.[15] Democratic institutions are also found to promote FDI indirectly by strengthening property rights protection.[16] Several empirical studies have shown that democracies have better property rights institutions and stronger contract enforcement[17] and "better property rights protection reduces the risks of expropriation, contract repudiation, and government corruption for private businesses, which is shown to improve the investment environment for foreign investors."[18]

Finally, there are those who contend that authoritarian regimes provide foreign companies with better monopoly profits and entry deals and thus can attract significant amounts of FDI.[19] Because popular pressures in democracies can lead to greater demands for redistribution, lack of it in authoritarian regimes makes authoritarian leaders more generous in the terms they provide for the companies.[20] Restrictions on political participation prevent losing groups from organizing and challenging the authority of the rulers. In democracies, FDI policies are exposed to a wider spectrum of societal influences and the opponents of FDI have better access to the policy-making process, which makes it difficult to ignore their interests in designing legislation and administrative rules that affect foreign investment. Further, the influence of foreign companies is diluted by various opposing groups in the system. Consequently, democratic institutions limit the generosity of the fiscal and financial incentives host governments can offer to attract foreign capital. In authoritarian regimes, on the other hand, leaders are insulated from popular pressures. As a result, they are more likely to cooperate than clash with the companies.

The dependency literature is replete with examples of the complementary interests of bureaucratic authoritarian regimes and international capital. Many of these studies link authoritarianism to the deepening phase of import-substituting industrialization, which over time reduced the need for democracy.[21] The appeal to the multinational corporations of authoritarian regimes in developing countries is seen to be in their greater

[15] Jensen 2003.
[16] Li and Resnick 2003.
[17] See North and Weingast 1989, Olson 1993, 2000, Bates 2001.
[18] Li 2006, 64.
[19] See Jessup 1999, Li and Resnick 2003.
[20] Janeba 2002.
[21] See O'Donnell 1973, Cardoso 1973, Evans 1979, Bennett and Sharpe 1983.

political capacity to insulate themselves from particularistic demands. According to Haggard (1990), especially in countries with strong labor traditions, authoritarian rule has been attractive to investors.

Even though the question of relative merits of authoritarian and democratic regimes continues to evoke intellectual analysis, as well as political passion, the general picture is inconclusive and contradictory. Just like the cross-national empirical research on the economic effects of regime types, studies on the relationship between democracy and FDI have yielded highly mixed results.

One of the reasons for the contradictory and inconclusive results is that the existing literature oversimplifies the relationship between FDI and regime type, and underappreciates the complexities of host country politics. The institutional structure that defines and shapes the relationship between the opponents and proponents of FDI is much more complex and intriguing than previously analyzed. The exclusive use of large data sets and generic regime labels oftentimes by itself does not capture the intricacies of relations between investors and host governments.

To refine the existing debate and make better sense of the mixed findings in the literature, this book improves on both methods and theory. Methodologically, I first provide an in-depth comparative analysis of investment environments across a small number of cases. By focusing on a single sector of FDI – the oil sector – I control for possible differences among foreign investors in terms of their sector-specific risk calculations and expectations. In addition to the qualitative analysis, I also provide a large-n statistical analysis to test the generalizability of the hypotheses I generate from the case studies. The use of both methods provides both depth and breadth to the analysis.

Theoretically speaking, rather than exclusively relying on an authoritarian versus democratic conceptualization and readily available numerical indices, I examine in depth the institutional structure that empowers and constrains domestic actors in policy making. This is in line with a new trend in the literature that finds basic comparison between authoritarian and democratic regimes as inadequate.[22] The minimal electoral definition of democracy to distinguish between these two regime types

---

[22] According to Collier and Levitsky (1997), there are more than 550 subtypes of democracy that identify specific institutional features or types of full democracy. As for variation among authoritarian regimes, Linz (2000) argues that authoritarian regimes range from sultanistic, and bureaucratic-military authoritarianisms where there are few if any channels of political participation to "organic statism," mobilizational authoritarianism in

is increasingly questioned.[23] Accordingly, despite free or relatively free elections, some democracies have authoritarian tendencies.[24] People are given the right to vote, elections take place, and political parties compete, but these regimes use procedures of questionable democratic legitimacy. Rights that do exist are often insecure, subject to arbitrary change or sudden withdrawal. Governments can ban political parties, access to media can be limited, judiciary may be under the aegis of the government and be used to control political opposition. Such variation in the degree of democracy as well as authoritarianism has brought a new wave of scholarly attention to the analytical importance of a third category of regimes – hybrid regimes – that is neither clearly democratic nor authoritarian.[25]

To be fair, some studies highlight the qualitative differences between old and new democracies in explaining economic performance in general and FDI in particular. For instance, Przeworski (1990) and Olson (2000) argue that the establishment of democracy does not necessarily lead to secure property rights and that *new* democracies may be predatory. Olson (2000:41) states that "the individual rights that a democracy provides cannot be secure if the democracy itself is not." Similarly, Resnick (2001) demonstrates that regime change heightens uncertainty for foreign investors and puts new democracies at a disadvantage in the struggle to attract FDI.

The problem with these "new" or "transitional democracy" classifications is the assumption that they are partial or diminished forms that are in the process of moving toward fuller versions of democracy. Consequently, scholars treat the group as a "residual" category and do not incorporate it systematically in their analyses.[26] Or when they do, as in the case of Resnick (2001), they find that it is the generic uncertainty accompanying change and not the institutional characteristics of

---

post-democratic societies, post-independence mobilizational authoritarianism, and post-totalitarian authoritarianisms with limited, controlled, or privileged political pluralism.

[23] The minimal standard definition of democracy presumes full contested elections with full suffrage and the absence of massive fraud, combined with effective guarantees of civil liberties, including freedom of speech, assembly, and association.

[24] According to Collier and Levitsky (1997), the concern with these authoritarian tendencies has led to the inclusion of other criteria to distinguish between the two regimes such as the effectiveness of governments to rule (Karl 1990, Valenzuela 1992) effectiveness of legislatures (Bollen 1980), checks on executive power (O'Donnell et al. 1986; Schmitter and Karl 1991), or social and economic equality (Jackman 1974, Muller 1988).

[25] Diamond 2002.

[26] For instance, even though Olson (2000) acknowledges problems with new democracies, he only focuses on two types of political regimes: stable democracies and dictatorships.

a specific regime that merit attention. It is, however, now apparent to many that a great many of these regimes are not democratic nor are they any longer "in transition" to democracy.[27] As a matter of fact, in recent scholarly debates, they constitute a regime category of their own and deserve attention in explaining different economic performances.[28] To overcome the conceptual stretching in the generic democracy versus authoritarian classification, I introduce a finer differentiation among regime types to isolate the effects of political institutions on the ability to attract FDI.

Executive Constraints and Political Competition

I distinguish among regime types in terms of the constraints they impose on the executive power and the opportunities they provide for political competition. These two variables – the level of executive constraints and the degree of political competition – tell us a lot about the nature of the policy-making process in a political system, that is, how much authority and flexibility an executive has to pursue a particular agenda/policy; how much control the other institutions of the state have to change that policy; how accountable the executive is for its policy choices; how effectively the other state actors can keep the executive policies in check; how much access societal groups have to policy-making; how they can affect the negotiations over policy etc. If we can distinguish among regimes in terms of these two variables, we can get a better sense of the distribution of power within the state as well as between the state and society when it comes to designing and implementing policy. While the strength of veto players indicates the degree of horizontal accountability within the state, the strength of political parties and interest groups reflect the degree of vertical accessibility to the state. These variables enable us to understand the quality of the investment environment because they demonstrate the relative strength of opponents and proponents of FDI, the level of their political participation and the institutional mechanisms that shape their interaction with the decision makers.

In the literature, the level of executive constraints is usually measured by veto players. Veto players are defined by George Tsebelis (2002:19) as "individual or collective actors whose agreement is necessary for a

---

[27] Carothers 2002.

[28] See Diamond 2002, Schedler 2002, Levitsky and Way 2002. Rather than seeing it as a diminished type of democracy, some in fact consider it a diminished form of authoritarianism and call it "competitive authoritarianism."

change of the status quo." Tsebelis' general argument is that more veto players lead to higher levels of policy stability and that legislative change takes place in countries with one or few veto players as opposed to those with multiple veto players.

In the analysis of FDI determinants, some studies have recently started to look at the impact of veto players. For instance, Luong and Weinthal (2001) argue that the degree and form of international participation in an oil-rich country is particularly constrained by the level of "political contestation" in the system. More specifically, Henisz (2000) argues that foreign firms' decision to invest in a market is conditional on the number of veto players. Accordingly, the constraints imposed on political leaders lead to higher levels of political stability by making the possibility of policy reversal more difficult. The result is more favorable policies toward multinationals. For instance, legislatures use statutes to safeguard investor rights against administrative discretion; an independent judiciary upholds contracts and property rights of investors and resolves conflicts between government and private investors. Politicians can win the trust of foreign investors by renouncing their discretionary powers and creating mechanisms for defining and protecting property rights, enforcing contracts, and resolving disputes.[29]

The problem with these analyses is that more and stronger veto players in the state do not necessarily always mean more "favorable" policies for foreign investors.[30] Increasing the number of veto players in the state could, in fact, lock in policies that are unfavorable to the investors. Policy stability may not always be preferred by investors who want to change the adverse terms of investment agreements.

I argue that the missing element in the veto player analyses of economic performance in general and FDI in particular is an understanding of the degree of political competition in the system. The existing analyses focus almost exclusively on the institutional balance of power among state veto players that are generally defined by the constitution of

---

[29] Mahon (1995) argues that in some Latin American cases the renunciation of discretionary power has been quite remarkable. In the early 1990s, governments of Mexico and Argentina deliberately limited their own sovereignty over economic policy in order to win the confidence of potential investors. Similarly, Maxfield (1997) argues that in order to signal their creditworthiness to international investors, many governments in the 1989–1993 period ceded authority to central banks.

[30] For instance, Jensen (2006) argues that we also need to look at the preference structure of veto players. He demonstrates that unless there is some degree of convergence between the preferences of investors and one of the veto players, market-friendly policies cannot be adopted.

that country to be the executive, legislative (both houses if a bicameral system), and judiciary branches of government. Without a doubt, opposition to investment policies oftentimes comes from these veto players within the state whose power and authority are curtailed as a result of regulatory changes in investment relations.[31] However, the veto player analyses do not take into account the competitiveness of participation and the institutionalization of that participation that in fact can regulate the very interaction among veto players. Opposition to pro-investment policies can also come from a range of societal actors such as nationalists, workers, environmentalists, and business groups that feel threatened by the advantages these policies give to foreigners. These groups influence policy when they form political parties and/or interest groups and pressure the veto players through electoral support, lobbying, campaign financing, and/or demonstrations.[32] If they have access to the state, they can affect the incentive structure of veto players as well as the interaction among them. Depending on their number and organizational capacity, they can discipline veto players, constrain them or force them to make compromises.

Therefore, in order to better understand the policy-making environment, we cannot only rely on the veto player theory. We have to also consider the competitiveness of the party system and interest groups. Investment terms are shaped not only by the number and strength of state veto players, but also by the number and organizational capacity of political parties and interest groups in society. The interaction of these two variables roughly correspond to three types of political regime, which produce three types of investment environment, which can then affect the level of FDI (see Table 3.1).[33] I argue that on a continuum, low levels of executive constraints (or in other words unlimited executive authority) and restricted

[31] In the political economy literature, many scholars stress that opposition to economic policies tends to come from state actors instead of or as well as societal actors (Geddes 1995, Van de Walle 1999, Kurtz 2004).
[32] Tsebelis (2002:79) refers to these groups as a second type of veto players: the partisan veto players. He argues that such veto players are generated inside the institutional veto players by the political game. For example, replacing a single-party majority by a two-party majority inside the parliament (an institutional veto player) transforms the situation from a single partisan veto player to two partisan veto players. This analysis, however, excludes all other societal groups that are not directly represented in the state but can pressure investment policies in many other ways. The political competition variable that I use in this book more broadly captures the stakeholders in a policymaking environment.
[33] Any two-variable model certainly creates at least a 2×2 matrix. However, in this book I collapse the analysis into one dimension because each of the cells on the forward diagonal,

TABLE 3.1. *Effects of Institutions on Investment Environment and*
FDI Flows

	Institutional Variation (Executive Constraints and Political Competition)		
	Low	**Partial**	**High**
Regime type	Authoritarian	Hybrid	Consolidated democracy
Investment environment	Flexible	Chaotic	Stable
Level of FDI	High	Low	High

competition produce a flexible investment environment. At the opposite end, high levels of executive constraints (or in other words constrained executive) and an institutionalized, open political competition can also produce an attractive investment environment; this time by offering stability. However, in political systems where some executive constraints exist but political parties and interest groups are weakly institutionalized, the investment environment tends to be chaotic and unstable, which tend to drive foreign investors away. An in-depth discussion of these variables allows us to go beyond the authoritarian versus democracy dichotomy and introduce a third regime category that becomes crucial in understanding the link between regime type and FDI.

High Executive Constraints and Political Competition

Neoclassical economic doctrine rests on the belief that constraints on government activity are needed to curb discretionary activities that produce suboptimal, inefficient outcomes for the market and society. State intervention in the economy is seen as an opportunity for rent seekers and, thus, the corruption of the state.[34] This school of thought views state autonomy as pernicious for economic performance and implies that the state is always ready to prey on society and that only democratic institutions can constrain it to act in the general interest.[35] When applied to the foreign investment environment, such logic suggests that

although constructed differently, results in roughly the same investment environment and both roughly correspond to hybrid regimes. As such, a one-dimensional authoritarian-hybrid-democracy continuum can capture the same explanatory model.

[34] See Krueger 1974, Buchanan et al. 1980, Bates 1983, Collander 1984.
[35] Przeworski and Limongi 1993, 57.

the more constraints state veto players exert on the decision makers, the more credible and secure the property rights and commitments to foreign investors become.

I argue that strong state veto players produce an attractive investment environment *only* under regimes that also provide competitive and institutionalized access to political power. Strong political parties and interest groups not only provide a representation of societal interests in investment policies but can also mediate among state-level veto players by forming enduring coalitions and providing formal channels of communication and conflict resolution among them. Robust and enduring societal organizations can overcome particularistic interests of the state veto players that produce suboptimal outcomes for society as a whole. In the absence of such institutions, groups organize not to advance collective welfare but to guarantee a disproportionate share of societal income for themselves.[36] Hence, weakly institutionalized and unchecked competition among heterogeneous interests in the state tends to create instability. Illustrated by Arrow's impossibility theorem,[37] social choice theorists posit that enduring institutions that form long and durable coalitions can solve collective-action problems by enforcing structure-induced equilibria.[38]

Empirical analyses have confirmed that consolidated democracies –where the rules of the game are institutionalized –develop stronger institutions to constrain executives than do the less democratic ones.[39] Consolidation is the process of achieving broad and deep legitimacy by a normative and behavioral commitment to the specific rules and practices of the country's constitutional system.[40] In consolidated democracies, governance is improved by horizontal accountability and representative functions are expanded by the strengthening of political parties and their linkages to social groups. These institutions protect investors against the banditry of predatory leaders. Moreover, as the feature of a routinized democratic polity, electoral cycles are less likely to be characterized by extensive mobilization, and conflicts among veto players are less likely to be posed in zero-sum terms. The result is a stable investment environment for foreign companies.

[36] Haggard 1990.
[37] Arrow 1951.
[38] See Riker 1962, Shepsle and Weingast 1982, Aldrich 1995.
[39] See Clague et al. 1996. As Tsebelis (2002) argues, even though the number and properties of veto players may change over time even in the same political regime, it is generally true that democracies tend to have more veto players than authoritarian regimes.
[40] Linz and Stepan 1996.

Low Executive Constraints and Political Competition

Reversing the logic suggested above implies that instability grows in the presence of weak executive constraints and restricted competition. Political regimes that have no or few veto players leave policy decisions at the discretion of the rulers. Such unchecked government power generally exists in authoritarian regimes, where legislatures either do not exist or are so thoroughly controlled by the ruling party that conflict between the legislative and executive branches is virtually unthinkable. The central and regional bureaucracies are recruited on the basis of personal loyalty to the leader and extensive patronage networks dominate government positions, providing very little, if any, constraints on the rulers. Moreover, vertical accessibility is weak in authoritarian regimes. Parties and interest groups, to the extent that they exist, tend to be centered on an individual, lack developed nationwide organizations, and have weak ties to society. As a result, the rulers are invincible in that "the electoral arena is little more than a theatrical setting for the self-representation and self-reproduction of power."[41]

Some would argue that such lack of checks and balances on the decision makers produces a less credible, transparent, and stable investment environment and accordingly authoritarian regimes face more difficulty in attracting FDI. This logic, however, does not capture the complexity of the relationship among the state actors, societal groups, and foreign investors. As Przeworski and Limongi (1993) correctly point out, the neoliberal literature overemphasizes the potential corruptive aspects of the state while underemphasizing the pernicious role of rational particularistic private actors in society.[42] They argue that both a corrupt state and particularistic interests can undermine property rights, and therefore the widespread usage of democracy (as opposed to consolidated democracy) as a proxy for guarantees of property rights is unjustifiable. Decision makers that are not constrained by particularistic interests in society and that have a certain degree of autonomy from policy pressures can have the flexibility to formulate investment terms that are favorable to investors and acceptable to themselves.[43] Like consolidated democracies, autocratic regimes are also able to bring about structure-induced equilibria, though through very different means.

---

[41] Schedler 2002, 43.

[42] Przeworski and Limongi 1993, 53.

[43] The experience of some developing countries helps confirm this point. It has been widely observed that the rule of law and representative institutions have generally become

Flexibility of decision makers is often underappreciated in the literature. What is ignored in this respect is that "the same mechanisms that make it difficult to impose arbitrary changes in the rules may make it difficult to enact sensible rules in the first place or to adapt the rules as circumstances change."[44] Flexibility in fact can result in innovative policy tools and allow decision makers to offer relatively secure property rights to foreign investors. This is where I differ significantly from studies that assert that property rights can be strong and secure *only* in democracies.[45] Foreign investors demand an environment that offers *them* (not necessarily other investors or societal actors) secure property rights and proprietary benefits. Consequently, in states whose legislatures cannot pass and courts do not uphold laws to guarantee investors' rights, flexible executives can proffer guarantees, arbitration, and commitments specifically embedded in licenses and contracts given to international foreign investors or can set up structures that are the functional equivalents of institutions that protect private property.

As Rodrik (2002:5) rightly points out, "[w]hat is relevant from an economic standpoint is whether current and prospective investors have the assurance that they can retain the fruits of their investments and not the precise legal form that this assurance takes." Rodrik cites China as the best example of a political leadership that has devised highly effective institutional shortcuts (such as the Household Responsibility System; Township and Village Enterprises; Special Economic Zones; and Two-Tier Pricing) so as to stimulate incentives for investment without a wholesale restructuring of the existing legal, social, and political regime.[46]

In addition to flexibility for decision makers, lack of constraints and competition in the regime can also offer foreign investors easy and informal access to decision makers. Foreign investors who have privileged access to decision makers in the executive have few reasons to concern themselves with the society-wide institutionalization of the rules of the game or the development of a robust legislature, judiciary, or civil society.[47]

---

weaker during periods of radical economic reform. There has been a remarkable surge of decrees and decree-like instruments in countries such as Peru, Argentina, Mexico, and Russia. In general, presidents have dominated the system in these countries, and a kind of "delegative democracy" has taken hold during times of major economic restructuring. See O'Donnell (1994).

[44] Levy and Spiller 1996, 5.
[45] Li and Resnick 2003.
[46] Rodrik 2002, 8.
[47] This is mostly true for big businesses that can afford to establish close links to governments. On the contrary, small businesses, which do not have direct and privileged access

Such investors are often satisfied with simple power structures and a lack of opposition to their "deals" with the government. Even though the insufficiency of solid institutional guarantees produces a nearsighted investment profile, some investors prefer informal access to institutionalized avenues of interest articulation. Dependency theorists provide ample examples of how foreign investors build "cozy" alliances with state elites that share a common interest in rapid capital and wealth accumulation at the expense of institution-building and society. Because investors want to sustain the existing favorable investment environment, they do not pressure autocratic executives to institute reforms to improve the conditions of the masses nor their representation.

In sum, authoritarian regimes with low levels of constraints and competition as well as consolidated democracies with high levels of those attributes can pursue successful pro-investment policies – albeit in vastly different ways. The theoretical model presented above refines and redefines the debate in the literature over the merits of regimes in attracting FDI. The question should not be whether FDI will favor democracy or autocracy but why some investors favor consolidated democracies, whereas others prefer authoritarian regimes. Foreign investors – given their sector- or firm-specific features and short-term versus long-term calculations – act differently when making their investment decisions. They may have different calculations of economic returns and assessment of political risks. Democratic and authoritarian regimes each have comparative institutional advantages in attracting FDI.[48] Given their specific institutional characteristics, these regimes vary in their abilities to make more credible or more flexible policies. The bottom line is that they both seem to have something that is attractive for investors.

Trade-offs Between Democracies and Authoritarian Regimes

Consolidated democracies with high levels of executive constraints and political competition provide long-term policy credibility, stability, and transparency. A credible commitment means a reasonable return on investment and protection against arbitrary government discretion and thus low levels of political risk, but it may also mean policy rigidity and low profits. Authoritarian regimes, on the other hand, with low levels of

to decision makers, may have an interest in making the government more accountable and bound by law.

[48] Zheng (2005) also confirms this argument in his analysis of sector- and firm-specific characteristics that affect multinationals' policy preferences.

institutional constraints and competition provide little policy credibility if any. Even if the autocrat has a long time horizon, the absence of an independent power to assure an orderly legal succession means that there is always substantial uncertainty about what will happen when the current autocrat is gone.[49]

An authoritarian leader can, however, compensate for that weakness by offering policy flexibility in the short run. Narrow elite control and insulation from public pressures facilitate quick decision making and help overcome collective-action problems. Flexibility and adaptability also give more discretionary powers to these leaders to provide exceptional incentives to foreign investors in the form of tax reductions, grants, subsidized loans, market preferences, or regulatory concessions. The provision of these incentives can lower the cost of initial sunk investment and bring imminent economic returns to foreign firms.[50] Hence, in this setting the political risks facing investors are high but so are the returns. The catch is that favorable conditions may last only for the ruling span of one or two dictators. The regime trade-off facing investors is one between credibility in the long-run versus flexibility and generosity in the short-run. Put another way, the trade-off is between low-return, low-risk opportunity and high-return, high-risk one.

Another trade-off between investing in a democracy as opposed to an authoritarian regime concerns the comprehensiveness of the investment environment. In consolidated democracies, the guarantees and incentives offered by the investment environment usually apply equally to all types of investors. In authoritarian regimes, on the other hand, there is selective targeting by the government. Not all investors face the same tax and regulatory rules and incentives. The country is partially attractive and welcoming to a select number of investors that the regime deems necessary for its survival and those that do not directly threaten its authority. The result in authoritarian regimes can be a two-tiered economy with different sets of rules and procedures for different investors.

Finally, due to the inclusive and participatory decision-making process, the investment policies in a consolidated democracy are more widely

---

[49] Olson (2000) argues that there is a strong and robust relationship between the time an autocrat has been in office and the quality of property and contract rights in his domain. He argues that an autocrat with a short-term horizon has no reason to consider the future output of his society and that his incentives are those of a roving bandit. However, an autocrat with a long-term tenure usually cannot gain from confiscating capital assets, because doing so normally means that there will be less investment and less income, and therefore less tax receipts in the future.

[50] Zheng 2005, 10.

supported than those in an authoritarian regime. Because investment policies tend to balance the interests of foreign and domestic actors, they are regarded as more legitimate and acceptable by broader segments of the population. This helps not only with the implementation of these policies but also with their sustainability and durability. In authoritarian regimes, on the other hand, support or acquiescence over investment policies is often on tenuous grounds. The powerlessness and the frustration that ordinary citizens feel as a result of not being included in the decision-making process can have the potential to produce social unrest not only over investment policies that over time are seen as handouts to foreign companies but also over the regime itself. While rewards of authoritarianism for selective investors are high, so is the potential of political instability in the long run.

In this analysis, I make the assumption that the governments in these political regimes *want* and *seek* FDI. Although global economic competition ties the hands of executives to some degree and forces them to adopt neoliberal policies of openness, leaders with strong protectionist tendencies can at times come to power and pledge to make the operations of foreign investors difficult. In authoritarian regimes the lack of constraints as well as political competition offers authoritarian leaders the ability to create obstacles for foreign investment if they so prefer. In consolidated democracies, however, these tendencies can for the most part be reined in and moderated by veto players that are pro-investment. This is another advantage of consolidated democracies over authoritarian regimes. Either way, though, negative attitudes toward foreign capital may constitute a significant FDI deterrent. Institutional characteristics are a necessary but not a sufficient explanation for variation in investment policies. Preferences of leaders, as well as some of the structural background conditions discussed below, matter as well. Having said that, this book demonstrates that given an interest in receiving FDI, the prospects of attracting it appear to be strongest in both authoritarian regimes and consolidated democracies.

Partial Executive Constraints and Political Competition

I also argue in this book that the real losers of FDI are not consolidated democracies or authoritarian regimes but, instead, are the hybrid regimes. The link between democracy and FDI is nonlinear, meaning that investors tend to prefer both consolidated democracies and stable authoritarian regimes but are reluctant about hybrid regimes. The institutional characteristics of hybrid regimes seem to provide the worst of both worlds: neither the flexibility of authoritarian regimes nor the policy credibility of consolidated democracies.

The new literature on hybrid regimes focuses mostly on the nature of electoral contests: the degree of fairness, inclusiveness and meaningfulness of elections. Levitsky and Way (2002) for instance argue that political systems descend into electoral authoritarianism when violations of the minimum criteria for democracy are so serious that they create an uneven playing field. In this book, I focus on the interaction of two variables other than elections to define hybrid regimes. Even though free and fair elections are a necessary condition for democracy, they are not sufficient. As Schmitter and Karl (1991) point out, elections occur intermittently and only offer narrow choices to voters. In between elections, however, the strength of veto players as well as political parties and interest groups has a significant impact on the policy environment. Hybrid regimes are not different from consolidated democracies and authoritarian regimes only by the nature of their electoral contests; they are also different in terms of the level of constraints and competition they provide in between elections.

Hybrid regimes generally provide some limitations on the executive but they lack strong political parties and interest groups that institutionalize and regulate competition.[51] As a result, these regimes witness higher levels of political mobilization and conflict. Compared to authoritarian regimes, the electoral arena is a genuine battleground in the struggle for power. As well, legislatures occasionally become the stage for opposition activity. In some cases, critics of FDI are also found in regional subunits, bureaucratic agencies, and domestic businesses or labor groups on the losing end of the change in regulatory framework or competition that foreign investors bring. Executives often cannot overcome the opposition of state veto players through exclusion and repression because the challenges tend to be formally legal and widely perceived as legitimate. In other words, executives are accountable to some veto players and not insulated from them completely. The greater access to political participation ensured by democratization significantly limits the generosity of the fiscal and financial incentives host governments offer to attract FDI.

---

[51] As discussed in fn.33, it is also possible that some hybrid regimes exhibit some level of political competition but weak executive constraints. In either case, I argue that the investment outcome is the same. The key distinction for hybrid regimes is the fact that they do not have the full insulation or the full accountability that authoritarian regimes and consolidated democracies have, respectively.

Compared to pro-investment groups in consolidated democracies, those in hybrid regimes can also have a hard time reaching consensus among state veto players on the terms of the relationship with foreign investors. Due to weak political parties and interest groups, differences among veto players may not be easily overcome. Consequently, in hybrid regimes political competition can be unrestrained, fluid, and often characterized by recurring, contentious interaction and shifting coalitions (i.e., Arrow's cyclical majorities). Veto players tend to engage in jurisdictional power struggles to the detriment of arriving at compromises. The result can be policy instability, deadlock, and, in most cases, chaos in the investment environment that weakens contract enforcement and property rights protection. Investors encounter arbitrary, conflicting, and aggressive legal and regulatory terms.

Therefore, given similar external pressures from global markets and a desire for FDI, both authoritarian regimes and consolidated democracies are likely to design investment policies that facilitate the flow of significant amounts of foreign investment. On the other hand, hybrid regimes render it problematic for pro-investment executives to overcome opposition to their policies, either in the state or in society. Distinguishing among political regimes in terms of executive constraints and political competition is useful in understanding the relationship between political regimes and the ability to attract FDI. An analysis of the oil investment environment in Azerbaijan, Russia, and Norway provides strong evidence for this relationship.

Can Structural Factors Explain the Attractiveness of Investment Policies?

Before I discuss how political institutions have shaped the investment environments in Azerbaijan, Russia, and Norway, I briefly entertain other possible explanations of why Azerbaijan and Norway were able to create favorable investment environments and therefore attract significant amounts of oil investment, and Russia could not. In explaining this variation, variables such as culture, ideology, prior integration with the world economy, geopolitics, and even country size can provide some background conditions and underlying trends. For instance, the historical, socioeconomic, and cultural development of some countries may make them more open to foreign capital. Positive attitudes toward foreigners may prevent the politicization of investment policies and make it easier for the decision makers to offer attractive terms to foreign investors.

In explaining the stability of the investment environment in Norway, many, for instance, emphasize the egalitarianism, consensus building, and harmony in the Norwegian culture in particular and the Scandinavian culture in general. Historically, lack of an aristocracy, the political mobilization of the peasantry in the nineteenth century and the socialist workers' movement in the twentieth century are seen as factors contributing to this egalitarian tradition in Norwegian society.[52] Many analysts have considered Norway to be a "community system" wherein social divisions are largely neutralized by "overarching sentiments of solidarity."[53]

In addition to the general features of the Norwegian culture, other analysts point out to the strong, traditional elite unity and consensus in order to explain the lack of major disruptive fluctuations in investment policies in Norway.[54] Accordingly, there have been three main elite settlements that have contributed to political and economic stability in Norway since the end of the nineteenth century. The adoption of parliamentarism in 1884 as a strategic move to distance Norway from the colonial governance of Sweden is regarded as the first of these settlements. Subsequent settlements in 1905 and 1945 united Norwegian elites against occupation by Sweden and Germany, respectively, by joining forces to work for national reconstruction. All of these events have significantly contributed to the creation of a basic consensus among the elites about the norms of the Norwegian political system and about the need to avoid strong partisanship.[55] It is argued in general that this tradition of consensus building among political elites is what prevented the politicization of oil issues and thus the unpredictable fluctuations in policy environment.

Finally, there are those who argue that Norway's geographic location and its historical openness to international markets can explain the favorable terms and conditions offered to foreign investors. For instance, Katzenstein (1985) writes that states in small western European and Scandinavian countries have historically been dependent on the international economy to survive and therefore have never been hostile to doing business with the outside world. Being small, Norway has of necessity been heavily involved in foreign trade and exposed to international competitiveness. For instance, some 40 percent of the total output of its goods and services was exported in 1970, and imports exceeded exports by 52

---

[52] Osterud and Selle 2006.
[53] Eckstein 1966, Elder et al. 1988.
[54] Author's interview with Trygve Gulbrandsen (researcher, Institute for Social Science), Oslo, January 22, 2001.
[55] Higley et al. 1976, Fredrik et al. 1999.

percent.[56] In 1990, the value of all Norwegian exports in commodities and services was as much as 44 percent of GNP.[57] Moreover, experience with foreigners at the beginning of the century in developing hydroelectric power and an aluminum industry, in addition to the important maritime sector, gave Norwegians an understanding of the market economy.[58] Hence, it is generally argued that the Norwegian culture, its size and strong economic relations with the outside world historically have created a business mentality that inhibits the politicization of investment issues and enables smooth formulation and implementation of legal, regulatory, and administrative rules governing investment relations with foreigners.

Conversely, many emphasize Russia's cultural uniqueness, its particular history, and geographic size in explaining the inhospitable attitude toward any foreign initiative.[59] The late and partial development of Russian capitalism, the weakness of the prerevolutionary middle class, and the indoctrinization of seventy years of Soviet rule are said to have left Russian citizens distrustful, individualistic, unconcerned with profits, and hostile toward private, especially foreign, enterprises. Russia's history, not just in the Soviet period but going back centuries, has been one of isolation from the West and distrust of the outside world.[60] This is often couched in terms of Russian national interests. The common fear is that Russia will allow itself to be "colonized" by Western investors and give away its national jewels to foreigners. In the extractive industries particularly, it is argued that a residual Marxist mentality engenders a zero-sum game orientation to joint projects, whereby any profit transferred to a foreign company is viewed as a direct loss to a corresponding Russian firm.

This cultural hostility is perhaps best expressed in Russian attitudes toward PSAs. Many argue that adopting an investment regime used by third world countries is embarrassing for Russia, especially because Russians had discovered most of their own oil and gas resources without foreign assistance and were not ready to admit that they may need outside help. Russian oilmen can remember having built a successful,

---

[56] Galenson 1986.

[57] Heidar 2001, 97.

[58] Author's interview with Daniel Heradstveit (professor of international relations in the Norwegian Institute of International Affairs), Oslo, January 17, 2001.

[59] Dyker 1995.

[60] Ogutcu 2002. As discussed in more detail in Chapter 6, Russia had in fact experienced a foreign investment boom prior to World War I, especially in the oil business but the war and the ensuing communist rule brought an end to it.

growing industry and resent being patronized by Western counterparts who, they argue, belittle their achievements.[61] Many also believe that given its significant financial and geostrategic value for the country, oil industry is considered a "commanding height" whose control should not be shared by foreigners. This stiff-necked Russian pride is explained by many as one of the most important obstacles to a friendly investment regime.[62]

In addition, some argue that Russia's sheer geographic size has created a more self-sufficient, inward-looking economy with few incentives to open up to the outside world. Russia's size has also historically created challenges of coordination between the center and the regions. As opposed to a small country, a large country like Russia has numerous gatekeepers, which makes consensus building on even the most basic government policy extremely difficult. According to this logic, the result is an environment where investment policies are highly politicized, decentralized, and uncoordinated.

There may also be geostrategic explanations for why some countries offer exceptional incentives and guarantees for investors and others do not.[63] For instance, in explaining the success of Azerbaijan in creating an attractive investment environment, some have emphasized the geostrategic objectives of the Azeri state.[64] In search of its identity in the aftermath of the Soviet Union's breakup, oil seemed to be the only viable solution to Azerbaijan's economic uncertainties as well as to its geopolitical isolation amidst an increasingly hostile neighborhood. Inviting foreign companies to develop its resources would meet many of Azerbaijan's strategic needs. For one, it would mean creating new alliances to get out of Russia's sphere of influence. In addition, the long-term presence of foreign oil companies could help to resolve the conflict over Nagorno Karabakh and improve the international image of Azerbaijan, which got significantly tarnished by the conflict. With independence, Azerbaijan found itself drawn into a bitter territorial struggle over this predominantly Armenian territory that wanted to secede from Azerbaijan. Soon becoming the main national security concern for this new state, Nagorno Karabakh pitted Azerbaijan against Armenia as well as Russia that was providing military and political support to

---

[61] Watson 1996, 451.
[62] Author's interviews with Richard Freeman (Texaco) and Jamal Quadir (Conoco), Moscow, August 22 and 25, 2000, respectively.
[63] Along similar lines, Loriaux et al. (1997) explain financial liberalization that took place in many countries in the 1980s as a result of their geo-political positions and the "predatory hegemony" of the United States.
[64] Hoffmann 2000.

Armenia. Azerbaijan also faced a critical United States that passed Section 907 of the 1992 Freedom Support Act to single it out as the only Soviet successor state not to receive any direct government assistance from the United States. Allowing foreign companies in its oil industry would mean a significant foreign policy and public relations victory for Azerbaijan.

Another strategic goal of Azerbaijan has been to gain the support of Western governments for its position on the legal status of the Caspian Sea. Compounded by the huge energy reserves lying under its seabed, the Caspian Sea became a lightening rod among the littoral states (Azerbaijan, Iran, Kazakhstan, the Russian Federation, and Turkmenistan) as they tried to legally determine their boundaries. Prior to its breakup, the Soviet Union and Iran relied on several agreements to govern their relationship in the Caspian. After 1991, the number of littoral states increased to include five, making these treaties null and void.[65] The main issue in the debate on the legal status of the Caspian has been whether it is a sea or a lake. Azerbaijan consistently insisted that the Caspian is a sea and that the United Nations Convention on the Law of the Sea should apply to it.[66]

Azeri leaders have also sought to get the support of Western governments in their attempts to diversify pipeline routes to export their oil to world markets. At the time of the breakup of the Soviet Union in 1991, Caspian oil was being transported through two pipelines: from Baku on the Caspian to either the Georgian port of Supsa or the Russian port of Novorossiysk on the Black Sea. From there, it was transported via tankers that had to pass through the increasingly congested Bosphorus Strait in Turkey. To minimize its dependence on Russia, Azerbaijan has been trying to change the region's energy flow from the existing north-south axis toward Russia to an east-west axis toward Europe.[67] In this effort, the Azeri leaders hoped to rely on foreign oil companies and their governments to help build and operate their preferred route, the Baku-Tblisi-Ceyhan (BTC) pipeline, which would start in Baku, Azerbaijan and go through the Georgian capital, Tblisi, all the way to the Mediterrenean Turkish city of Ceyhan, bypassing Russia and the congested Turkish straits.[68]

Given all these geostrategic goals, signing long-term investment contracts with foreign oil companies were in the interest of Azeri leaders. It can be argued that the government's decision to develop the technically challenging offshore deposits in the Caspian and its decision to invite as

[65] Bahgat 2005.
[66] For more information on the legal status of the Caspian, see Bayulgen (2009).
[67] USEIA 2003.
[68] For more information on the pipeline routes from the Caspian, see Bayulgen (2009).

many foreign oil companies as possible to international consortiums are reflective of this desire to marry foreign commercial interests with the geostrategic interests of the government and turn oil into an effective diplomatic currency.[69] Along this line, some argue that even the opposition groups believed that the timely development of Azeri oil and gas resources was a national security issue and that given the difficulties of the transition to a new state and market economy, Azerbaijan had no choice but to open its industry to foreign investment.[70]

These structural and cultural factors certainly shed light on the opportunities, constraints, and challenges that host governments face in their interaction with foreign companies. But by themselves these explanations cannot account for how an attractive investment environment is or is not created. Not only are these explanations partly deterministic but they also do not explain different interests in society, how interests change over time, and what policy outcomes are derived as a result of the interaction among various interest groups. Hence, they tend to ignore how domestic political struggles constrain economic policy and shape state responses to the external environment. They too readily assume that states are unitary actors and that there is consensus about how they should behave given certain geographic, cultural, or historical constraints and opportunities.

An in-depth study of the investment environment in each country reveals that there was in fact very little consensus on attitudes toward foreign investment. In Norway, except during the early years of oil development when the Norwegian society was very skeptical and uncertain about the actual levels of oil resources it possessed, issues related to oil and foreign involvement were extremely politicized. In the early 1970s, with the discovery of the Ekofisk field, oil investment policy became an integral and contested part of Norwegian politics.[71] Groups that historically benefited from economic openness were in favor of foreign investment; others displayed considerable mistrust and suspicion toward foreigners, citing the long foreign domination in the past. The latter believed that industrial growth should be owned and managed by Norwegians,

---

[69] More than 33 companies from 15 countries were invited to take part in the Azerbaijan oil development. The high number of embassies in Baku is proof of the saying 'flag follows trade.'

[70] Vitaly Begliarbekov (Azerbaijan State Oil Company – SOCAR – department manager) interview with the author, Baku, July 15, 1999 and Assim Mollazade (Popular Front Party of Azerbaijan) interview with the author, Baku, July 13, 1999.

[71] The early 1970s was a period of great political upheaval in Norway. The debate over Norwegian membership in the European Community had created an intense questioning of general values and societal goals. This political climate together with the oil crisis of

consistent with their socialist, environmental, or conservationist values.[72] Especially as the country's vulnerability to global oil market fluctuations grew, the nationalistic stance against foreign investment became ever stronger. As will be further discussed in Chapter 7, the role of the state oil company, the rate of oil production, and oil taxation were three principal issues over which fierce political struggles erupted between the proponents and opponents of foreign investment.

Similarly in Russia, the structural constraints discussed above did not produce consensus on negative attitudes toward foreign investment in oil. Although some groups have used cultural, ideological, and geostrategic reasons to oppose foreign investment, others have consistently favored partnerships with foreign companies and supported the adoption of the necessary policies to attract them. Thus, suspicion of Western involvement has not been as widespread as defenders of cultural arguments posit. Rather, opposition to the West depended on the type of investment project being considered and the extent of stakeholder control. When the Western side made finance and technology available to the Russians without seeking to obtain an equity stake in the project for itself, it was normally welcomed with open arms. However, the idea of Western participation in the form of a joint venture or production sharing agreement tended to arouse wariness. Such direct participation was permitted only when there were significant, usually nonfinancial barriers to the independent development of resources by the Russian entity.[73]

Moreover, some argue that the Russian nationalists and communists have used cultural and ideological rhetoric against foreign investment in order not to lose control over the resources that provided them with political and financial leverage.[74] What is more interesting is that the PSAs that these groups so strongly opposed have been also promoted and used by Russian oil companies within and outside Russia. This is a clear sign that

---

1973–74 strengthened interest in the oil industry (Andersen 1993, 98). The period also corresponds to the Labor Party's taking office again.

[72] Many Norwegians saw the attitude of American companies toward labor relations as problematic and as reflective of a "cowboy mentality." Author's interview with Kjell Roland (managing director of the Center for Economic Analysis), Oslo, January 22, 2001.

[73] The Sakhalin projects, for instance, need sophisticated offshore technology that the Russia does not have and they cover fields in a region, which is not an integral part of the country's energy complex. Similarly, the Timan Pechora project requires major investment in transport infrastructure and that is why it was less contentious to use foreign investment in this region.

[74] Author's interview with Glenn Waller (Petroleum Advisory Forum-PAF-), Moscow, May 10, 2001.

opposition to PSAs has been due less to cultural hostility than to political and economic interests. In fact, in late 1998, when the responsibility to prepare the PSA amendments was transferred from the Duma's Natural Resources Committee (headed by a Yabloko deputy) to the Committee on Industry, Construction, and Transportation, which would be headed by someone close to the Communists, PSAs became a "communist issue" and received more support in parliament.[75]

Finally in Azerbaijan, the structural explanations mentioned above assume consensus on a range of issues regarding oil development. In fact, an in-depth analysis of the political discourse demonstrates that the policy objectives of the ruling elite have not been viewed as representative of the interests of the Azeri people in general. The secrecy of negotiations with foreign oil companies; the pace at which oil contracts were signed; the mysterious disappearance of bonus payments to the government at the signing of the contracts; some of the contracts' unfair terms for Azeri employees, and below-average tax rates for oil investors have been some of the complaints voiced by opposition groups continuously.[76] Even though opposition parties have not been completely against foreign investment in principle, they have had serious objections to the terms and procedures of oil agreements, which – if listened to – could have significantly delayed and/or altered the rate and form of FDI.[77]

General conclusions based on culture, ideology, or country size significantly limit our understanding of why some countries are more

---

[75] Author's interview with Vladimir Averchev (former Duma member), Moscow, April 19, 2001.
[76] Ahmedbeili 2005. Magerram Zulfugarov (National Independence Party) during his interview with the author in Baku, July 3, 1999, argued that the terms of the contracts that were signed during the Elchibey presidency were much more advantageous to the Azeri society than the contracts under Aliev. A common argument that is shared by all opposition parties is that the government has squandered oil bonus payments by the investors. They complain that the bonuses are never reported to the parliament and that there are no official documents stating where these bonuses are spent. They all suspect that the bonuses "end up in the pockets of several top officials." Assim Mollazade (Popular Front Party) during his interview with the author also criticized the secrecy of the government in its relations with foreign investors and wondered why the government has been hiding these documents from opposition groups if there was nothing wrong in them for the Azeri society. Moreover, most of the opposition parties believe that the revenues from the first contracts should be used to improve the national oil industry and that Azerbaijan should be able to develop these resources in the future on its own.
[77] Author's interview with opposition party representatives Magerram Zulfugarov and Nazim Imanov of the National Independence Party; Sulhettin Akperov of Musavvat

successful than others in creating attractive investment environments. These explanations, at best, are useful in understanding the preferences and interests of certain groups regarding foreign investment. They do not however take into account the institutional capacity of various actors in either pushing for or resisting pro-investment policies. They cannot inform us about policy outcomes.

In this book, I argue that politics and political institutions, instead of underlying cultural and structural considerations, have been more influential in shaping state responses to foreign capital. Regardless of their disparate backgrounds, governments in all three countries considered here have become convinced of the need to make changes in their investment regimes in order to attract foreign investment. But, despite the similar objectives, outcomes have varied considerably. The issue, then, has not been the existence or absence of the will to adopt investment-inducing policies but the ability of pro-investment groups (most notably the governments) to do so in the face of opposition.

A Comparison of Political Regimes in Azerbaijan, Russia, and Norway

Azerbaijan is a typical example of an unconstrained, uncompetitive political regime. It survives not by including opposition groups in policy making but by excluding them. Even though there is electoral contestation, the regime has many characteristics of "sultanism."[78] Control of the state apparatus is vested in a small group of personally connected individuals, at the core of which sits a presidential clique. The clique consists of the president's most trusted kinsmen, who monopolize the most sensitive and lucrative positions. There are no veto players within the state because the parliament is a symbolic and inchoate institution, and because central and regional state administrations have no voice in policy making. Moreover, societal interests lack the organizational capacity to overcome collective-action problems and resist exclusion by the dominant political

---

Party; Ali Kerimov, Assim Mollazade of the Azerbaijan Popular Front Party; and Mahir Asedov of the Azerbaijan Democratic Party.

[78] According to Linz (2000), a sultanistic regime is a type of authoritarian regime in which "the ruler exercises his power without any restraint at his own discretion and above all unencumbered by rules or by any commitment to an ideology or value system. In many respects the organization of power is similar to traditional patrimonialism as described by Weber (1968). But the lack of constraint derived from tradition and from continuing traditional legitimacy distinguishes it from the historical types of patrimonial rule."

elite. To the extent that there are any interest group organizations, they are either weak and powerless or heavily dependent on the autocratic state. Finally, party organizations are too weak and too detached from society to form policy coalitions and constrain state policies.

This regime has had a profound impact on the ability of Azerbaijan to attract a significant amount of foreign investment in its oil industry during the 1990s. First, the Azeri parliament has rubberstamped every PSA contract into law without discussion or delay, and the bureaucracy had little input to the PSA process. There was not even a Ministry of Energy until June 2001. The near-monopoly role of the state oil company, SOCAR, of which President Heidar Aliev's son was vice president until he himself became the president of Azerbaijan, prevented bureaucratic interference at the higher levels of government and provided policy insulation. This insulation created a conflict-free environment in which political elites operated. With no critical institutional checks coming from the Azeri parliament, bureaucracy, regional administrations, or business groups, the ruling elite has been able to negotiate with foreign investors with the utmost discretion and flexibility. Foreign investors, for their part, have enjoyed the guarantees and incentives provided to them.

Unlike Azerbaijan, Russia was an example of a hybrid political regime in the 1990s. Constraints on the executive were much more effective than in Azerbaijan. Despite President Yeltsin's significant powers in the formulation and execution of policy, the federal and regional legislatures, regional and local governments, and bureaucratic agencies have at times exerted some veto power over executive decisions throughout the 1990s. Adding to this limited pluralism within the state was a lack of strong political parties and interest groups that could effectively represent various societal interests, mediate among state veto players, build policy coalitions, and resolve conflicts among them. The party system lacked institutionalization. Parties' financial and organizational debilities prevented them from mobilizing different interests in society. Their attenuated ties to their constituencies made it difficult to aggregate different interests into policy coalitions and to constrain the behavior of legislators. Severe jurisdictional struggles were commonplace. As a result, divisions among state institutions as well as government ministries and agencies contributed to the chaotic and incoherent policy-making process during the 1990s.

Given this institutional mix and the enormous stakes in the control of oil resources, a PSA regime was presented as the only solution to the oil industry's investment problems. Despite its importance, the PSA issue immediately became what observers have called a "political football." State actors had conflicting interests over the procedures of assigning subsoil rights in the PSAs and the control over PSA tax revenues. The institutional system that assigned veto powers to the parliament as well as to the regional and central bureaucracies made strategies of co-optation or exclusion for the government that championed PSAs less likely. The PSA process, which crystallized the problems associated with the creation of a stable investment environment, failed in Russia due to the weakness of a hybrid regime that gave some power to state-level veto players in the absence of organized societal interests that could keep state actors in check.

Norway, as a contrast, is an example of a consolidated democracy. Its regime over the years has produced a stable investment environment for foreign investors by including opposition groups in the policy-making process and by providing institutional channels of mediation among them. First of all, the parliament, comprising strong, coherent parties, acted as a significant check on the executive branch. Second, regional governments and legislatures exerted important constraints on the government. Even though the country has a unitary political system, power is geographically dispersed. The political system has three levels: the national level (national assembly and state bureaucracy); a regional level (democratically elected assemblies and regional bureaucracies); and local-level municipalities with their own assemblies and bureaucratic administrations. Historically, the central bureaucracy has acted as a strong veto player in the political system. In addition to government ministries, numerous parastatal organizations with different agendas and interests have created a highly competitive policy environment.

Despite these constraints on the executive branch, policy disagreements among state actors have been overcome thanks to strong and coherent political parties and interest groups. In the oil policy arena over the past four decades, the powerful representation of societal interests in the state, such as environmentalists, labor unions and business groups, has pressured the Norwegian decision makers into mediating among different veto players and making compromises during the negotiations over investment policies. The resulting balance of power moderated radical opposition to government policies by emphasizing consensus building and co-optation. As Chapter 7 delineates in more detail, Norwegian decision makers made many compromises to co-opt different veto players into investment policies aimed at attracting investors. One example was the tax reform in 1986 that scaled back the role of the state oil company, abolished the "sliding scale" mechanism of profit distribution, and put in a robust set of safety regulations.

Conclusion

In this chapter I make a theoretical case for why politics and more specifically political institutions matter in explaining the quality of investment environments and to a large extent the resulting FDI patterns. Although the relationship between political regimes and FDI is gaining increasing attention in the literature, the results from various studies provide mixed and inconclusive results. We can, however, overcome this problem by introducing a finer institutional distinction among political regimes based on the level of constraints on the decision makers as well as the degree of political competition in society.

I also provide, in this chapter, a brief analysis of how the three cases in this book fit the theoretical model presented above. I argue that even though variables such as culture, ideology, prior integration with the world economy, the size of reserves, geopolitics, and country size have been useful in understanding the preferences and interests of certain groups in these countries, it is mostly the political institutions that determined the success or failure of these states in creating a favorable investment environment.

The next chapter provides a discussion on how FDI and the revenues that are generated by FDI affect socio-economic and political development. Challenging the unidirectional arguments about the effects of FDI, I emphasize once again the importance of political institutions in disentangling the complex impact of foreign capital, especially in oil-rich countries. The institutional analysis that was presented in this chapter contributes to the literature not only by revealing which political regimes may be more compatible with foreign capital but also by projecting on how these revenues are managed consequently.

4

Curse or Blessing? Effects of FDI on Development

Foreign capital, once invested, can have significant effects on the economic and political development of a host country. Foreign Direct Investment (FDI) and its developmental effects have assumed greater importance in the context of increasing globalization and the likewise increasing discontent with it. There is a significant body of political economy literature that examines the impact of FDI on economic growth, distribution of wealth, governance, social wellbeing, and political structure. Even though determining the exact effects has proven to be remarkably contentious and complicated, one can generally discern two competing approaches. The first sees FDI as having direct and indirect positive effects on a host country economy and as promoting democracy. This neoliberal approach centers on the logic of modernization, which assumes an inherent link between increased economic interdependence, socio-economic development, and democracy. The second approach, influenced by dependency theories, focuses on the negative impacts of foreign capital as retarding economic development and producing significant social and political costs.

In between the benign and malign models of FDI, many studies have started to emphasize that the effects of FDI are neither uniform nor automatic. The UNCTAD World Investment Report (2007), for instance, finds that the direction and intensity of FDI's influence depend on the characteristics of the foreign companies that are involved, the form of their involvement, the international market conditions and commodity prices, among other things. I argue in this book that perhaps equally important, FDI's influence depends on the way governments manage and use these external resources. The type of political institutions matters significantly in shaping and implementing the policies that regulate the relationship between foreign investors and host governments. An analysis of political regimes is useful not just for understanding which countries are more successful in attracting FDI but also for identifying which countries are better at managing foreign capital once it is invested in the economy.

This chapter draws attention to this reverse relationship between FDI and political institutions in understanding the prospects for development. It briefly discusses the literature that outlines the positive and negative effects of FDI on economic and political structures. It pays special attention to the burgeoning literature on the management of oil wealth to depict the direct and indirect role oil-FDI may have on the development of oil-rich societies. Finally, it provides a summary of the experiences of Azerbaijan, Russia, and Norway to demonstrate the effects of diverse political institutions. These cases are discussed in more detail in the chapters that follow.

FDI as a Catalyst for Development

There is widespread belief among policymakers and some scholars that FDI enhances the productivity of host economies and promotes economic development. As one of the main tenants of the Washington Consensus, this belief stems from the observation that FDI provides direct capital financing to governments and the private sector. Especially for large-scale extractive projects, significant amounts of funds are necessary. Oftentimes the governments and/or domestic companies do not have the financial sustainability to undertake such investments. The involvement of foreign investment is one of the ways to overcome financial constraints.[1]

In addition to their financial contributions, foreign investors also bring a bundle of additional assets, in the form of technology, management, and know-how. Through these externalities, FDI inflows can potentially break the vicious cycle of underdevelopment by easing capital, technology, and knowledge constraints in the host economy.[2] They can raise efficiency, improve management, expand output, generate employment and

---

[1] Alternatives for accessing funds, such as borrowing from international financial organizations, are available but they oftentimes generate huge foreign debt for host-country government.
[2] Narula and Portelli 2004, 5.

skills, and increase production and income.[3] Furthermore, they can be valuable for sharing the risks associated with exploration and extraction activities as well as for boosting exports by expanding production and providing access to global markets.

As an extension of this logic, many have also argued that foreign capital plays an important role in promoting political development and improving democracy. Those in the neoliberal tradition declare that foreign capital sows the seeds of democracy by bringing economic growth, increasing the size of the middle class, promoting education and reducing income inequality.[4] Moreover, it is argued that foreign capital has the power to curb discretionary powers of authoritarian governments by disciplining the business environment, cutting patronage, by promoting transparency, accountability, and institution building.[5] Others argue that foreign capital can be an impetus for democratic transition by promoting pluralism and thus changing the composition, vitality and political character of entrepreneurial groups and encouraging capital accumulation in the private sector.[6]

FDI as an Obstacle to Development

Challenging the neoliberal view of FDI, many in the development literature question the positive impact of foreign capital on economic and political development. At the macroeconomic level, various cross-sectional empirical studies have found little support that FDI has an exogenous effect on

---

[3] Caves 1974, Cardoso and Dornbusch 1989, Blomstrom 1990, Gillis et al. 1996, Djankov and Hoekman 1999, UNCTAD 2007.

[4] See Schumpeter 1950, Held 1992, Weitzman 1993, Lipset 1994, Bhagwati 1994, Muller 1995.

[5] See Lindblom 1982, Mahon 1995, Stallings 1995, Frieden and Rogowski 1996, Block 1996, Henry 1996, 1998, Winters 1996, Maxfield 1997, De Soysa 2003. A seminal contribution to this idea has been put forth by Hirschman (1978) in which he outlines the role of "movable property" as a restraint on the government's freedom of maneuver by checking on despotic and predatory rule. Maxfield (1997) provides another good example of the need to make institutional changes to get credit and investment from international investors. She proposes an investor-signaling model of central bank interdependence according to which governments cede authority to central banks in order to signal their creditworthiness. Frieden and Rogowski (1996) also depict the pressures exerted on governments in regard to trade policies. They argue that as transaction costs decline, governments face increasing pressures from internationally oriented sectors to liberalize trade. The prospective winners of trade press for institutional reforms that reduce access to groups seeking exemptions.

[6] See Chaudry 1997, Henry 1998.

economic growth.[7] Their findings indicate that local conditions, such as the development of local financial markets, the educational level of citizens, the level of human capital and the physical infrastructure, play an important role in allowing the positive effects of FDI to materialize.[8] The argument is that host countries cannot capture the full benefits associated with FDI until a threshold level of capabilities is achieved. These studies emphasize that the positive spillover effects that neoliberals attribute to FDI are found mostly in advanced economies.

Especially the adherents of dependency school have argued that FDI in developing countries could in fact lower domestic savings and investment by extracting rents and siphoning off capital through preferred access to local capital markets. Several case studies of FDI in manufacturing or extractive industries have shown that the operations of foreign companies support a small oligarchy of indigenous partners and suppliers, driving other domestic producers out of business.[9] According to this argument, foreign companies' tight control over technology, higher management techniques and export channels prevent spillovers to local businesses, create monopolies, and increase the level of inequality in host countries.

Dependency theorists have also repeatedly pointed out to the antidemocratic effects of FDI. Accordingly, in competing for foreign capital, governments design policies that benefit foreign investors at the expense of ordinary people. Some see this as dependent development which creates a particular transnational class coalition, a "triple alliance" between state elites, foreign firms and local firms, all of whom share a common interest in rapid capital accumulation.[10] Others regard this as governments losing their capacity and willingness to provide for welfare programs.[11] It is often argued that this change in the priorities and capacity of governments has the potential to affect the process and quality of democracy in two ways: (1) by weakening the accountability and responsiveness of

---

[7] Borensztein et al. 1998, Xu 2000, Saggi 2000, Zhang 2001, Carkovic and Levine 2002, Alfaro et al. 2003, Hermes and Lensink 2003, and Durham 2004.
[8] Narula and Portelli, 2004, 9.
[9] See Cardoso 1973, Evans 1979, Bennett and Sharpe 1983.
[10] The "new wave" of dependency theory provides multiple examples of how foreign capital causes distortions in the political system of host countries. Dependency theorists who developed their thinking primarily with reference to the large Latin American NICs share many basic assumptions with writers on imperialism, proponents of a world-systems perspective, and some structuralist theories of international political economy. For a more detailed description of the main tenets of this theory, see Haggard (1990).
[11] See Gill 1995, Sassen 1996, Cox 1996, Rodrik 1997, Cammack 1998, Diamond 1999.

elected officials to citizens and (2) by leading to social unrest and thus the radicalization of the political discourse as a result of the ensuing income inequality and class polarization from the neglect of social programs. The rise of antidemocratic groups may, in turn, encourage weak governments to resort to authoritarian and repressive measures in order to contain challenges to the regime, which dramatically weakens the legitimacy of the regime and the quality of democracy.[12]

FDI in Oil

In developing their natural resources, many countries often face constraints with respect to capital, technical and managerial capabilities and access to markets and distribution channels. By enabling and boosting production, foreign companies can help overcome these constraints and influence the overall economic performance of the host country in terms of its macroeconomic stability, growth, and income distribution. However, the role of FDI in development is compounded in extractive industries, and especially in the oil sector, by the linkages between natural resource dependence, poor economic performance, poverty, bad governance, conflict, and authoritarianism. While it would be wrong to assert that many of the underlying determinants of economic and political performance of oil-rich countries are directly related to FDI, the involvement of foreign companies in the oil industry may hamper the achievement of various development objectives by accelerating a vicious circle of negative results. There can be significant drawbacks to FDI presence in oil-rich countries related to their ownership and control over production and revenues, limited local procurement and linkages as well as the unequal bargaining power of host-country governments vis-à-vis the foreign companies. By their mere presence, they may directly or indirectly support or strengthen the existing order.

   In order to understand the possible effects of oil-FDI on development, first it is necessary to discuss the consequences of oil-led development in general. There is an extensive body of literature that provides evidence to the "curse" that oil dependence brings to oil-rich countries. The experiences of most of these countries illustrate that in the economy, oil-led development generates slower growth than expected, barriers to economic diversification, high levels of poverty, inequality and unemployment, and poor social

---

[12] See O'Donnell 1994, Haggard and Kaufman 1995, Muller 1995, Cox 1996, Martin and Schumann 1997.

welfare performance. Moreover, oil-dependent countries tend to witness exceptionally poor governance, high corruption, a culture of rent-seeking behavior, as well as high incidences of conflict and societal tensions. Finally, oil dependence is argued to have significant effects on political structures. Many believe that oil and democracy do not generally mix and that there is a robust and statistically significant relationship between oil dependence and authoritarianism given the exceptional rents accrued and the ways these rents are spent. I develop each of these arguments in some detail below.

Oil Dependence and the Economy: Dutch Disease and Resource Curse

The literature on rentier states, or more specifically petro-states,[13] overwhelmingly asserts that there is a negative relationship between natural-resource-based exports and economic growth.[14] The argument is that a high degree of energy dependence usually creates serious structural problems in the economies of oil-rich countries – also known as the "Dutch disease."[15] Typically in the first stage of this disease, as the rents flow into the economy, national currency becomes very strong in relation to the U.S. dollar. Imports then become cheaper, and local products become more expensive and noncompetitive in international markets. The result is that most branches of the national economy, other than the booming mineral sector and nontradable sectors such as retail trade, services, and construction, soon deteriorate. The move to the nontradable sector accelerates domestic inflation. The reduced competitiveness in agriculture and manufacturing crowds out other productive sectors and makes the diversification of the economy particularly difficult. The decline of the manufacturing industry also retards economic growth by decreasing the demand for and supply of skilled labor.

Moreover, such dependence on oil rents may cause the economy to become vulnerable to changes in world oil prices as they go through

---

[13] According to Karl (1997), petro-states can be considered a special subset of mining states. The main characteristics shared by all petro-states are (1) dependence on a single, depletable resource that is capable of generating extraordinary rents and (2) state's ability to capture those rents.

[14] Gelb 1988, Shams 1989, Auty 1993, Mikesell 1997, Sachs and Warner 1999, Auty 2001, Auty and De Soysa 2006.

[15] This phenomenon is called the "Dutch Disease" because it was first identified when the Netherlands became a major exporter of natural gas in the late 1950s. The classic model describing Dutch disease was first developed by Corden and Neary (1982). For an extensive analysis of the negative economic effects of oil revenues, see Gelb (1986).

cyclical booms and busts. This volatility is partly due to the fact that natural resources typically have low price elasticities of supply. Any significant drop in oil prices leads to a sharp decline in government revenues and exerts a strong negative influence on budgetary discipline and control of public financing. Extreme volatility of oil prices also increases the incentive for excessive borrowing, leading to huge debt burdens during the bust period. Finally, despite increasing government revenues, oil development typically does not improve the job market since energy development projects are technology- and capital-intensive and require only a few qualified engineers and workers after the initial construction period. Furthermore, the productive linkages between this sector and the rest of the economy tend to be weak and so opportunities for technology diffusion are very limited. Together, all of these factors slow growth, limit the diversification of the economy away from oil dependence, and produce what is known as the "resource curse."

Oil Dependence and State Capacity: The Rentier State

In addition to weakening the economy and making it vulnerable to global price fluctuations, oil windfalls can also change the structure and capacity of states to govern effectively.[16] Oil dependence is found to skew the institutional development of the state because oil rents weaken accountability and restraint. First, thanks to easy oil rents, oil states do not have to build the institutional capacities to extract resources from their populations. As such they are denied the incentives for innovation within a civil service. Second, due to the centralization of oil rents in the state (especially a weak state), rent-seeking behavior increases, the state gets captured by special interests and the public sector looses the cohesiveness and authority necessary to exercise effective public policy. State actors focus on capturing the resource rents rather than on wealth creation and favor the development of institutions geared toward rent seeking rather than entrepreneurship. Third, the availability of easy and direct rents makes government elites and their supporters who benefit from these rents reluctant to introduce reforms that can empower new groups and threaten the status quo.[17] This is most evident in the drastic decline in the

---

[16] Leite and Weidmann 1999, Ross 1999, Auty 2001.
[17] These elites do in some cases introduce reforms that are mostly tailored to foreign investors because of the need for Western capital and expertise to jump-start the energy development. As energy resources become more developed, however, one would expect to see

ability of these governments to enforce tax collection and maintain even minimal levels of public services and social welfare protections. In these societies, tax authorities are often disbanded or weakened since they appear to be no longer necessary. Moreover, despite available resources, governments spend less and less on health care and education. In addition to causing an inability to reform, oil rents also allow incapable, incompetent state institutions to endure and ineffective policies to persist.

Perhaps one of the most obvious characteristics of rentier states is their extraordinarily high levels of corruption. Exceptional levels of profit associated with oil extraction increase the temptations for abuse and weakens restraint. The extent of corruption and weak governance deforms policy choices and results in high levels of poverty, and weak development indicators for these societies despite the availability of resources. Where huge oil rents are present, officials tend to favor larger public sectors with overly excessive regulatory interventions that enhance opportunities for rent-seeking. Unproductive infrastructural projects (also known as "white elephants") and defense projects are generally favored over health and education expenditures, thereby reducing the quality of public services as well as lowering the quality of public infrastructure.[18]

Oil Dependence and Conflict: Petro-Violence and Social Unrest

Several studies have also found a strong link between dependence on natural resources and the risk of inter- as well as intra-state conflicts.[19] "Point resources," such as mineral deposits, are potentially easier to monopolize so struggles to control them are more likely to be zero-sum. Concentrated rents are likely to give rise to greater polarization and fiercer, more contracted control struggles.[20] Hence, oil revenues, given high profit margins, can be the main catalyst for going to war. Similarly, they can fund and prolong conflicts that break out for various other reasons, especially during times of economic crises. Wars are expensive to pursue and oil rents can be used both by governments and rebel groups to finance their

---

reform incentives weaken. For more information on how availability of resource rents influences a government's propensity to liberalize, see Dalmazzo and Blasio (2001). Also for a comparison of reform progress between energy-rich and energy-poor countries of the former communist states, see Esanov et al. (2001).

[18] Karl 2007.

[19] Collier and Hoeffler 1998, Wantchekon 1999, De Soysa 2000, Collier and Hoeffler 2005, Snyder 2006.

[20] Tompson 2005.

armies. Some studies have found secessionist wars to be statistically more significant in oil exporters than in non-oil exporters. Many of the violent civil wars in the developing world, such as the ones that took place in Algeria, Angola, Indonesia/Aceh, Yemen, the Sudan, Nigeria, Iraq and the Republic of Congo are examples of petro-violence.

Oil revenues and the high expectations that are associated with it can also trigger social unrest, if not an outright war. The discovery of oil in poor countries initially gives the citizens a sense of entitlement and rising expectations that they will be able to benefit from the oil windfall and overcome poverty that has constrained them for so long. However, as discussed before, oil profits also increase the rent seeking incentives and behavior in a society that does not have strong institutions to reign in the greed and corruption and to allocate the wealth of the nation equally and fairly. The resulting income inequality and the perception of unfair distribution of oil profits can in turn contribute significantly to social tensions and unrest.

Oil Dependence and Political Regime: Authoritarian Curse

Lastly, the rentier state literature extensively demonstrates how dependence on a resource that is capable of generating extraordinary rents also reinforces authoritarian tendencies by concentrating state power in the hands of a few ruling elites.[21] Michael Ross (2001) in his seminal article discusses the three reasons for why oil has antidemocratic effects. He calls the first one the "rentier effect," which suggests that resource-rich governments use low tax rates and patronage to relieve pressures for greater accountability. Because they live from oil rents rather than direct taxation, they are likely to tax their populations less or not at all. As a result, they are unaccountable to their population and their populations are less likely to demand representation in government; hence the idea: no taxation, no representation. Moreover, oil wealth increases spending on patronage, and the state buys political consensus through the distribution of rents. The use of the resource for patronage tends to result in a politically motivated expansion of the state bureaucracy as well as in the creation of a social constituency with a vested interest in the status quo.

The second effect, according to Ross, is the "repression effect," where resource wealth retards democratization by enabling governments to boost their funding for internal security. In order to retain control over

---

[21] See Mahdavy 1970, Hughes 1975, Delacroix 1980, Gelb 1986, Shafer 1994, Chaudry 1997, Karl 1997, Ross 2001, Jensen and Wantchekon 2004, Ulfelder 2007.

resources and prevent opposition groups from getting access to it, states spend much more money and a greater percentage of their revenues on their military and security forces. Increased repression and militarization help further consolidate and entrench authoritarian regimes. Some have found that oil wealth is robustly associated with regime durability.[22] Higher levels of oil rents translate into higher levels of support for incumbent politicians, making political change very difficult.[23]

Finally, Ross discusses the "modernization effect, which holds that growth based on the export of oil and minerals fails to bring about the social and cultural changes that tend to produce democratic government."[24] Because of the concentration of enormous capital and technological resources, foreign companies become a dominant social force and create huge entry barriers for the domestic entrepreneurial class. The special advantages enjoyed by foreign companies leave few opportunities for domestic capitalist class to develop on their own. Thus, instead of strengthening the middle class, which is considered an agent of democratization, oil-related economic growth creates a privileged elite group that is dependent on oil rents and the political power arrangements that distribute them through patronage. Oil dependence also compromises the formation of broad-based urban working class. Because oil employs relatively few workers with high skill levels, dependence on oil fosters a type of labor aristocracy which in turn provides little in the way of holding the government accountable and demanding representation.

Prior Political Institutions

Whether or not oil revenues and the participation of foreign companies in generating those revenues have pernicious effects on the socioeconomic and political development of oil-rich states depends on the quality of government policies and institutions that accumulate, manage, and allocate these resources in the first place.[25] Despite the assumptions of the neoliberal and dependency theories, neither FDI nor oil

---

[22] Smith 2004.
[23] Jensen and Wantchekon 2004.
[24] Ross 2001, 326.
[25] In the literature, some also point out that poor policy performance may actually have been caused not by resource abundance but instead by the structures of ownership and control that resource-rich countries often choose for their sectors (Ross 1999, Luong and Weinthal 2001, 2006, Auty 2004).

as a commodity has automatic, unidirectional effects on development. Their effects are mediated by the choices that politicians make and the strategies they use within a certain institutional framework. Host country politics is crucial in shaping the relationship between foreign investors and various domestic stakeholders, influencing the behavior of foreign investors and determining how the resource rents will be distributed. There are an increasing number of studies that examine various government strategies in using and distributing resource wealth and their effects but very few of them shed light on the institutional origins of those choices and strategies.[26] The analysis in this book starts to illuminate some of the ways in which political institutions prior to the infusion of foreign capital shape the way oil revenues are managed later on.

The most positive outcomes for resource development and management have been achieved in countries with well-functioning institutions.[27] In consolidated democracies, given the institutional constraints on government and the intense competition by political parties and interest groups, FDI and the accruing oil revenues have the potential to increase national and individual wealth, generate employment, provide extensive social services to meet the needs of the current and future generations, and increase the legitimacy of the democratic regime by strengthening its accountability and representative functions. In authoritarian regimes, on the other hand, given the lack of executive constraints and political competition, FDI and oil revenues have the potential to lead to a weak and vulnerable economy, poor and inadequate social services, a corrupt and unprofessional government, huge societal disparities and an entrenched authoritarian regime. A weak institutional structure limits the ability of these regimes to reap the potential benefits from the entry and operation of foreign investors. Finally, the effects of FDI and oil wealth tend to be negligible in hybrid regimes due to the fact that – as argued in the previous chapter – such regimes have a harder time attracting FDI and/or pursuing effective oil development strategies. In order to compete for and attract foreign investment, however, hybrid regimes tend to move towards either more authoritarianism or more democracy, with the respective consequences discussed above.

---

[26] See Collier and Hoeffler 1998, 2005, Wantchekon 1999, De Soysa 2000, Ross 2001, Bagirov et al. 2003, Smith 2004, Jensen and Wantchekon 2004, Snyder 2006.
[27] UNCTAD 2007, 153.

A Comparison of Azerbaijan, Norway, and Russia

The Azeri case is illustrative of the negative effects of FDI and oil revenues on development. It demonstrates how an authoritarian regime that has been successful in attracting FDI cannot use the oil wealth to create a strong and diversified economy that meets the needs of all its citizens. As will be further discussed in Chapter 5, the Azeri case shows how easy access to oil rents in an authoritarian regime reduces the ability and willingness of the government to maintain even minimal levels of public services and social welfare protections. For instance, in terms of the amount of government expenditures on health care and public education, Azerbaijan for more than a decade has performed very poorly even when its revenue streams increased thanks to oil and gas exports. Moreover, an abundance of petrodollars in government hands has been increasing the incentives for rent-seeking behavior and corruption, leading to huge disparities in income and consequently intense popular dissatisfaction. Various international corruption indices rank Azerbaijan nearly at the bottom of all countries in terms of level of corruption. Even the Special Oil Fund of Azerbaijan (SOFAZ), which was set up by a presidential decree to manage the oil wealth and to avoid the negative experience of other petro-states, lacks formal and clear operating rules, and gives the president the sole authority to use the funds.[28] Finally, FDI in oil has contributed to further strengthening of the authoritarian regime by directly providing Aliev and his ruling clique a certain degree of legitimacy and indirectly by generating additional resources for them to suppress the opposition groups and buy off supporters through patronage networks. FDI in Azerbaijan has clearly deepened the oil curse.

The Norwegian case, on the other hand, is regarded by many as one of the best examples of resource management. Thanks to its already mature democratic institutions and practices prior to the development of oil resources, Norway was able to set up an equitable, transparent, accountable, and ethical framework for managing its oil wealth. Today, its Oil Fund is considered the world's largest retirement fund, which uses strict ethical guidelines in its investment decisions and saves considerable amount of revenue for its future generations. The Norwegian democracy was also able to transform the influx of oil revenues into an ever expanding system of social services and welfare, including education, medical care, and child and elder care. Guided by democratic

---

[28] Bagirov et al. 2003, 108.

principles and respect for human rights, the Norwegian political system has also used oil revenues to further its humanitarian mission in the world and become a respected international player. Finally, as opposed to the democracy-impeding effects of foreign capital in Azerbaijan, in a consolidated democracy like Norway economic success brought on by the inflow of foreign capital has increased the legitimacy of decision makers and strengthened the foundations of the democratic welfare state. Foreign capital in this context has had a positive effect on the further consolidation of democracy.

To sum up, even though Azerbaijan and Norway both had success in creating the favorable conditions for investment and attracting significant amounts of FDI, they differed dramatically in the way they have made use of foreign capital and the oil wealth generated from the development of their resources. Their nearly polar opposite regimes have provided these countries with different constraints and opportunities and thus different resource management strategies.

What is similar in these two cases is that FDI seems to have had a "reinforcing effect" on the political regime. The success of attracting significant amounts of foreign capital into the economy has strengthened and consolidated the existing regime regardless of its nature. Foreign capital has not only provided additional resources to state coffers but also gave control and/or legitimacy to the ruling regime.

The comparison of Azerbaijan and Norway contributes specifically to our understanding of rentier states. In the literature the general assumption is that oil rents – through the 3 effects mentioned above – impede democratic development. As some scholars have also acknowledged, this assumption is not always empirically substantiated. Karl (1997), for instance, emphasizes the salience of institutional settings prior to the flow of oil rents. She argues that "stateness" is a crucial determinant of how oil rents will affect domestic politics. Challenging the determinism in the rentier state literature, she contends that oil profits do not necessarily always make a state more rent seeking and authoritarian. Even though she emphasizes the importance of certain political variables – such as a professional bureaucracy, effective courts and regulatory institutions – in mitigating the antidemocratic effects of oil rents, she falls short of providing a causal model for why political effects of oil rents are different across oil-rich countries.[29] In this book I argue that FDI deepens

[29] Similarly, Ross (2001) in his analysis of the political effects of oil rents fails to account for prior political regimes. Just like Karl (1997), he acknowledges the variation in political

the resource curse in political regimes that are already authoritarian. In mature democracies, on the other hand, FDI can lessen the detrimental effects of oil on development and in fact help strengthen the economic and democratic foundations of the regime by providing funding and legitimacy to government policies.

Finally, the Russian case provides an interesting case study of how FDI and oil revenues affect prospects for development in a hybrid regime. As discussed before, Russia in the 1990s could neither attract much FDI nor realize its oil potential effectively given the partial executive constraints and political competition that its hybrid regime produced. As a result, effects of FDI on Russia's development – either negative or positive – have been negligible. Even though Russia has largely been able to avoid the negative impact of oil rents during this period, it is very difficult – if not impossible – to discern the exact impact of FDI, or lack thereof. The irony is that Russia's move to a more authoritarian regime in the 2000s made it successful in terms of attracting FDI but seems to have hurt its chances of using oil resources for the benefit of the society and democracy. In recent years with the oil industry increasingly captured and dominated by the state, Russia has been witnessing slightly more corruption and restrictions on the political freedoms of its citizens. Essentially, it has moved closer to the Azeri model of resource management, with similar consequences on development.

Conclusion

An analysis of the institutional structure in a country helps us understand whether or not that country can create an investment environment that is stable and/or flexible enough to attract foreign investors. Such an analysis also informs us about how foreign investment affects economic and political development in that country. This book contributes to that extensive debate about the connections between FDI and development, as well as between oil and development, by calling attention to the missing variable of political institutions.

To that end, in this chapter I started out with an overview of the literature on the economic and political effects of FDI as well as oil dependence.

responses to oil rents but explains it with differences in per capita income. Results of his empirical test demonstrate that "large oil discoveries appear to have no discernible antidemocratic effects in advanced industrialized states, such as Norway, Britain, and the United States, but may harm or destabilize democracy in poorer countries" (Ross 2001, 333).

In sorting out the conflicting causal theories in the literature, I offered the logic of focusing on the prior institutional setting. I finally concluded the chapter with a brief comparison of the developmental effects of oil-FDI in Azerbaijan, Russia and Norway. What follows in the next three chapters is a more in-depth analysis of each case.

5

Azerbaijan: One-Stop Shopping

Since the collapse of the Soviet Union, most of the former Soviet republics have been striving to become part of the global economy as new sovereign states. Among these states, Azerbaijan's performance in terms of attracting foreign investment has been the most impressive. According to the UNCTAD (2006), Azerbaijan has shown an "above potential" investment performance in more than a decade of its independence. In terms of the inward Foreign Direct Investment (FDI) performance index, of approximately 140 countries, Azerbaijan ranked the third highest during 1994–1996 and eighth highest during 1998–2000.[1] FDI constituted approximately 65 percent of gross fixed capital formation in Azerbaijan between 1995 and 1999.[2] Since the "contract of the century" in September 1994, Azerbaijan signed more than twenty oil contracts with 33 companies from 15 countries.[3] According to some accounts, in the 1990s it has attracted the most FDI per capita of any state in the former Soviet Union.[4] It was soon dubbed by many as the former Soviet Union's "showcase" for the art of doing business, the "frontier of global capitalism," and a "united nations of oil."[5]

The untapped oil and gas reserves of Azerbaijan – onshore and offshore in the Caspian Sea region – certainly explain the initial interest of international oil companies. Azerbaijan has approximately 7 billion barrels of proven oil reserves (with additional *possible* reserves at 32 billion

---

[1] UNCTAD 2002a, Azerbaijan was ranked the highest in 2004 (UNCTAD 2006).
[2] UNCTAD 2001.
[3] USEIA 2006.
[4] Wagstyl 2000.
[5] Goldberg 1998, 57.

barrels) and 30 billion barrels of proven gas reserves (with additional possible reserves at 35 billion barrels).[6] These figures represent 0.6 and 0.8 percent of the world's oil and gas supply, respectively, making Azerbaijan almost on par with Norway in terms of oil and gas potential (0.8 and 1.3 percent, respectively).[7]

Another apparent reason for the high levels of FDI in Azeri oil is the U.S. geostrategic interest in the Caspian Sea region. In the aftermath of the Cold War and 9/11, the United States has seen the development of these resources as part of its national security objectives. To bolster the newly independent states in this region against the hegemony of Russia and to isolate Iran in the new balance of power emerging in Eurasia, the U.S. government has encouraged U.S.-based oil companies to heavily invest in the region. In addition, more recently the war on terrorism has made foreign investment more of a strategic tool for the United States to win allies in the region. Finally, investments in the Caspian Sea region were encouraged to help the United States counterbalance its excessive dependence on the Middle East, diversify its resources and ensure energy security. As Ian Bremmer rightly asserted, in the post-Cold War era, the Soviet Union has been eclipsed by the Caspian basin as an American strategic priority.[8]

Although Azerbaijan's attractive natural resource endowment and the U.S. government's geostrategic considerations are possible explanations for the high levels of FDI in Azerbaijan, they cannot by themselves account for the Azerbaijani government's impressive FDI performance in the past decade. First, oil companies do not necessarily base their investment decisions on the geostrategic calculations of the home governments.[9] Before companies decide to invest in a certain region, they consider and weigh in many commercial risks involved.

---

[6] USEIA 2006, BP 2006. Possible reserves are less precisely quantified than proven reserves and are defined by USEIA (2006) as including other reserves found through extensions, divisions, and new discoveries.

[7] BP 2006. Azerbaijan's oil reserves are expected to last for roughly thirty years. Production is expected to peak around 2010. According to (Bagirov et al. 2003, 102) after 2012, unless new reserves are discovered, a rapid decline will drop production to a quarter of the peak level by 2024.

[8] Bremmer 1998.

[9] During his interview with the author, Gerald Tilk (Economy/Energy Officer in United States Embassy in Baku), Baku, July 6, 1999, pointed out that there is much tension between oil companies and the U.S. government. He argued that companies make strictly commercial decisions – at times at the expense of the objectives of the U.S. government – because they are accountable to their shareholders. They see it as a matter of economics rather than politics. Their decisions to invest depend on the existence of markets, competition and the investment environment.

Second, even though the Caspian region is a prospective oil province and companies need to secure a share of it to diversify their assets, commercially it has not been an easy place to do business in the 1990s. Oil investors faced many exploration and transportation challenges especially during low oil prices. For one, industry sources have cited several drilling disappointments in the Caspian, particularly in the Azeri sections, casting doubt on the commercial attractiveness of the region.[10] Moreover, the landlocked geography of the Caspian Sea required the construction of new pipelines that would pass through some contested, unstable territories, increasing significantly the risks of investing in this region. For instance, since 1988, Azerbaijan has been engaged in a bitter territorial dispute with Armenia over the latter's claim to the Azerbaijani area of Nagorno-Karabakh. The conflict grew into a full-scale war and resulted in the occupation of over 17 percent of Azerbaijan's territory, the death of thousands of people and the dislocation of almost a million people from their homes. Even though military actions have stopped with a 1994 ceasefire agreement, the unresolved, frozen conflict between the two countries and the risk of resumption of hostilities create significant uncertainties for the oil companies.[11] These risks add significantly to the cost of production and put the Caspian oil at a disadvantage compared to oil regions elsewhere.[12] For instance, while oil in Saudi Arabia can be produced for less than US$3 a barrel, the transport costs of Caspian oil would mean that oil companies would need about US$13 a barrel to make a profit from their Caspian oil exports.[13] Finally, the dispute over the legal ownership of the Caspian Sea has made the initiation and development of oil projects quite risky for investors.[14]

The interesting question, then, is given these commercial costs and risks, why did foreign oil companies continue to show interest in the Azerbaijani oil industry? In other words, what other factors counterbalanced these risks and allowed the region to still be attractive for foreign companies? In this chapter, I argue that the ability of the political regime to create a flexible investment regime was what kept investors in

---

[10] Manning 2000, Rasizade 2005.

[11] For instance, despite the fact that it is one of the most secure pipelines in the world (as it is buried under ground), as the main export route of the Azeri oil, the Baku-Tblisi-Ceyhan (BTC) is often threatened by various terrorist organizations.

[12] For a detailed analysis of "pipeline politics" in the Caspian region; see Goble 1995, Roberts 1996, Forsythe 1996, Ebel 1997, and Ruseckas 1998.

[13] Manning 2000, 18. According to others, such as Ebel 2003 and Rasizade 2005, a price of at least US$20 is needed to justify overall Caspian investment.

[14] For more information on the legal status of the Caspian Sea, see Feifer 2002, Lelyveld 2002, Askari 2003, Rasizade 2005, Bahgat 2005, and USEIA 2007.

Azerbaijan. The geostrategic interests of the U.S. government in addition to the commercial interests of the companies emphasize the external actors' incentives more than the ability of the Azeri government to create an attractive investment environment. Not every country with significant amounts of oil resources is able to attract foreign investment. Even though there are also many cultural and strategic explanations of why Azeri leaders have been willing to open their oil industry to foreign investment (as discussed in Chapter 3), I argue that the ability to realize these objectives depended mostly on the characteristics of the political regime.

In this chapter, first I briefly discuss the history of oil development in Azerbaijan and the relations between the government and foreign companies. Then I analyze the characteristics of the Azerbaijani political regime that made the investment environment attractive for foreign oil companies. Finally, I turn to the implications of foreign capital and the accruing oil revenues for economic and political development of Azerbaijan and I emphasize the role of political institutions in managing these vast resources.

History of Relations between Investors and the Government

The Nineteenth Century

The history of oil in Azerbaijan is long and rich. In the thirteenth century, Marco Polo reported hearing of a substance that came from the ground near Baku and that was "good to burn."[15] By the early nineteenth century, a small oil industry had developed in Azerbaijan. In 1806 there were 50 oil wells, by the middle of 1860s, the number had reached 218. The first oil well to be drilled in Azerbaijan took place in the Bibi-Heybat field in 1844, eleven to twelve years earlier than those drilled in the United States. In 1873, Baku's true oil rush began when the first gusher occurred on this field. This was the oil boom that made Baku the world's most productive oil province by the turn of the century.[16]

At the end of the nineteenth century, Baku became the center of attention for foreign investors. A large refining industry had also sprung up to turn crude oil into kerosene. In addition, the completion of the Baku-Batumi railroad in 1883 connected Baku to world oil markets. During the 1870s and 1880s, the Rothschild family and Nobel brothers financed the oil industry in Baku. By 1883, the Nobels owned half of Baku's oil

[15] Yergin 1998, 50–51.
[16] Ibid.

exports. At the same time, Russian and Armenian companies started to play an important role in the Baku oil business. Baku was the primary oil source of the Russian empire. In 1890, 97.7 percent of Russian oil came from Baku.[17] Azerbaijan was the first in the world in the total amount of oil produced from 1899 to 1901, extracting 100.9 million tons per year, more than half of the world's production. Annual oil production in the United States at the time amounted to only 9.1 million tons.[18]

Soon, however, oil production in Azerbaijan started to decline. Around the revolutionary year of 1905, strikes, ethnic conflict, and general chaos in the Tsarist Russia engulfed Baku. Exports were cut off and the local oil industry quickly lost its momentum. Between 1904 and 1913, Baku went from supplying 31 percent of the world's petroleum exports to less than 8 percent.[19] Even as, there was still enough attraction to Azeri oil, especially from the Germans during World War I. Germans came all the way up to Georgia in June 1918, but the war ended before they could reach Baku.

The Soviet Period

After an abbreviated period of Azerbaijani independence (1918–1920), the Soviet state took control of the Azeri lands in 1920. With the takeover, the oil industry immediately became nationalized. Stalin abolished all joint ventures with foreign oil companies. Azeri oil, however, did not lose any of its significance. Seeing oil as crucial to fueling economic growth, the Soviet government increased the production levels to a record-high 23.4 million tons and built a new pipeline to export oil to the West. During this period, Baku became the center for production of oil equipment in the USSR.[20]

The World War II turned Baku once again into a prize for the Germans as Hitler became preoccupied with gaining control over its oil fields. Fearing a German victory in the Caucasus, the Soviet state ordered much of the region's infrastructure to be dismantled and sent north and east to the more secure Volga-Urals region, which geologists had identified as a promising oil province. They called the region the "second Baku." Equipment, factories, skilled personnel, and even the Baku-Batumi pipeline were moved to Tatarstan and Bashkiria, where they provided the basis for postwar oil boom.[21] "With the discovery of various other fields, such as those in

[17] Nassibli 1999.
[18] Yusifzade 1999, 63.
[19] Ibid., 50.
[20] The first oil-industry machine-building works, now known as Sattarkhan Works, was founded in Azerbaijan in 1922.
[21] Yergin 1998, 51.

western Siberia in mid 1960s, the percentage of the Azeri contribution to
total Soviet oil production dropped from 71.6 percent in 1940 to 2.4 percent in 1980. In terms of output, oil production declined from 21 million
tons during 1964 to 13 million tons in subsequent years."[22] Because of the
impoverishment of the oil fields onshore, the Soviet government started
to extract oil in the Azerbaijani sector of the Caspian Sea in the 1940s.
Despite the decrease in oil production, Azerbaijan remained the center of
production of oil industry machinery in the Soviet Union. Baku was also
famous in this period for training petroleum engineers and conducting
petroleum research. The city was called the "Oil Academy."[23]

The relaxation of foreign economic relations during Gorbachev's perestroika opened the doors of Baku oil to foreign investors once again.
Initial attention of foreign companies was on three untapped offshore
deposits: Chirag, Azeri, and Gunesli in the Caspian Sea bed off Baku. In
January 1991, the Azerbaijani Republic issued a decree soliciting bids for
the exploration of the three fields and in June a consortium was formed
under the leadership of Amoco to develop them.[24]

Oil in a New State

With the independence of the Azeri republic from the collapsing Soviet
Union in October 1991, a new era in Azeri oil began. The disintegration of the union led to a breakdown of the all-union Soviet market,
which had negative repercussions for the economy in Azerbaijan as well
as in the other newly independent states. Disruption of trade links was,
in fact, a principal reason for the very sharp fall in production, which
was particularly intense in Azerbaijan. The slump resulted directly from
the republic's strong orientation toward the production of raw materials which rendered it heavily dependent on the other Soviet republics
for other goods. GDP fell by more than 60 percent between 1991 and
1995. Budget deficits increased to as much as 10 percent of GDP. In
1994, the currency depreciated by 1,300 percent and inflation soared,
increasing consumer prices by 24,000 percent between 1991 and 1995.[25]
Azerbaijan's economic troubles were compounded by the war with
Armenia over the disputed territory of Nagorno Karabakh. As a result of
the macroeconomic instability inherited from the Soviet state, oil came

[22] Ogan 1993, 17.
[23] Nassibli 1999, 104.
[24] Ibid.
[25] Bagirov et al. 2003, 91.

to dominate the economy and became the industry on which hopes for a richer future were pinned.

Acknowledging the dismal situation the oil industry and the economy were in, the first democratically elected leader of Azerbaijan, Abulfez Elchibey, started to actively promote foreign investment in the oil industry. He believed that remittances from oil contracts in the form of direct investment, bonus payments, and oil sales presented the best hope for improving the industry and securing the much-needed capital for the economy at large. In May 1993, six agreements were signed creating joint ventures for the development of oil deposits. In the same month talks about the oil contracts and the possibility of having Elchibey sign them were planned in London. However, Elchibey was replaced in June 1993 with a former Azerbaijan Communist Party First Secretary Heidar Aliev. Some argue that the expansionist circles in Russia, fearing Elchibey's close relations with Turkey and the West, forced him from power before he could sign the contracts. Yet others argue that Western oil companies, British Petroleum and Amoco were instrumental in instigating the insurrection that resulted in Elchibey's ouster in order to renegotiate more favorable terms for the contracts.[26]

After Aliev became the president of Azerbaijan in 1993, at first, he halted all talks with foreign oil companies, stating that he wanted to "review" the agreements. Soon though, he began meeting with representatives of the companies, assuring them that the deal would go through. After three months of negotiations with the companies, in September 1994 Aliev signed what was called the "contract of the century" with ten foreign companies.[27] The contract entailed the development of three offshore fields Chirag, Azeri, and Gunesli with US$8 billion foreign investment over the course of thirty years. To coordinate the consortium's joint

---

[26] "BP accused of backing 'arms for oil' coup" *The Sunday Times* (U.K.). March 26, 2000.
[27] The division of stakes among the signatories were: Azerbaijan State Oil Company (SOCAR) 20%; British Petroleum 17%; Amoco (USA) 17%; Lukoil (Russia) 10%; Pennzoil (USA) 9.8%; Unocal (USA) 9.5%; Statoil (Norway) 8.5%; McDermott International (USA) 2.5%; Ramco (Scotland) 2%; Turkish State Oil Company 1.8%; Delta-Nimir (Saudi Arabia) 1.7%. SOCAR subsequently transferred 5% of the total shares to the Turkish State Oil Company and an additional 5% to Exxon when SOCAR proved unable to come up with the necessary investment capital. It is interesting to note that in the original negotiations, no Russian oil company was given a stake. To appease Moscow, Aliev allocated to the Russian company Lukoil a 10% stake. Aliev, in November 1994 also tried to transfer 5% of SOCAR's stake to Iran, which like Russia had originally been excluded. However, faced with the US objection, Azerbaijan International Operating Company blocked this move. For more details, see Bolukbasi (2004).

operations, the Azerbaijan International Operation Company (AIOC) was created in early 1995.

Aliev's eagerness to sign these contracts had a lot to do with the economic, political and geostrategic challenges his new regime faced in 1994. Being cut off from the former Soviet economy, the Azeri economy was suffering a deep recession, the loss of Nagorno Karabakh was draining resources as well as the morale of the country, and there was a political vacuum as the country swung from one coup to another. Given this background, Aliev sought to use the alliance of foreign oil companies to fortify himself against his enemies, secure his position, and build legitimacy around his new regime.

The trend of constituting new consortiums continued after this first contract. By the end of 1990s, Azerbaijan had signed more than twenty contracts with foreign oil companies. Investment in the oil sector over time increased to 37 percent of total FDI in 1995 and 97.6 percent in 2004.[28] By some accounts, foreign investment in the oil sector between 1994 and 2000 has been around US$4 billion.[29] In addition to investments in oil extraction, the country also became the recipient of investments for pipeline construction. By one estimate, the construction of the Baku-Tblisi-Ceyhan pipeline brought in US$150 million investment into Azerbaijan.[30] Fueled by these investments, the country began a period of steady growth in the latter half of the decade. The bonuses that followed the signing of the first contract helped government reverse the devaluation of its currency and the ensuing inflation. As FDI grew, so did the GDP. Azerbaijan's GDP rose by almost 6 percent in 1997 and 11.4 percent in 2000.[31]

Aliev's Investment Policy

Azeri leaders enacted several pieces of legislation relating to foreign investment in general: the *Law on Protection of Foreign Investments* (1992), the *Law on Investment Activity* (1995), the *Law on Privatization of State Property* (2000), and the *Law on International Arbitration* (2000). These laws have provided investors with currency convertibility, guarantee of stability of the legal framework, the right to repatriate funds, and free access to international arbitration. Despite these laws and a number of regulations regarding foreign investments in all sectors, Azerbaijan has

[28] USEIA 2006.
[29] Economist Intelligence Unit 2002.
[30] Cornell and Ismailzade 2005.
[31] Business Information Services for the Newly Independent States (BISNIS) 2000.

also created a separate legal framework for investors in the oil industry in the hopes of minimizing their risks and expediting oil projects.

For its investment regime regarding the oil industry, President Aliev chose production sharing agreements (PSAs) as the principal mechanism for attracting foreign capital. As discussed in Chapter 2, these contracts outline the regulatory, financial, organizational, legal, and compensatory relationship between investors and host governments. Under a PSA, contractors are granted the sole and exclusive exploration, development, and production rights within the contract areas. The PSA law and regulations, which constitute the PSA regime, provide that the state is bound by the contractual obligations to the investor and should be liable for breach of contract.[32] Under a PSA, the scope of the state's obligations and investors' rights can be freely negotiated to the extent permitted by law. This is characteristic of a civil relationship, where the parties act more or less as equals in a commercial context.[33] In addition to leveling the legal playing field, a PSA also provides a stand-alone tax regime, in which the investor enjoys a predictable tax liability, completely independent of the general tax regime of the state. Therefore, replacing the existing tax regime with a PSA secures for the investor the stability of the investment regime over the term of the contract's validity and an individual and flexible approach to particular projects.

There are many different PSA models used around the world. The "innovative" aspect of the Azeri PSA regime has been that instead of a generic PSA law, each contract after being ratified by the Azerbaijan parliament (Milli Majlis) assumes the force of law and prevails over any other existing or future law or decrees whose provisions differ from or are in conflict with the contract. Hence, each contract contains detailed stability provisions, assuring that the contractor's rights and interests under the contract are not subject to any change, modification or restriction without prior consent by the contractor. The contract also contains detailed arbitration provisions generally accepted in international practice.

Moreover, as opposed to standard tax and royalty schemes, PSAs provide physical mechanisms for rendering to the Azerbaijani state its share of profits, while allowing foreign energy companies to recoup their investments. Foreign participants recover their capital and operating costs in the form of a share of crude production at the beginning of the production cycle. The remainder of a field's oil output is then split between the state and its foreign partners according to a formula

[32] Blinn 1978, Smith and Dzienkowski 1989.
[33] Johnston 1994.

agreed upon for each individual PSA. For instance, for Azerbaijan's biggest block of fields, the Azeri, Chirag and Gunesli (ACG), 50 percent of the profits are used by the consortium partners for cost recovery up until the time the companies have recovered their investments plus interest. Once capital recovery is complete, 50 percent of the profits go to State Oil Company of Azerbaijan (SOCAR), as the representative of the government. The other 50 percent is available for profit sharing between the government and consortium partners, based on an index that takes into account transport costs and rate of return. Under this index, the government's share increases as the rate of return to the investor increases.[34]

Finally, the only tax levied on the contractor is the profits tax payable at a fixed rate for each PSA.[35] Currently, all PSAs provide for profits tax at either 25 or 32 percent depending on when the agreement was signed. The PSA provides detailed definitions of each item of income and deductible expense, and therefore provides a clear mechanism for profit-and-loss accounting. It also offers protection against future increases in the profits tax rate. The contractor is exempt from all other existing or future taxes, duties, excise taxes, including export and import duties or taxes.[36]

Through the PSA framework, the government also provides the oil contractors numerous guarantees, including but not limited to exclusivity of rights to the contract area; protection against any infringement by the government in the rights and interests of the contractors; the right to full and prompt compensation of any right, interest, and property of contractors expropriated, nationalized or otherwise taken by the government; enforceability of government obligations to provide licenses, approvals, visas, and any other permissions necessary for the investors to carry out their activities in Azerbaijan; and the right of contractors to access onshore construction facilities, supply bases, and all necessary transportation and infrastructure facilities. PSAs also stipulate that all rights to sovereign immunity are waived by the government.[37] Overall,

---

[34] Bagirov et al. 2003, 102.
[35] Contractors are also subject to social security contributions with respect to local employees.
[36] Currently two types of tax regimes are applicable in Azerbaijan: the statutory tax regime and the oil consortia tax regime. The statutory tax regime applies to all foreign investors operating outside of production sharing agreements. The oil consortia regime applies to all foreign investors involved in PSAs, including foreign oil companies functioning as contractor parties and foreign-service companies providing services to the contracting parties or the operating company.
[37] Baker and Mamedov 1998.

in terms of experience in applying the PSA regime to the oil and gas industry, Azerbaijan is considered a "world leader."[38]

Despite the generally accepted advantages of PSAs for creating an attractive investment environment, not all oil-producing countries have been able to formulate and implement an effective PSA regime to reduce investment risks for oil companies. As discussed above, the Azeri leaders had plenty of political, economic, and geostrategic reasons to push for these contracts. However, the key is not what they wanted but instead what they could do given the institutional context they operated in. As will be discussed in the next chapter, the Russian leaders were not able to create an attractive investment environment in the 1990s even when they understood the importance of PSAs and pushed for them. To explain how the Azeri leaders were able to create such an attractive PSA regime despite the serious concerns and objections of opposition groups, next I offer an analysis of the political regime in Azerbaijan.

Azerbaijan's Political Regime

In the limited literature on Azerbaijani politics, there is very little consensus on the regime characterization for Azerbaijan. The categories range from neopatrimonial dictatorship[39]; sultanistic[40]; authoritarian[41]; to decaying semi-authoritarian[42]; sultanistic semi-authoritarian[43]; hybrid[44]; and partially democratic.[45] Despite the different terminology, all accounts consistently point out to the low levels of institutional constraints and competition in the political system due to a lack of effective state veto players and strong political parties and interest groups.

Unconstrained Executive

State power has been concentrated in the president since Heidar Aliev came to power in 1993.[46] The president appoints the prime minister and

---

[38] Deloitte 2006.
[39] Lash and Remick 2002.
[40] Lieven 2000, Shevtsova 2001.
[41] Roeder 1994, Mamed-zadeh 2001.
[42] Ottoway 2003.
[43] Gulliyev 2005.
[44] Cornell 2001, Rasizade 2003.
[45] McFaul 2002.
[46] Heidar Aliev spent his early career in the KGB, eventually becoming the first Azeri to head the KGB of Azerbaijan. A Brezhnev protégé, he served as first secretary of the Communist Party of Azerbaijan from 1969 to 1982, and then under Yuri Andropov, was

the cabinet, issues decrees, and signs laws. The president can also dissolve the parliament and call for new elections to the legislative body. Although the Azerbaijani constitution of 1995 established a system of government based on a nominal division of powers between a strong presidency, a legislature with the power to approve the budget and impeach the president, and a judiciary with limited independence, in reality these state institutions bolster rather than moderate the power of the executive.[47]

The three nominally independent high courts-the Constitutional Court, the Supreme Court, and the High Economic Court- have been subject to executive influence and control and have been staffed primarily with judges loyal to Aliev.[48] Lower-level judges have also been directly elected by the president. The judiciary in essence has become subordinate to the president's office.

Similarly, the parliament exercises virtually no legislative initiative or oversight independent of the executive. Some call it merely an "appendage" to the executive.[49] Much of the initiative on legislation comes from the executive in the form of decrees, with the parliament acting like a rubber stamp. For instance, the parliament does not have any effective control over public finance. Parliament can neither draft nor amend the annual budget, but can only approve or reject the budget submitted to it by the Ministry of Finance, which is directly subordinated to the president. In 2001, the budget was approved after only twenty minutes of discussion.

The lack of checks and balances in the state stems partly from the flawed parliamentary elections of 1995, 2000, and 2005. In 1995, for instance, almost three-quarters of the candidates who represented opposition groups were denied registration. In rural areas, proxy voting and block voting were common. Even in urban areas, there were incidents of one member of a family voting on behalf of the whole family. As a result, a total of 8 political parties gained representation in the 1995 parliament. Of the 125 seats, only eight were occupied by the political opposition, the rest going to the president's Yeni Azerbaycan Party (YAP), allied progovernment parties, and primarily progovernment unaffiliated candidates.[50]

---

elevated to the central party leadership as a full member of the Politburo. In 1987, under Gorbachev, he fell from favor and was removed from his post. He returned to Azerbaijan and for a time headed the local parliament in his home province of Nakhchevan until his presidency in 1993.

[47] The president himself presided over the commission charged with drafting the constitution; many articles related to the powers of the executive reflect Aliev's own preferences.

[48] Hoffman 2000, 61.

[49] Arifoglu and Abbasov 2000.

[50] Progovernment parties included the Azerbaijan Democratic Independence Party, the Motherland Party, the Democratic Entrepreneurs Party, the Alliance in the Name

The 2000 parliamentary elections were another missed opportunity for democratic development in Azerbaijan. The U.S.-based National Democratic Institute (NDI) stated that the 2000 elections represented "a continuation of a pattern of seriously flawed elections in Azerbaijan that fail to meet even minimum international standards."[51] One of the major problems was once again the registration of candidates. Even though a total of 13 parties qualified to register in the party-list election, the Central Election Committee rejected the applications of 8 of these on dubious grounds. The situation was no different for the single-member constituencies, where more than half of the candidates were refused registration.[52] In addition, numerous abuses were noted on election day from ballot-stuffing to intimidation of voters and opposition members of electoral commissions. This election was characterized by the Office of Democratic Institutions and Human Rights (ODIHR) as a "crash course in the different methodologies of manipulation."[53] As a consequence, leaders of the main opposition parties were left out of the 2000 parliament. The ruling party received more than 70 percent of the votes, but only one opposition party was announced to have passed the 8 percent threshold. When this situation led to boycott of the parliament by the opposition, Aliev's regime reacted by reducing the ruling party's official election results and declaring that two other opposition parties had passed the threshold.[54]

The 2005 election was likewise marred by serious irregularities and abuses. Along with the use of intimidation and administrative resources, the election saw sharp increases in the practice of vote buying. Observers reported numerous instances of harassment, obstruction, and unwarranted detention by local officials and police. Attacks on media freedom rose too. The outcome was the further weakening of the parliament as an institution. YAP won 56 of the 125 seats in the parliament, with a further 50 or so seats going to YAP-aligned independents. The genuine opposition, including the Azadlig and Yeni Siyaset blocs, won a total of just 8 seats.[55]

Executive dominance in Azerbaijan is sustained not only by the weakness of the judiciary and legislative branches of government but also by the

---

of Azerbaijan, and the Azerbaijan National Statehood Party. The Popular Front, the Musavat Party and the Azerbaijan National Independence Party provided the main opposition.

[51] Quote taken from Cornell (2001:128).
[52] Ibid., 126.
[53] Organization for Security and Cooperation in Europe 2001.
[54] Cornell 2001, 128.
[55] Alieva 2006.

absence of serious challenge from the regional administrations. Azerbaijan comprises 59 regions (rayonlar), 11 cities, and the Autonomous Republic of Nakhcivan.[56] The president appoints and dismisses governors, who head the rayon governments. Without a voice in state decisions, regional authorities have no formal powers to keep the executive branch in check.

Finally, the Azeri government bureaucracy can neither exert any constraints on the decision makers nor act as a bridge between various veto players in the state. It has virtually no input in decision making. Policy making is restricted to a close circle of senior ministers, advisers and aides to the president. Bureaucrats are recruited on the basis of personal loyalty to the leader, not according to any objective and professional criteria. Ministry appointments and promotion are based on informal, patronage networks, the most prominent being the regional tribe composed of Azeris from Armenia (Yeraz) and the Azerbaijani enclave of Nakhichevan. President Heidar Aliev himself was from the latter and most of his inner circle came from this regionally defined tribe.[57] Networks are also based on kinship. For instance, Heidar Aliev placed family members in important positions: his two brothers and his son Ilham Aliev were put in the political council of YAP, and his son was made the vice president of SOCAR from 1994 until he became the prime minister and then the president of Azerbaijan.

Another important patronage network consists of bureaucrats and new businessmen who were Soviet-era associates of the president. Much of Heidar Aliev's political power in the earliest part of his presidency depended on the ties he formed during the Soviet years. Moreover, Aliev was able to sustain his unchallenged rule by controlling the "power ministries": the army, the Ministry of Internal Affairs, and the Ministry of National Security. These institutions that were staffed with Aliev loyalists protected the president from overt coup attempts and manipulated public political discourse in the president's favor through media censorship and suppression of political dissidents. In exchange for their political support, they were allowed to pursue profitable economic ventures.

Restricted Competition

In addition to weak state institutions, political parties and interest groups have also been weak in Azerbaijan, restricting political competition. Parties tend to be centered around an individual with a strong personality

[56] For more information, see Commission of the European Communities (2005).
[57] Hoffman 2000, 62.

and/or sufficient wealth to establish a power base. Programs and party platforms, if they even exist, are generally vague, consisting of little more than idealistic declarations. Few parties have developed nation-wide organizations. The majority are small and unknown to the public. Membership is almost always very modest in number and restricted in social range, drawing predominantly on a network of personal contacts and acquaintances.[58]

Party politics, then, does not play a significant role in either parliamentary or presidential elections: most candidates at both levels run and are elected as independents rather than as representatives of a particular party. All parties and other types of political groupings must be officially registered; if they are not, they are declared illegal and liable to prosecution. The preconditions for registration are arduous and are almost impossible to fulfill without government backing.[59] Parties have even more difficulties in the outlying regions, away from Baku, where local executive committees prohibit large-scale meetings, assemblies, and public relations activities.[60] The notion of loyal opposition oftentimes is employed as "noncritical" or "cooperative" opposition rather than the opposition parties' loyalty to a democratic system. Toleration for opposition and criticism within the party system remains low.[61] The absence of a visible presence or organization outside the parliament means that parties in Azerbaijan tend to resemble parliamentary factions more than established institutionalized parties.[62]

Interest-group development in Azerbaijan has a record similar to party development. The main interest-group organizations are concerned with human rights issues, gender rights and ecological problems. In general, they are closely supervised by the authorities. Registration for NGOs (nongovernmental organizations) for instance is routinely denied, often without an explanation. Their activities are also hampered by the fact that they have limited and usually short-term funding. Like the political parties, they attract very little public support and are frequently regarded with suspicion, mostly due to the fact that they rely heavily on financial support from international donor organizations.[63] Their influence on government policies is very limited. For example, in terms of unionized

---

[58] Akiner 2000.
[59] Ibid., 102.
[60] Freedom House 2003.
[61] Altstadt 1997.
[62] Herzig 1999, 34.
[63] Akiner 2000, 103. According to Freedom House (2003), only 11.5 percent of the public in 2001 was aware of the term NGO and could name at least one NGO.

activity, Azerbaijan's interest groups are debilitated. There are a few trade unions, such as the Azerbaijan Free Trade Unionist Confederation, the League of Protection of Labor Rights of Citizens, and the Trade Union for the Protection of the Rights of Oil Workers. However, their activities are neither free nor extensive. Trade unions in Azerbaijan do not have a major role in the political decision-making process and do little advocacy for their members.[64]

Given the first few years of the newly independent state, perhaps it is not surprising that interest groups have been routinely excluded from participation. Until Aliev came to power in 1993, Azerbaijan was enveloped in political turmoil and instability. Between its independence in 1991 and 1993, politics was characterized by a series of coups, ethnic conflict in Nagorno-Karabakh, and several separatist movements in other parts of the country. During this period, the country had four presidents.[65] Having come into office during circumstances fraught with instability, Aliev soon consolidated his power and started state-building by systematically purging his opponents and their civil society organizations. Coercion maintained public support for the regime through manipulation of the media and selective use of laws as a means to curb opposition. Violations of human rights in connection with the suppression of political opposition were rampant. Opposition groups have had their rights abused through arrest and imprisonment, violent disruption of political rallies, and the arbitrary exclusion of individuals and parties from the political process.[66]

Despite the seemingly apparent weak executive constraints and competition in the political system, some scholars have classified Azerbaijan as a semi-authoritarian regime for having – at least on paper – a constitution, elections, and some semblance of a civil society.[67] I argue in this book that Azerbaijan is actually a de facto authoritarian regime with

---

[64] Freedom House 2003.
[65] On August 30, 1991, Azerbaijan's Communist regime headed by Ayaz Mutalibov declared its independence. In September 1991, he was elected, unopposed, as president. At the beginning of March 1992 Mutalibov was forced to resign as president following the massacre of Azerbaijani civilians at Khojali in Nagorno-Karabakh. After him, Iagub Mamedov served as an interim president until June 1992, when Abulfaz Elchibey, the leader of the Azerbaijan Popular Front, won new presidential elections with 57 percent of the votes cast. In June 1993, a coup by Colonel Surat Husseinov unseated Elchibey and paved the way for the ascension of Heidar Aliev. When new elections were held in October 1993, Aliev won by a landslide.
[66] Herzig 1999.
[67] See Cornell 2001, Ottoway 2003.

sultanistic tendencies. Politics has been revolving around one person with unchecked discretion and an immense personality cult.[68] Loyalty to the ruler has been motivated by a mixture of fear and of rewards given to his collaborators. The patrimonial governance and nepotism, traits of sultanistic regimes, have been abundantly present in Azerbaijan. Family, cronies, clans, and patronage have been more influential social constructions than formal legal institutions have been.[69]

Finally, dynastic succession, which took place in Azerbaijan in 2003, is also emblematic of sultanistic regimes. In 2002, Heydar Aliyev organized a referendum – a presidential prerogative – which further weakened the opposition by abolishing the proportional representation system for parliamentary elections and by establishing mechanisms for a "constitutional" dynastic succession. Succession to the presidency, should the incumbent die or become incapacitated, was shifted from the parliamentary speaker to the prime minister. A year later, the ailing President Aliev issued a decree appointing his son Ilham as prime minister, which was adopted by a 102–1 vote in the parliament. During the final phase of his father's illness, Ilham Aliev was named acting president. Despite his illness, the father maintained his own candidacy in the 2003 campaign alive until just two weeks before the election so as to deter elites from defecting until it was effectively too late. The "flawed" referendum and the power of the presidential decree gave the son an unfair electoral advantage and ensured the dynastic succession.

In addition to the undemocratic nature of the selection process, the 2003 presidential election failed to meet international standards. Violations began during the campaign and culminated with significant irregularities during voting and counting and tabulation of the ballots.[70] After the election, police and internal security units used force to break up opposition rallies protesting the fraud. Officially Ilham Aliev won 77 percent of the vote and reappointed his father's entire cabinet.[71] The October 2008 presidential election in Azerbaijan continued the consolidation of political power. Ilham Aliev won a resounding victory gaining nearly 89 percent of the vote, with the remaining 6 candidates each receiving about 1–3 percent of the vote.[72]

---

[68] Heidar Aliev was often cast in the role of sage father to the young nation. He has had numerous portraits in public places and adulatory commentaries in the official media.
[69] Guliyev 2005.
[70] Bouckaert 2004.
[71] Freizer 2003.
[72] Nichol 2008.

Politics of Oil Investment Policy

Oil, FDI and politics are closely linked in Azerbaijan. The success of the Azeri state in attracting significant amounts of foreign investment over the past two decades can be attributed to the flexible investment environment its political regime has provided for investors. The absence of significant veto players and strong political parties and interest groups has insulated the ruling elite from any opposition to investment policies and offered foreign investors easy and direct access to decision makers. The regime provided "one-stop shopping" for investors; oil companies could negotiate the terms of the investment agreements with a few actors and bypass any potential opponents to those terms.

The decision-making structure in the oil industry best depicts the benefits this regime has been able to offer foreign investors so far. The authority and ultimate responsibility to design and implement the oil investment policy of Azerbaijan lies solely with the president. To assist the president in controlling and managing this industry and its relations with the foreign investors, the State Oil Company (SOCAR) was founded by a presidential decree in 1992. Until 2001, when the Ministry of Fuel and Energy was established, SOCAR functioned as a government ministry (as well as a vertically integrated state oil company) and its president acted as a minister and reported directly to the president. Bypassing the formal government hierarchy and administrative bodies that had official responsibility for regulating investment activities in general, SOCAR, with its special ties to the president, maintained a virtual monopoly over the management of the oil industry. SOCAR president Natik Aliev (no relationship to President Heidar Aliev); SOCAR vice president Ilham Aliev (President Heidar Aliev's son and the current president); and the director of the Foreign Relations Department Valekh Alekperov made all the top decisions regarding oil investments in the 1990s, in consultation with President Heidar Aliev. The exclusive and narrow elite control prevented any possible bureaucratic infighting and red tape that typically stall projects in many other developing countries.

In an attempt to separate the regulatory and operational functions of SOCAR, President Aliev reorganized the industry and in 2001 established the Ministry of Fuel and Energy, which was renamed in 2004 the Ministry of Industry and Energy. Even though now the responsibility for the preparations of PSAs and the negotiations with companies officially reside with this ministry, SOCAR is still involved in the negotiations as a party to all of the international consortia developing new oil and gas projects.[73] The ultimate roles to be played by SOCAR and the ministry are still evolving. Meanwhile, the previous powerful actors have changed their titles but still almost exclusively dominate the industry. The former vice president of SOCAR, Ilham Aliev, is now the president of Azerbaijan, and the former president of SOCAR, Natiq Aliev, has been the energy minister since 2005.

In addition to SOCAR's role and proximity to the President, the actual procedure of adopting PSAs is indicative of the political structure in Azerbaijan as well. PSAs are initiated by either SOCAR or the companies themselves. In the first method, rarely used, SOCAR opens a tender and companies bid. Unless SOCAR sees a high interest in a very attractive area, companies become proactive and show their interest in a field or structure.[74] Before both sides proceed with negotiations, the offer is taken to the president of Azerbaijan for his approval. Only after he gives consent in the form of a decree, do the negotiations resume.[75] At this stage, the top officials of SOCAR and foreign-company representatives negotiate the terms of the agreement.[76] Once they reach an agreement, the President's approval is needed again before it is sent to the parliament for ratification. Meanwhile, for technical, legal and "grammatical" inspection, the draft is sent to the Petrochemical Department of the Government, which works in collaboration with the legal and tax advisors. Here, except for some typo corrections, nothing actually gets changed. The only contribution of this department is the signature of the department chairman on a statement of "government guarantees," already mutually designed and negotiated by the president and the foreign companies.[77] The president then

---

[73] USEIA 2006.

[74] Author's interviews with Fred Marshall (government affairs manager in Exxon), Baku, July 6, 1999; Sabit Baygirov (first ex-president of SOCAR), Baku, July 7, 1999; and Vitaly V. Begliarbekov (SOCAR), Baku, July 15, 1999.

[75] Author's interviews with Unal Bayram (Mobil), Baku, July 2, 1999, and Vitaly Bagliarbekov (SOCAR).

[76] Author's interview with Vitaly Begliarbekov (SOCAR department manager), Baku, July 15, 1999. According to Begliarbekov, the criteria that Azerbaijani side uses to award a license to a company include: the size of the project area, financial capacity of the company, bonus payments it is willing to make, and the Azeri content, i.e., company's presence in Azerbaijan, its premises, its desire to hire local personnel, to form joint ventures with local partners for infrastructure, and the social investments (in education, health etc.) that the company pledges to make.

[77] Author's interview with Rasim Dadasov (head of the Petrochemical Department in the government of Azerbaijan), Baku, July 3, 1999. Dadasov stated that the contents of the contracts were kept secret from the media and opposition parties. He argued that usually the foreign oil companies and not the government made this request.

forwards the document to the parliamentary Commission on Mineral Resources, Energy and Ecology the day before the ratification session in the parliament. The commission spends roughly a half hour, at most an hour on the draft.[78] Without making any changes, the chairman of the commission and the head of the Foreign Investment Department in SOCAR brief the parliament on the terms of the agreement. Again in a very short amount of time the deputies are asked to vote yes or no on the draft proposal, after which the agreement is ratified.[79] Despite the powers given to it by the constitution, the Parliament does not exercise any oversight powers over the PSA process.[80] If any indication, in the 1990s, the parliament has not once rejected or even returned for review an oil contract put before it.[81] After the parliament's rubber stamp, once again the contract goes to the President for final approval and then becomes law when he signs and officially declares it. The process is so fashioned that nobody other than top SOCAR officials and the president has any input in the decisions.

The absence of checks and balances in the process of PSA adoption has been seen as a blessing by foreign investors, at least in the short run. SOCAR's strong position in the system and proximity to the seat of political power has made it a favorable partner to oil investors. During the negotiation and implementation of the contracts, foreign investors feel no pressure to defend their intentions to opposition parties or interest groups. Despite their many concerns with the format and content of the oil contracts, opposition groups do not have any substantial power to contribute to the decision-making process, let alone pressure the government or the foreign companies in any certain way.[82]

---

[78] Author's interview with Asia Manafova (chairwoman of the Mineral Resources, Energy, and Ecology Commission in the Azeri Parliament), Baku, July 8, 1999. Manafova was a member of the Yeni Azerbaijan Party at the time.

[79] Author's interview with Nazim Imanov (National Independence Party), Baku, July 7, 1999.

[80] Magerram Zulfugarov (National Independence Party), during his interview with the author in Baku, July 3, 1999, depicted the parliament as "a branch of the president."

[81] Sulhettin Akperov (Musavvat Party) during his interview with the author in Baku, July 5, 1999, indicated that the contracts that were given to deputies were not the same as the original contracts; they were either a very short version or a narrowly selected part of it.

[82] Fred Marshall (Exxon Government Affairs Manager) during his interview with the author stated that as a foreign oil company, Exxon has not had much of a relationship with the parliament and opposition parties. He argued that that responsibility to deal with foreign companies resides with the government and that being a commercial entity, the company tries not to get involved in politics and take sides.

Foreign investors have been satisfied with the simple power structure and absence of opposition to their contracts. They know where the political power lies. Whether or not they like it, the knowledge gives them assurances that their voices will be heard.[83] The process, according to some foreign investors, also isolates them from corruption and manipulation by petty officials and bureaucrats.[84] The PSAs, as one company representative put, provide them with "a suit of armor in terms of being able to walk through what would otherwise be dangerous and difficult."[85] He added that the single most attractive thing about investing in Azerbaijan – apart from the presence of hydrocarbons – is the PSA framework under which companies and the government mutually set the rules.

Even though officially foreign companies assert that they have no regime preferences, they nevertheless have had good relations with the Aliev family. Heidar Aliev and his aides have been praised by some investors as being "far-sighted individuals"[86] and for maintaining "stability in a dangerous neighborhood."[87] Despite the undemocratic and repressive nature of the dynastic succession, foreign investors and foreign governments viewed the succession as critical to the stability of billions of dollars of investments in the country's energy sector.[88] They seemed eager to embrace the new President Ilham Aliev and wasted no time in congratulating him.[89] "When news broke of the planned succession, an unnamed Western executive in Baku was quoted by the French news agency AFP as gloating, 'we are about to crack open the champagne in the office'."[90]

For their part, government officials have been proud of their innovative, "genius" style of doing business with foreign investors.[91] Even though, a generic PSA law has been, and still is, in the works,[92] the President and

---

[83] Unal Bayram, Mobil.
[84] This is a very interesting comment considering that foreign investors regard corruption by lower level bureaucrats as disruptive and problematic but consider high-level corruption as manageable and even to a certain extent acceptable.
[85] Author's interview with Peter Henshaw (BPAmoco representative), Baku, July 20, 1999.
[86] Fred Marshall has repeatedly commented on the importance of individuals and how they by themselves can make a difference.
[87] Weir 2006.
[88] Bouckaert 2003.
[89] According to some news sources, President W. Bush sent an unusually long letter of congratulations to the new Azeri president.
[90] Wheelan 2003.
[91] Author's interview with Rafig Abdullajev (SOCAR, Assistant of President), Baku, July 1, 1999.
[92] Mahir Asedov (Azerbaijan Democratic Party) during his interview with the author, in Baku, July 16, 1999, argued that this generic law was prepared as a result of collaboration

his oil team have preferred meanwhile to continue this process of turning each contract into law in order to win time and avoid any hurdles in coming up with a general law.[93] In this way, they also believed that they could provide a significant amount of flexibility to themselves and the investors. Each contract has given them opportunities to maneuver, depending on the specifics of the project.[94] "Only if those in Russia were smart enough to do what we have been doing here" said a SOCAR official, "they would have reaped the benefits of foreign investment just like us."[95]

Implications of Oil FDI on Development

Distortion in the Economy: Dutch Disease

The government's overriding objective has been the promotion of the oil industry, which is Azerbaijan's main source of income and international interest.[96] In the past decade, thanks to large infusions of foreign capital, the Azeri oil industry witnessed record-high growth rates with output increases of more than 200 percent.[97] By many accounts, Azerbaijan has already become a petro-state, in terms of oil dependence. One typical indicator of this dependence is the percentage of fuel exports in total exports, which for Azerbaijan has been on average 78 percent between 1996 and 2004.[98] These figures are similar to those of major oil-producing countries

of several deputies, including opposition deputies like himself, in the first years of the republic, but Heidar Aliev purposely never allowed it to be discussed and passed in the parliament. Asedov further argued that this had nothing to do with inexperience or timing as some government officials assert. Instead, he argued that this case-by-case process increased Aliev's control over the contracts and was an obvious attempt to bypass the parliament, which would have been responsible for developing the legislation. He found it outrageous that an oil-rich country such as Azerbaijan still does not have general legislation on oil.

[93] The difference between a generic PSA law and case by case contract law is that under a body of law, everybody is playing by the same rules, and using the same criteria. However, in a case-by-case approach, each negotiation and contract is different. The terms of each contract may reflect different priorities. However, this does not necessarily mean inconsistency in legal provisions. Usually the differences among contracts are in the commercial framework. Contracts have different models of profit distribution, participating interests etc. Otherwise they are very similar in the legal guarantees they provide.

[94] During the interview, Rafig Abdullajev also pointed out that this method gave enough flexibility for the government to increase its share of revenues with each new contract.

[95] Interview with Rafig Abdullajev.

[96] Economist Intelligence Unit 2002.

[97] Bagirov et al. 2003, 93.

[98] It is important to note that the nonfuel exports include export of natural gas. If we treat natural gas as we treat oil- which should probably be the case because it is becoming more closely linked to oil- the share of the nonfuel sector would decrease even further.

like Venezuela and Iran: 81 and 85 percent, respectively, on average during the same period.[99] In all, exports have remained concentrated on oil and have not diversified. Further, the energy sector has accounted for more than half of budget revenues and more than 30 percent of the GDP since 2002.[100] In general, the Azeri economy has grown strongly as a result of rising oil exports generated by FDI. Considering that oil and natural gas production are expected to increase dramatically in the near future with operationalization of the newly constructed pipelines from the region, even under conservative oil and gas reserve and price estimates, the revenue windfall over the next twenty years will be substantial.[101]

As demonstrated in more detail in Chapter 4, such a high degree of energy dependence usually creates serious structural problems in the economies of oil rich countries – also known as the "Dutch disease." Even though its oil and gas production levels are not yet at full capacity, Azerbaijan is already showing signs of this disease.[102] For instance, the agricultural and nonfuel industrial sectors have already suffered significantly since the collapse of the Soviet Union. As a percentage of GDP, agriculture value added fell from 32 percent in 1991 to 12 percent in 2004. The appreciation of the national currency against the dollar has also become quite visible. For instance, the Azerbaijani manat appreciated over 6 percent in nominal terms against the U.S. dollar in 2005, and an additional 1 percent in 2006.[103] Moreover, inflation has been showing signs of increase in the last couple of years in part due to higher levels of public spending as a result of higher oil revenues. For instance, in Azerbaijan, inflation was reported at 9.6 percent in 2005 and 11 percent in 2006.[104] Experts warn that a further increase into double digits can jeopardize the growth potential of the economy.

---

[99] World Bank 2006.

[100] USEIA 2006.

[101] According to International Bank for Reconstruction and Development (2006), long-term revenue projections, based on an average oil price of about US$43 per barrel for the next 20 years, suggest gross revenues of about US$340 billion from Azerbaijan's oil and gas fields plus pipeline transit fees before operating costs. After operating costs, state fiscal revenues are expected to reach about US$175 billion, of which about US$20 billion will accrue to the state budget in the form of corporate tax revenues and the remainder will accrue to the State Oil Fund (SOFAZ) in the form of royalties. The oil consortia are expected to rapidly repatriate some US$40 billion of invested capital, plus profits. According to the report, this implies an annual oil windfall of US$1,000 per capita for the next 20 years.

[102] Esanov et al. 2001, Cohen 2006, O'Lear 2007.

[103] Global Insight 2006.

[104] See U.S. Department of State, Background Note (July 2007). Available online www.state.gov/countries.

According to IMF, these inflationary pressures are likely to increase as the oil export volumes increase and the non-oil sectors contract.[105] Furthermore, despite economic growth in recent years, employment opportunities have not expanded. The oil sector represented only 1 percent of employment in Azerbaijan in 2002.[106] The 34 percent drop in employment in non-oil industry from 1995 to 2001 resulted in a loss of 110,000 jobs.[107] For instance, in the second-largest city Ganja, of the total population of 300,000, only about 18,000 inhabitants officially had jobs in 2003.[108]

Finally, high dependence on oil makes the Azeri economy extremely vulnerable to price fluctuations and supply cycles. According to International Development Association (2005), Azerbaijani oil production is expected to reach a peak in 2010 at 59 million tons annually (roughly four times current production) and then decline rapidly from 2012 onward, effectively coming to an end by 2030. The slowly diminishing pace of oil production can slow down or even reduce the growth rate and force the government to use the oil fund to sustain the level of spending which existed during peak production years.

Weak Governance, Corruption, Inequality

In addition to weakening the economy and making it vulnerable to global price fluctuations, oil windfalls are also affecting the structure and capacity of the Azerbaijani state to govern effectively.[109] First, the availability of easy and direct rents is making government elites and their supporters who benefit from the rents reluctant to introduce reforms that in the long run can empower new groups and threaten the status quo.[110] This is most evident in the drastic decline in the ability of the Azeri government to enforce tax collection. For instance, a recent International Monetary Fund (IMF) paper concludes that in ten years of reforms Azerbaijan has made no progress and has even backtracked on electricity reform, a large source

---

[105] Cohen 2006, 14.
[106] International Development Association 2005.
[107] Holsen 2003.
[108] Rasizade 2003, 358.
[109] Leite and Weidmann 1999, Ross 1999, Auty 2001.
[110] The few reforms that are introduced are mostly tailored to foreign investors because of the need for Western capital and expertise to jump-start energy development. As energy resources become more developed, however, one would expect to see reform incentives weaken.

of potential tax revenue for the state.[111] This is typical of rentier states, where oil revenues precipitate the decline of the extractive and regulatory institutions. Unlike welfare states, which are redistributive, rentier states do not exist by extracting surplus from the local population because oil revenues enable them to cease taxing altogether.[112] Hence, with no revenue-gathering motive, these states are financially autonomous from their citizenry and therefore are not accountable to it.[113] The weak fiscal structure in Azerbaijan delays the development of a modern consciousness of the state and contributes to the perpetuation of traditional concepts of authority as the personal patrimony of the ruler.

Second, easy access to oil rents is also reducing the ability and willingness of the government to maintain even minimal levels of public services and social welfare protections. Social welfare is a relatively low priority for government spending. The amount of government expenditures on health care and public education in more than a decade demonstrates that Azerbaijan on average spent less (as a percentage of GDP) even when its revenue streams increased thanks to oil and gas exports. For instance, public expenditure on health care in Azerbaijan as a percentage of GDP dropped from 3.1 percent to 1 percent between 1991 and 2003. Similarly, public spending on education fell from 8 to 3 percent between 1991 and 2004.[114] In consequence, according to many experts, in the past several years, public education in Azerbaijan has broken down, health care has deteriorated, pensions have gone unpaid, and a relatively egalitarian social structure has been destroyed for the most part.

Third, an abundance of petrodollars in government hands has been increasing the incentives for rent-seeking behavior and corruption in Azerbaijan. A 2001 study by the European Bank for Restructuring and Development (EBRD) shows that total energy rents from 1992 to 2000 have ranged from 20 to 50 percent of GDP in Azerbaijan and some of the other former Soviet republics, and that a significant portion of these rents has been used to support subsidies to special interest groups favored by incumbent governments rather than being allocated to productive areas.[115] The report shows as well that in several instances, the leaders of

[111] Cohen 2006, 15.
[112] Mahdavy 1970.
[113] Chaudry 1997.
[114] By comparison, Norway's public expenditure on education and health care stands on average 7.5 percent and 7.8 percent of its GDP during the same years (World Bank Group 2006).
[115] Esanov et al. 2001.

these countries have appropriated export rents outside the state budget for the benefit of their closest entourage.[116]

The Transparency International Corruption Perception index, which ranks countries according to perceptions of the degree of corruption as seen by business people and country analysts, puts Azerbaijan nearly at the bottom of the list with low corruption perception index (CPI) score, indicating a high level of corruption.[117] For instance, in 2006, among 163 countries, Azerbaijan was ranked 130th. Similarly, a study conducted by the World Bank and European Bank for Reconstruction and Development shows that among twenty countries with transitional economies, 59.3 percent of the companies in Azerbaijan spend from 8 to 10 percent of their annual income on bribery, a figure that puts Azerbaijan in the lead.[118] The weekly news magazine Hesabat concluded that nine of Azerbaijan's ten wealthiest men were in the government.[119]

Corruption is, of course, nothing new in the former Soviet republics; in fact, it is a legacy of the Soviet regime. In its declining years the Communist system lived on bureaucratic fiddling. These former Soviet republics "inherited political institutions that entailed near-universal state ownership of property and a bureaucracy imbued with an autocratic and interventionist mentality."[120] The Soviet legacy of centralized power was further strengthened after independence in 1991. The persisting elites from the communist era have acquired the right to set the rules of the game for energy development in an environment where the necessary regulatory institutions were painstakingly absent.

The bonuses that foreign companies pay when oil contracts are signed are a perfect illustration of corruption in these countries. For instance in Azerbaijan, many believe that even though there is a Special Oil Fund set up to keep oil revenues from being inappropriately used, some bonus payments are pocketed by officials and that foreign companies are turning

---

[116] According to Rasizade (2003), during Heidar Aliev's rule, his brother Jalal Aliev owned the national fuel-station cartel called Azpetrol, and his son, as the vice president of SOCAR, controlled every shipment of crude oil produced in Azerbaijan. Rasizade reports that every year SOCAR exported via the Georgian Black Sea ports of Batumi and Poti about 6.5 million tons more oil than was officially reported by the government, bringing into the pockets of the presidential clan around US$1 billion annually.

[117] The CPI scores range from 1 to 10, indicating the most and least corrupt, respectively.

[118] Hellman and Schankerman 2000.

[119] Chivers 2005. According to the article, the number-one wealthiest man heads the State Customs Committee; number three is the nation's top police official, whose troops have been beating protesters with batons; and number four was the health minister, now under arrest.

[120] Schroeder 1996, 12.

a blind eye to this diversion. A comparison of figures from oil contracts and the National Bank of Azerbaijan indicates a misbalance and confirms these suspicions.[121]

In Azerbaijan, despite the recent economic growth generated by the energy windfall, corruption and weak governance have resulted in high levels of poverty, and weak development indicators for the Azeri society. So far, the energy wealth has not translated into material comfort for the general population. In Azerbaijan the rate of poverty soared in 2002 to 44.6 percent poor and 26.9 percent very poor. Even though it has decreased over the past years, it is still widespread at roughly 33 percent (poor and very poor combined) of the population.[122]

Moreover, life expectancy at birth in Azerbaijan – already low – has been declining, the result of high infant, child, and maternal mortality rates and a dismaying prevalence of preventable diseases. Despite having one of the highest rates of GDP per capita among the former Soviet republics due to its oil wealth, Azerbaijan has the second-highest share of undernourished people.[123] In 2002, nearly one-quarter of the children in Azerbaijan were malnourished and two-fifths were suffering from anemia. Drinking water was available for only 54 percent of households countrywide and for 17 percent in rural areas.[124] In terms of the Human Development Index (a composite measurement of educational level, life expectancy and income) in 2006, among 177 countries, Azerbaijan was ranked 99.[125]

Corruption and weak governance has also widened the income and consumption gaps between the haves and the have-nots in these societies. In terms of the gini coefficient, which measures inequality in a society (a value of 0 represents perfect equality; a value of 100, perfect inequality), inequality in Azerbaijan has been steadily increasing. There have been wide gaps between the richest and poorest segments of the Azeri society during the 2000s when rents from energy projects started to accrue. Even though on average monthly wages have been increasing, this growth in wages has been unevenly distributed in favor of employees in the oil sector and related sectors, and has not been realized in other sectors of the economy.[126] Since relative deprivation drives group mobilization, especially when the distribution of wealth is considered unfair and the

---

[121] Central and Eastern Europe Bankwatch Network 2002.
[122] International Development Association 2005.
[123] Bagirov et al. 2003, 97.
[124] Central and Eastern Europe Bankwatch Network 2002.
[125] United Nations Development Program 2006.
[126] O'Lear 2007, 212.

system is perceived to be engulfed in corruption, such a wide gap does not bode well for Azerbaijan. According to some experts, disproportionate standards of living are likely to contribute to domestic instability by exacerbating existing social and ethnic conflicts between oil-producing enclaves and other regions in the country.[127]

Foreign oil companies have traditionally been criticized for turning a blind eye to the resource curse and for not pressuring the governments to foster good governance and development. Even though BP, as the leading foreign company in the country, has developed corporate social responsibility policies, such as local community health and education projects, business development, and infrastructure projects, the fear of falling out with the authorities has discouraged it and other foreign companies from addressing macro-level issues such as corruption, spending, inequality and lack of transparency.[128] In some cases, the presence of foreign companies and the projects they initiated have negatively affected the lives of communities. For instance, many NGOs have accused foreign companies of causing pollution, infrastructure damage, as well as social and economic disruption throughout the construction of the Baku-Tblisi-Ceyhan pipeline. It was argued that in some areas, as a result of these projects, local authorities have illegally purchased or forced people to give up their lands. In addition, local residents employed at the construction of BTC have complained about being mistreated in terms of labor rights and medical treatment.[129] Foreign companies were seen as perpetuating the powerlessness of local communities.

AntiDemocratic Tendencies

As much as the level of FDI is affected by the existing political regime, foreign capital and revenues that are generated from it can also significantly affect a country's political regime. As the Azerbaijani case demonstrates, the success of an authoritarian regime in attracting FDI – especially during a period of state building – has a reinforcing and perpetuating effect on the regime. In this section of the chapter, I argue that foreign capital in Azerbaijan has been shaping the political regime and state building in two ways. First, directly, foreign investors have been legitimizing the authoritarian regime in the international scene by endorsing and praising it for

---

[127] Kurbanov and Sanders 1998.
[128] Gulbrandsen and Moe 2007.
[129] Cornell and Ismailzade 2005.

being stable and attractive for investors. Second, indirectly, increased oil production spurred by large sums of FDI is producing an oil windfall and a consequent dependence on oil, which – as also demonstrated in the literature – is having the effect of further solidifying the authoritarian regime.

Development based on energy resources produces a classic alliance between foreign companies and local rulers to sustain each other's interests.[130] Oil companies want to secure contracts and ensure the profitability of their projects and the governments want to control oil production and rents. The alliance contributes to the centralization of power and exclusion of potential opposition groups. To ensure their stay, foreign companies protect the status quo and turn a blind eye to violations of democratic principles and practices.

In Azerbaijan the alliance was most evident in the PSA process. The secretiveness attached to the PSAs has created suspicion among the Azeris that foreign oil companies sustain a corrupt and unaccountable system. As discussed above, it is been regularly asserted that some bonus payments that companies made before the start of their projects are pocketed by corrupt officials and that the companies turn a blind eye to this practice even though they are very well aware of it. [131] According to some surveys, the Western oil companies in Azerbaijan are aggravating rather than ameliorating the culture of corruption because collaboration with a corrupt regime is itself corrupting.[132] A saying among the Azeris asserts that "the name of oil belongs to us but the taste of it belongs to others"[133] meaning that the people own the oil resources but the benefits accrue to others. Generally people believe that foreign capital has contributed to the zero-sum nature of Azerbaijani politics and widened the gap between elites and masses. A 2004 survey across Azerbaijan shows that despite the influx of oil investments into the Azeri economy, most people have not seen a parallel boost in their family's economic situation.[134]

---

[130] The stability that is so consistently praised by foreign investors is not seen by opposition groups as real stability contributing to the welfare of the society. Magerram Zulfugarov of the National Independence Party, during his interview with the author, called it "police stability."

[131] Assim Mollazade of the Popular Front Party (during his interview with the author in Baku, July 15, 1999) stated that due to this corruption, there has been a capital flight of US$80 million from Azerbaijan in the 1990s.

[132] Heradstveit 2000.

[133] Author's translation of *"Neftin adi bizimdir, tadi baskalarinindir."* Interview with Ismayil Musayev (a professor of political science from Baku State University), Baku, July 14, 1999.

[134] O'Lear 2007.

Moreover, opposition leaders accuse Western governments of selling out Azerbaijan's freedom for oil. They blame the West for having a double standard and for failing to be assertive in promoting democracy in Azerbaijan. The Western reaction to human rights violations, fraudulent elections, and opposition protest movements in the aftermath of the elections is considered by many to be clearly reflective of the desire to sustain the authoritarian regime.[135] For instance, despite fraudulent elections and blatant harassment of opposition leaders, the Council of Europe admitted Azerbaijan in January 2001 and in January 2002, President Bush suspended Section 907 of the Freedom Support Act, which had placed sanctions on Azerbaijan for its alleged aggression against Armenia in the Karabakh region. In April 2006, President Bush invited President Ilham Aliev to the White House and legitimized his rule by declaring him a key ally and a valued partner of the United States.[136] More recently, in September 2008, the U.S. Vice President Dick Cheney arrived in Baku to highlight Azerbaijan's importance for U.S. energy security. The visit was the first such high-ranking visit by a U.S. official.

In addition to endorsing the authoritarian regime and contributing to its persistence, I argue that foreign capital and the ensuing oil rents have also been indirectly affecting the course of democratic development in Azerbaijan. The rentier state literature extensively demonstrates how dependence on a resource that is capable of generating extraordinary rents reinforces authoritarian tendencies by concentrating state power in the hands of a few ruling elites, by reducing the incentives for political reform, and by strengthening corruption and patronage networks in the system.[137] For instance, a recent study of oil-exporting countries from 1960 to 1999 shows that oil wealth significantly decreases the likelihood of regime change.[138]

By many accounts, this is a pattern that is becoming apparent in Azerbaijan.[139] With so much money flowing into the economy, the stakes are raised for the ruling elites to continue to dominate the political system and control the energy resources. As a result, despite the rhetoric of change and democratic reform, the ruling elites are tightening their grip on society to prevent any challenges from the opposition. The regime is paying closer attention than ever before to the campaign period, elections,

---

[135] See Lobe 2003, Bouckaert 2003, Wheelan 2003, Alieva 2006.
[136] O'Lear 2007.
[137] See Mahdavy 1970, Hughes 1975, Delacroix 1980, Gelb 1986, Shafer 1994, Chaudry 1997, Karl 1997, Ross 2001.
[138] Smith 2004.
[139] See Rasizade 2003, Freizer 2003, Guliyev 2005, Alieva 2006.

and the immediate aftermath of elections, especially in the context of "colored revolutions" engulfing some of the other post-Soviet states. Despite the close monitoring by international observers, the Azeri leadership is increasing its use of methods to pressure, constrain and harass the opposition parties, civil society organizations, and the media. The 2002 referendum, for instance, abolished the proportional party list elections, severely weakening the chances of opposition groups to be represented in the parliament. Moreover, as discussed earlier, the 2003 presidential, 2004 municipal, and 2005 parliamentary elections all witnessed sharp increases in the practice of vote-buying, intimidation, and use of force. The government resisted any change that it thought would threaten the ruling elite's grip on power, insisting in particular that the composition of election commissions remain unchanged despite the fact that elections failed to meet OSCE and Council of Europe standards.[140]

Especially the use of excessive force by the police in the aftermath of the 2005 elections underlines the regime's determination to prevent a "color revolution" at all costs and to ensure that the control of energy resources remains in the hands of the ruling elite. Increasing consolidation of power in Azerbaijan in the past few years is perhaps best depicted by the drop in freedom ratings for Azerbaijan from "partly free" to "not free."[141]

Increased military spending, another indicator of repressive effects of oil rents that are commonly found in resource rich states, is easily observable in Azerbaijan. The Azeri leaders have poured a substantial amount of the new-found petrodollars into the defense budget, which has increased about 1480 percent from US$125 million in 1992 to $1.85 billion in 2008.[142] Even though military spending as a percentage of total expenditures as well as a percentage of the GDP has stayed pretty consistent over the years, the massive amount of military spending due to rising oil revenues has undeniably been helping to consolidate the regime against internal as well as external enemies.[143]

---

[140] Alieva 2006.

[141] Individual countries are evaluated based on a checklist of questions regarding political rights and civil liberties that are derived in large measure from the Universal Declaration of Human Rights. Each country is assigned a rating for political rights and a rating for civil liberties based on a scale of 1 to 7, with 1 representing the highest degree of freedom present and 7 the lowest level of freedom. The combined average of each country's political rights and civil liberties ratings determines an overall status of Free, Partly Free, or Not Free.

[142] International Crisis Group 2008.

[143] Military spending has traditionally been around 11–14 percent of total expenditures and military expenditures as a percentage of GDP has on average been at 2–3 percent (International Crisis Group 2008, World Bank 2009).

Furthermore, despite the restructuring in the oil industry since 2001, the control of the industry still is in the hands of a few elites. The Special Oil Fund of Azerbaijan (SOFAZ), which was set up by a presidential decree to manage the oil wealth in a more efficient and transparent way, lacks formal and clear operating rules, and gives the president the sole authority to use the funds.[144] The executive director, who is appointed and can be dismissed by the president, operates the fund. All strategic decisions are made by the president, including the decision to liquidate the fund altogether. In other words, the president and his closed circle of loyalists still hold near-total control over the way energy contracts are written, the way energy projects are carried out, and the way energy revenues are spent.

Overall, then, foreign capital in an authoritarian regime presents a paradox. The very regime that makes it possible to attract investment gets emboldened by the actual investment and the endorsement foreign investors give it. Foreign capital also indirectly affects the regime trajectory by enabling the oil rents and dependency that further centralize political authority. Authoritarianism and foreign capital keep feeding each other in a vicious cycle.

The Azeri case clearly demonstrates that the success in attracting foreign investment in the oil sector does not automatically translate into success in the efficient use of oil revenues. "Successful efforts to use petrodollars wisely depend on the presence of countervailing political and social pressures strong enough to curb "petrolization," a process by which states become dependent on oil exports and their polities develop an addiction to petrodollars."[145] Such countervailing pressures include transparent democratic institutions, powerful enough to rein in the alliance between multinational oil interests and political leaders. A consolidated democratic regime can constrain the centralizing tendencies that petroleum exploitation leads to and limit the powerful alliance between rulers and oil companies that initially takes place when oil revenues gets allocated without strict controls. Without stable democratic institutions, it is highly unlikely that the effects of an abundance of oil money will extend beyond a small, politically and regionally connected subset of the Azeri population.

To facilitate the management of oil revenues and to prevent the resource curse that has been so widely experienced in developing countries, the

[144] Bagirov et al. 2003.
[145] Karl 1997, 38.

Azeri leaders have been taking certain steps, albeit small and limited. As mentioned earlier, President Aliev signed a decree to set up the State Oil Fund of the Azerbaijani Republic (SOFAZ) in 1999. In addition, Azerbaijan volunteered to become the pilot study for the Extractive Industries Transparency Initiative (EITI) that was internationally created to increase the transparency with which developing and transitional states manage revenues from oil, gas, and mining. The purpose of EITI is to increase public knowledge and transparency of natural resource revenues, to help empower citizens and institutions to hold their governments accountable, and to create a more attractive business environment for foreign investment.[146] Despite these attempts, however, the Azeri government has a long way to go before establishing transparent, professional and efficient institutions to manage the influx of foreign capital and the ensuing oil profits. The fact that the Azeri president still holds ultimate control of the Oil Fund surely does not help.

Trade-offs Facing Investors

Even when foreign investors benefit from and acquiesce to the repressive and corrupt authoritarian regimes, they still face certain trade-offs from investing in such regimes as opposed to more established, stable democracies. They undertake significant long-term risks in exchange for short-term rewards. Oil dependence in an authoritarian regime has the potential to create social unrest and instability in the longer run, which can threaten the profitability and sustainability of foreign investment projects.

In addition to the risk of long-term instability, foreign companies also face the risk of selective targeting by the government. Not all investors face the same tax and regulatory rules and incentives. The country is attractive and inviting to only a select number of investors that the regime deems necessary for its survival and those that do not directly threaten its authority. The favorable conditions and legal protection created for foreign investors in the oil sector are noticeably absent in other sectors. One can argue that oil investments have been ring-fenced through production sharing agreements signed with the government. This special framework has kept the big oil companies immune to the difficulties of everyday business life experienced by smaller companies.

Azerbaijan, in fact, has proved to be a minefield for other foreign companies trying to establish operations in the country. Outside of the

---

[146] O'Lear 2007.

oil sector, monopolies still dominate most of Azerbaijan's economy and many are run by associates of the President.[147] Investors in other sectors face a multitude of difficulties with outdated legislation and bureaucratic hurdles. The prevalence of corruption undermines the development of the non-oil sector, the revival of which is essential to Azerbaijan's long-term economic development. In a survey of 555 non-oil foreign firms operating in Azerbaijan, the Foreign Investment Advisory Service found the investment climate in the oil sector was significantly better than in the non-oil sector. The impression of prevalent corruption was the reason most frequently cited by businesses that chose not to invest in Azerbaijan.[148]

Therefore, the success of the oil sector demonstrates the limited capacity of the Azeri state to attract selective foreign investment. An authoritarian state is useful only to the extent that it can provide isolated stability and flexibility for certain industries that generate enormous rents. Azerbaijan's shot at globalization is sector-specific and investors clearly face a two-tiered economy.

Conclusion

The commercial and geostrategic importance of Azeri oil has been a necessary but not a sufficient condition for attracting significant amounts of foreign investment. What has been pivotal in turning the potential interests of the oil companies into actual investment projects was the flexible investment environment that offered investors generous incentives and guarantees.

In this chapter, I have argued that the political regime in Azerbaijan and the flexible investment environment it produced can explain the high levels of FDI into the Azeri oil industry. Thanks to weak executive constraints and political competition, the Aliev family was able to exclude any potential opposition group and equip itself with the utmost discretion and flexibility to negotiate with foreign investors. The sultanistic regime created a perception of stability for foreigners and reassured them that the terms of their investment relationship would be guaranteed by the president and a rubber stamp parliament through the duration of their projects. The Azerbaijani case demonstrates that authoritarian regimes that provide for policy flexibility can be as successful in getting a

---

[147] Cohen 2006.
[148] Foreign Investment Advisory Service (FIAS) 2002.

share of the international investment as consolidated democratic regimes. This case challenges conventional theories that assume an inevitable relationship between globalization and democracy.

I have also argued that given its negative impact on the political and economic development of the country, Azerbaijan's ability to attract significant amounts of foreign investment in a very short amount of time should be approached with skepticism and not be hailed as a success that should be emulated by other oil-producing countries in the post-Soviet region or in other developing countries. One of the dilemmas of global capitalism for developing countries lies in the choice between immediate economic success, i.e., the ability to attract foreign investment in this case, and long term socio-economic and democratic development. The experience of Azerbaijan offers a sobering example of the trade-offs facing both developing countries and international investors.

In the next chapter, I analyze the investment environment in another oil-producing post-communist state, Russia. Considering that both Azerbaijan and Russia started the development of their oil resources at the same time in the beginning of the 1990s, the differences in their performance over the course of a decade are striking. While Azerbaijan was able to create favorable conditions for investors to invest significant amounts of capital in its oil resources, Russia failed to establish an attractive legislative and regulatory framework and, as a result, received very little investment capital throughout the 1990s. This occurred despite the fact that in the 1990s Russia had been considered one of the top potential destinations for FDI.

6

Russia: Two Steps Forward, One Step Back

In its first decade of independence, Russia received far less foreign investment than it could have received, both relative to the size of its economy and compared to other emerging markets. According to the World Investment Report, Russia has shown a "below potential" investment performance throughout the 1990s.[1] In terms of the inward Foreign Direct Investment (FDI) performance index, among approximately 140 countries, Russia ranked the 108th and 104th highest during 1992–1994 and 1998–2000, respectively.[2] FDI constituted approximately 6 percent of gross fixed capital formation in Russia between 1995 and 1999.[3] In per capita terms, Russia's poor performance in attracting FDI is revealed more starkly. Between 1989 and 1997, Russia attracted a cumulative inflow of FDI per capita equivalent to only US$63; this figure contrasts with an inflow of US$1,667 per capita in the case of Hungary; and US$823 per capita in the case of the Czech Republic. Russia's overall performance in attracting FDI ranked twentieth out of twenty-five countries in the post-Communist region in terms of FDI per capita.[4]

The oil sector has not been much of an exception for Russia in terms of attracting FDI. The amount of foreign capital inflow to this sector paralleled its poor investment performance in other sectors. For example, during the 1990s, with almost ten times the oil reserves of Azerbaijan, Russia received approximately one tenth the FDI for each barrel of its oil reserves than Azerbaijan received for its (see Table 1.1).

[1] UNCTAD 2006.
[2] UNCTAD 2002a.
[3] UNCTAD 2001.
[4] European Bank for Restructuring and Development 1998.

Russia's lackluster FDI performance in the 1990s was certainly not due to a lack of interest on the part of the foreign investors. Nearly all the major oil companies and many smaller ones expressed interest in participating in the exploration and development of Russia's oil and gas reserves and a willingness to commit modern technology and billions of dollars of capital on a long-term basis.[5] In the beginning of the 1990s, some analysts put the total amount of potential FDI that Russia could receive in the oil sector by the end of the decade at around US$60–70 billion.[6] This is because Russia is very attractive commercially. Its oil wealth is enormous: proven reserves alone stand at 74 billion barrels, approximately 6.2 percent of the total world reserves.[7] In addition, the proximity of several of its oil provinces to growing markets in the Asia-Pacific region makes Russia very attractive to multinational oil companies, as do its skilled labor force and existing infrastructure.

Even more important, opportunities for investment in the Russian oil industry have been ample. Following the collapse of the Soviet Union, Russia's oil industry, which accounted for approximately 90 percent of the former Soviet Union's oil output, fell upon hard times due to the breakdown of inter-republic trade, decreased domestic industrial demand, low oil prices, and a decline in drilling and capital investments.[8] From 1992 to 1998, oil production plummeted 23 percent, from 7.86 to 6.07 million barrels per day (bbl/d). To develop new fields, extend the life of existing oilfields with exhausted and low-yield reserves, undertake neglected capital expenditure programs, and thus to reverse the decline in production, huge sums of investment capital were needed.[9] The Ministry for Fuel and Energy calculated the total investment needs of the industry between 1992 and 2000 at about US$35 billion.[10] A World Bank study in 1995 put the amount of combined operating and capital expenditure required to maintain Russian oil production at US$13 billion annually.[11] Given the fact that during the low oil prices of 1990s, only a few Russian oil companies were willing to use their profits to invest in exploration and new drilling projects and that there was in fact a capital flight from

[5] Ogutcu 2002.
[6] Konoplyanik and Lisovsky 1992.
[7] BP 2006.
[8] According to Locatelli (2006), investment in exploration dropped by some 60 percent between 1988 and 1994.
[9] According to the Ministry for Fuel and Energy, the drilling of between 40,000 and 76,000 new wells were needed to stabilize production in the 1990s (Sagers 1993).
[10] Dienes 1993.
[11] Gyetvay 2000.

Russia, the much-needed investment capital was expected to come mostly from external sources in the form of FDI.[12]

Foreign oil companies' interest in Russia's resources and its investment opportunities were further reinforced by Western governments' geostrategic interest in creating and sustaining a healthy Russian oil industry that would reduce their dependence on the volatile Middle East oil, ensure energy security for the foreseeable future, and enable a moderate and pro-Western government to stay in power in Russia. Since the collapse of the Soviet Union, Western governments have not only actively encouraged Western oil companies to invest in Russia but have also used every bilateral and multilateral diplomatic opportunity to pressure the Russian government to liberalize its investment regime.

Despite the investment potential of Russia as well as the clear interest of foreign oil companies and Western governments in the Russian oil industry, FDI levels remained surprisingly low throughout the 1990s as demonstrated above. I argue that Russia's poor performance in attracting foreign investment was due to the instability of its investment environment, caused largely by its hybrid political regime. Russia has consistently fallen short on investment conditions compatible with international practice, such as a clear and reasonable tax regime, a stable set of rules, and equal opportunity to obtain and exercise rights to the oil fields. Moreover, the convulsive transformation of the ownership structure of the Russian oil industry in the 1990s made it extremely difficult to provide a unified, consistent, and stable domestic industry as a counterpart and partner to the foreign investors.

In the first section of this chapter, I discuss the history of relations between foreign investors and the Russian state. After describing the characteristics of the oil investment environment – and specifically the PSA regime – in the 1990s, I analyze the links between Russia's political regime and its oil policy. I trace the sources of instability in the investment environment to the limited institutional constraints and competition that its hybrid regime produced in its first decade of existence. The following section focuses on the recent developments in the investment environment since the beginning of 2000s. I once again analyze the relationship between the Russian state and investors as a function of the changes in the

---

[12] According to Dienes (2004), most Russian companies throughout the 1990s concentrated on maximizing extraction from the best reserves already developed in the Soviet era. Essentially they were "skimming off the easiest oil" to boost their short-term cash flow rather than develop new fields that required extensive capital and technology (p. 339) It has been estimated that in the period from 1992 to 1995 capital flight from the Russian oil industry amounted to a total of US$7 bn. (Tikhomirov 1997).

international oil industry as well as Russia's political regime in the 2000s. I end the chapter with a discussion on whether or not Russia's economic and political development has been negatively affected by foreign investment as well as production and export of oil. The study of Russian oil illuminates not only the general problems with the investment climate, but also the changing role of the Russian state in the economy as well as the contours of Russia's overall economic relations with the West.

History of Relations between Investors and the Government

The Soviet Period

Early oil during the Russian Empire was produced in Baku (then part of the empire) by Western investors who dominated the domestic Russian market and supplied oil to Western Europe. After the Bolshevik Revolution of 1917 and until 1987, however, as part of the communist anti-imperialist policy, all forms of foreign capital were banned and all foreign assets were nationalized in Russia. During only two periods in Soviet history were foreign investors invited to form joint ventures (JVs) with the Soviet state (albeit in only export-oriented sectors). The first was during Lenin's new economic policy (NEP) in the 1920s. Although numerous Western oil companies protested the forced nationalization of the industry and refused to cooperate, others, such as Standard Oil of New York, continued to invest in Russia. During this brief period, Western technology and investment enabled production to recover and by 1923 oil exports to Europe rose to their prerevolution levels.[13] After Lenin, however, Stalin abolished and outlawed JVs.[14] Not only was foreign capital strictly forbidden, but even the mention of the word "capital" was deemed intolerable.[15]

---

[13] Obut 1999.
[14] Ironically, even though the Soviet state did not permit foreign capital to operate in the Soviet Union, Russian capital was permitted to participate in joint ventures in several parts of the world. After WWII, for instance, German shares in some of the companies in Eastern European countries were transferred to the Soviet state. Another such incident took place in the 1960s when the Soviets formed joint ventures in fishing enterprises in Africa.
[15] Author's interview with Ninel Voznesenskaya (professor at the Institute of State and Law), Moscow, April 20, 2001. According to Voznesenskaya, for instance if a scholar had to use this word, he had to put it in a negative context by adding that foreign capital brings with it the exploitation of workers. This is why in most of the Soviet texts of that period, one is likely to see words like "resources", "income," and "funds" in lieu of the word "capital." This imposition by the state symbolizes the negative attitude toward foreign investment at the time.

In the 1930s, 1940s, and early 1950s, Russia's domestic consumption of oil grew rapidly, causing a fall in oil exports. The late 1950s saw resurgence in exports due to massive domestic investments in the newly discovered Volga-Urals oil province. By the early 1960s, the country had replaced Venezuela as the world's second-largest oil producer and had once again become a major competitor of the West. In the 1960s and 1970s, the Russians discovered the Tyumen and Samotlar oil basins in western Siberia and their output by 1980 increased rapidly to make that region the principal producer in the Soviet Union.

The Soviet state viewed an uninterrupted supply of oil as crucial to its economic progress. Under the command economy, the country's energy sector was bound by law to provide oil to domestic industries and consumers at prices significantly below those of the world market. The oil industry was regulated by a group of ministries that exercised total control. This centralized control over oil assets led to overproduction of existing fields to meet production quotas without regard for proper reservoir-management practices. The Soviet state favored the exploitation of big reservoirs with inefficient techniques such as water flooding, which resulted in permanent damage to oil fields. Moreover, in the absence of market-driven incentives to improve operating efficiency, the state chronically underinvested in technology. These systemic problems arising in Soviet-era policy, combined with the continued deterioration of the western Siberia reserve base eventuated in a steady decline in Russian oil production from late 1980s onward.[16]

To reverse the dramatic decline in oil production, in January 1987 Gorbachev issued a short decree permitting formation of JVs with foreign capital and outlining the basic principles of foreign investment. However, the decree specified neither the details of the legal relationships nor many of the issues critical to the industry, such as taxation, freedom of export, transportation, and government participation.[17] Subsequent to the decree, Government Act number 48 permitted organization of JVs with socialist countries and Act number 49 permitted creation of JVs with capitalist and developing countries. Not only was this arrangement problematic when an investor from each group was included in a JV, it was also significant in demonstrating the lingering mentality of separating the socialist camp from the rest of the world. Even though from a legal standpoint, there was not much difference between these

---

[16] Obut 1999.
[17] Nelson 1996.

two acts, symbolically they reflected a continuation of the discrimination against *Western* foreign investment.[18]

Without applicable corporate legislation and clear-cut specifications as to the type of legal entity created and how it was organized, the initial interest of foreign investors turned into disappointment. Many JVs were formed initially, yet very little capital actually entered the economy in the last years of the Soviet Union. Some described the initial euphoria aroused by talk of partnership arrangements at this period as "foam."[19] As Thane Gustafson noted more than a decade ago, the dominant characteristic of the energy sector in Soviet times – which lingered into the 1990s – was that of "crisis amidst plenty."[20] The pattern of "lost opportunities" did not suddenly appear in Russia in 1991.

Oil Investment Policy of the New Russian State-Early 1990s

In 1991, the new Russian state passed the Foreign Investment Law (FIL), which allowed the creation of other forms of investment in addition to the JVs that were legalized by Gorbachev in late 1980s. Together with this law, the state also developed a substantial body of laws and regulations governing oil exploration and production.[21]

The fundamental legislation in regard to natural-resource development in Russia was the Law on Underground Resources (LUR), adopted in February 1992. In the early 1990s, except for some service contracts, the only regulated form of investment in the petroleum sector was through a legal entity, typically the JV, which had to be granted a license to carry out all petroleum activities. The LUR provided the general framework for licensing exploration and development activities relating to minerals and other subsurface resources, including hydrocarbons.

---

[18] Author's interview with Ninel Voznesenskaya.
[19] Ibid.
[20] Rutland (1997) quoting from Gustafson (1991).
[21] For instance, commercial relations were generally regulated by the Civil Code (November 1994), which set forth the applicable principles governing contracts, international transactions, forms of legal entities, and other matters. Procedures for licenses were governed by a variety of regulations adopted at the federal and local levels. Environmental issues arising from the exploration and production of oil were governed by the Law on Environment Protection (December 1991) and the Law on Ecology Expertise (November 1995). The use of land arising in connection with the exploration and production of oil was governed by the Land Code (April 1991), and by several presidential decrees as well as federal and local regulations. Taxation was governed by a comprehensive set of laws and regulations. The financing of exploration and of production ventures by foreign sources was subject to foreign-currency regulations in the Law on Foreign Investments (July 1991) and the Law on Foreign Currency Regulation and Control (October 1992).

Under this law, petroleum exploration, development, and production could take place as a result of a license issued jointly by the Russian Federation Ministry of Natural Resources and the legislative authorities of the territory in which petroleum operations were to be conducted.[22] In terms of the financial aspects, the LUR laid out the fees that were to be paid by those who explored for and extracted subsurface resources. Usually the payments were designed for issuance of a license, the right to use subsurface resources, for resource replenishment, and for excise taxes.

Despite its myriad laws governing oil and gas activities in particular and foreign investment in general, Russia lacked comprehensive and effective natural-resource legislation. The licensing regime depicted in the LUR did not provide sufficient guarantees, stability, or incentives for foreign investors. In fact, it raised a number of concerns stemming from the fact that licenses and the licensing procedures were based on administrative law rather than on contractual rights and obligations. This implied that foreign investors were subject to state legislative action that could unilaterally change and modify the license. They had no right to prevent or influence the process. As well, they were subject to possible change by new laws and regulations that did not include provisions for compensating the licensee. For instance, existing law and applicable regulations allowed a license to be terminated by the licensing agency in a wide range of situations beyond the licensee's control, that is, force majeure circumstances, without adequate protection against the abuse of these powers by the agency. Adding to this difficulty were provisions defining the duration of the license. There were no assurances that the licensee could extend the term of the license depending on particular field conditions.

Moreover, the legal hierarchy established under the 1993 Constitution was not very clear as to the distribution of authority between the Federation and its subjects, where oil reserves were located. Article 72 assigned ownership and use of subsurface resource matters to the jurisdictions of both federal and regional governments. Even though it also stated that regional laws pertaining to such joint jurisdiction were subordinated to federal law, ambiguities remained concerning the power of

---

[22] In July 1992, the parliament of the Russian Federation approved the Regulations of the Procedure for Licensing the Use of the Subsurface. These regulations addressed the licensing procedure in greater detail than the LUR. Accordingly, licenses were to be granted by means of competitive tenders or auctions. A license to engage in geographic exploration could be issued for a period of up to five years while a license to produce hydrocarbons could go up to twenty-five years.

the regions to bypass federal laws. As such, investors were exposed to tax laws, regulations, excise fees, and licensing requirements at both the federal and local levels that often contradicted or duplicated one another.

Finally, the tax burden under these laws made the investment environment unattractive. Many taxes – most notably the export tax – were levied not on profits but on revenues. This was problematic for foreign investors, who were often pursuing projects with high costs and low margins in fields that had been declared uneconomic by Russian production associations. A 1993 estimate suggested that the total tax burden on some Western oil-producing operations was as high as 65 to 70 percent of revenues.[23] Moreover, the frequent and unpredictable changes to taxation added significantly to the tax burden.[24] Export duties, for instance, have changed at least a dozen times under this regime. Exporters struggled with cumbersome and restrictive quota and licensing requirements, and they were further confused when the restrictions were lifted with ambiguous procedures for fair access to overburdened pipelines.[25] Even though in February 1995, the State Duma approved some amendments to the LUR, (which took effect in March 1995) most of these problems with licensing procedures, legal hierarchy, and tax burden persisted.[26]

As a result, JVs failed to become the main conduit for foreign investment in the Russian oil and gas industry. In 1998, there were 42 oil-producing JVs that produced a meager 6 percent of the total oil production and 7 percent of total oil exports.[27] Many of the JVs that were established in the early 1990s produced technical achievements in the sense that they succeeded in raising production in the fields.[28] However, they were not considered by foreign investors as economic successes. By the end of 1990s, not one JV had recovered its capital

---

[23] Watson 1996.
[24] For instance, when the White Nights JV was formed in 1991, it was subject to only four taxes; by early 1993, this had risen to eleven, radically altering the economics of the project. Similarly, Gulf Canada cut off all additional investment in an oil field near the Arctic Circle, where it had already committed US$60 million. The company stated that its Russian tax bill exceeded its total revenues. Author's interview with Jamal Quadir (Conoco), Moscow, August 25, 2000.
[25] Hober 1997.
[26] Author's interview with Alexander Levshov, Moscow, March 14, 2001.
[27] Heinrich et al. 2002.
[28] Some of the most important joint ventures were the U.S. firm Phibro Energy's *White Nights* venture with the West Siberian production association Vareganneftegaz; Conoco and Arkhangelskgeologiya's *Polar Lights* project to develop fields in the Timan Pechora region of northern Russia; and Occidental's partnership with the West Siberian company Chernorneft.

costs. This was largely because the fiscal terms on which the investments had been made were later arbitrarily changed. Inevitably, many of these JVs closed and some Western companies left Russia, especially after the 1998 economic crisis.[29] As a JV senior executive told Reuters in 1999, "The Russian government absolutely strangled the life out of every nascent joint venture right at the beginning."[30]

Another form of FDI that was tried in the Russian oil and gas industry in the 1990s was the foreign equity investment. But this, too, was confronted with many political and legal restrictions and was unsuccessful in attracting much-needed foreign capital. The state opposed the sale of larger stakes to foreigners for fear of selling out to foreign interests. Moreover, Russian managers were unwilling to share control of their companies. Foreigners were excluded from the mass privatization of 1992–94 and 1995–97. A presidential decree restricted foreign ownership in major Russian oil companies from 1992 until 1997 to 15 percent. The minority status of foreign investors made it very difficult to counter the decisions of the Russian management when those decisions clearly hurt their interests. Heinrich et al. (2002) argue that "the practices of share dilution, transfer pricing and asset stripping effectively robbed most minority shareholders of their entitlement and left them with huge losses on their investments."[31] As a result, among the four main foreign equity investments that took place in the 1990s, two failed, one had a mixed record and only one met the demands of the foreign investor.[32]

Given these problems with the two forms of foreign investment, production-sharing agreements (PSA) presented an attractive alternative to solving the foreign investment challenge. PSAs were preferred by foreign investors because they would put the investors in a much more secure position and would protect their property rights for the life of the projects.[33] Unlike the LUR, which provided a "take-it-or-leave-it" arrangement between the licensee and the state – in that the licensee's rights

---

[29] Author's interview with Jamal Quadir (Conoco), Moscow, August 25, 2000.

[30] Quote taken from "Firms wait on laws in Russia's black gold rush." *The Russia Journal* 21: 64 (June 5, 2000).

[31] Heinrich et al. 2002, 503.

[32] For more detailed analysis of these investments, see Heinrich et al. (2002).

[33] It is important to note that concessionary licensing in general is considered commercially more profitable for both the host government and the investors. Opting for a PSA regime is a political and psychological need for stability. If a reasonable tax system is in place and the investors trust that it will not be changed arbitrarily, then the investors generally prefer the concessionary licensing. As discussed in detail in Chapter 2, PSA is mostly a developing-country phenomenon.

derived from a nonnegotiable license, – the PSA law would bind the state to its contractual obligations and make it liable for breach of contract.[34] It would allow the foreign investor to circumvent the existing legal environment and acquire guarantees of certainty and protection directly from the state. A PSA Law would also provide a clear and transparent regulatory framework for oil contracts by establishing which government agency would be responsible to formulate contracts with foreign companies, and most important, how exactly the project would be protected from subsequent changes in other laws. Finally, a PSA would permit the investor to submit disputes to binding arbitration in an international tribunal.

Like the investor, the Russian state would also enjoy certain benefits under the PSA framework. Its chief benefit would be greater national control over natural resources and oil companies.[35] Under a PSA, the state would keep title to the land and resources and retain a significant portion of the natural resource product. By creating a stable and transparent system, the state would guarantee payments on the part of the investors and ensure a reliable stream of revenues – an opportunity that was certainly not secured by the licensing regime that existed in Russia at the time.[36] Furthermore, the enactment of the PSA law would strengthen the capacity of the federal government by creating new opportunities for cooperation between the center and the regions where PSA projects take place.[37] Given these characteristics, it was believed by various groups that the PSA legislation in Russia could "jump-start" the oil and gas investment process by immediately establishing a special legal regime for PSAs to insulate investors from many of the risks that JVs faced.

The Evolution of the PSA Regime: "Progress Stalled Again"

The PSA regime, with all the necessary laws and regulations, could not be developed smoothly and in a timely fashion in Russia. In fact, its development proved very problematic. It probably would not be an exaggeration

---

[34] Note however that PSA investors and producers are still required to obtain a license. The difference, in theory, is a mandatory formality on the part of the government rather than a discretionary administrative act.

[35] Author's interview with Daniel Lefebvre (Yukos), Moscow, April 23, 2001.

[36] For instance, as of January 2000, investors in the only working PSA projects in Russia – Sakhalin 1 and Sakhalin 2 – had paid more than US$100 million to the federal and local budgets, and the state's revenues from existing PSA projects was around US$350 million. PSAs give governments profit share from the first production. Under the licensing regime, however, the host government receives nothing until the company as a whole makes a profit.

[37] Subbotin 1996.

to argue that the restructuring of the oil industry, as reflected in the PSA process, has been one of the fiercest struggles that the new Russian state had to go through in its first decade of existence.

Russia was a textbook setting for the use of PSAs in the 1990s. It was rich in hydrocarbon resources but lacked the financial and technical means to develop new reserves efficiently. Moreover, its tax system and legal regime were too unpredictable and burdensome to attract large-scale, long-term non-PSA investments. In addition, the possibility that PSAs could bring benefits to both the state and the investors made this a win-win situation and appealed to both liberal reformers and conservatives. However, despite the pressing need for and the potential appeal of it, a full PSA regime could not develop in Russia over the course of a decade.

Russian lawmakers had begun preparing for PSAs even before the breakup of the Soviet Union. In the new Russian state, the PSA process started on December 24, 1993 when Yeltsin signed the Presidential Decree 2285. This decree outlined the general features of PSA enabling legislation, and called on the new parliament, the State Duma, to pass it.[38] Galvanized by investors' continued dissatisfaction with the JVs, the Russian authorities focused on creating an adequate PSA law. Over the course of the following year, three special working groups set out to draft the new legislation.

Directed by, Ruslan Gennadievich Orekhov, the head of the Legal Department of the Presidential Administration, and his executive officer Alexander Sergevich Pashkov, the first group released an initial draft in early summer 1994. The draft was submitted for comments to a wide range of individuals, among them foreign legal specialists. The second group to draw up draft PSA legislation was headed by the deputy minister Vadim Anatolievich Dvurechensky of the Ministry of Fuel and Energy (MFE). By the end of 1994, the MFE group joined forces with the first group from the presidential administration to author a common draft, which came to be known as the "government draft."

Finally, the third group, called the inter-ministerial working group, was led by Andrei Aleksandrovich Konoplyanik and several technocrats from different ministries. In addition to drawing up the enabling legislation, this group drafted normative acts, which would be the instructions to be used by ministries in implementing the general precepts of a PSA law. This group also fashioned a "model PSA" contract as a guide for actual

[38] Kennedy 1995.

contracts. Soon the Yabloko Party in the Duma sponsored this draft, and labeled it as the "Duma draft."

The competing drafts were submitted to the Duma for debate in December 1994. The failure of their backers in reaching an agreement was the key factor delaying initial parliamentary approval of the Law on PSA.[39] The session of February 24, 1995 adopted the "Duma draft" after the first reading: 162 to 19 with 7 absentions. The draft also passed its second and third reading on June 14, 1995, but failed to get an approval by the upper chamber, the Federation Council, on October 3.[40] Because it had not gained the necessary number of votes in the Federation Council, it passed to the Duma for a new consideration. As a response, a conciliatory commission was set up to reconcile the differences between the two houses of the parliament. Finally on December 6, the Duma adopted the revised PSA law. Then, on December 19, it was approved by the Federation Council, and on December 30 it was signed by the president. The PSA law was finally published on January 11, 1996.

Despite the PSA law, foreign investors still did not find the investment environment stable enough to initiate their projects. For instance, Exxon in a press release stated that the law "will not provide the stable foundation upon which the legal framework required to attract foreign investments can be developed."[41] A Texaco spokesman concurred by saying that "it is not a law that you can depend on in terms of your exports, your tax rates, your ability to gain a reasonable economic return."[42] Western oil companies raised their concerns with the Russian authorities and legislators at such forums as the Gore-Chernomyrdin Commission meetings, the Petroleum Advisory Forum, and the Congressional U.S.-Former Soviet Union Energy Caucus.[43]

[39] "Too many cooks: Competing drafts slow progress of PSA legislation." *Russian Petroleum Investor* (February 1995): 13–16. The issues on which these drafts differed included licensing regulations, taxation, and the nature of entities to which the laws apply.

[40] According to many accounts, although most deputies finally agreed to the passage of the PSA Law on the second and third readings in the Duma, it came down to the actions of one man, Irik Amirov, the then-executive director of the Russian oil company Yukos. When the second reading was over, with only slightly more votes in favor, the Duma deputies hurried out of the hall without waiting for another round of dull proceedings. Amirov, who was one of the draft's authors, rushed to the doors and blocked the exit, loudly begging the deputies to stay for a few minutes more and cast their votes during the third reading. That's how the passage of the law in the Duma was finally possible. "A Reason to Stay: Passage of PSA Legislation Important for Its Symbolism, Not Its Substance," *Russian Petroleum Investor* (July/August 1995): 15.

[41] Quoted in Senecal and Daly (1996).

[42] Ibid.

[43] Pugliaresi and Hensen 1996.

In explaining the weaknesses of the investment environment in Russia, foreign investors cited the shortcomings of the core PSA law on the one hand, and conflicts between the core PSA law and various subsoil use, tax, customs, and foreign trade laws on the other. The core PSA law was not consistent on key contractual issues such as the priority of civil-law arrangements, the transfer and pledge of PSA rights, and dispute resolutions. The drafters did not clearly classify the relationship between the state and the investor under a PSA as purely contractual. Article 1.3 of the draft provided that the rights and obligations of the parties to a PSA would be governed by the federal law and the civil legislation of the Russian Federation. According to some, this implied that certain rights and obligations of the parties to the PSA would not be civil in nature and, as such, would be governed by administrative law principles. On its face, the text of the law was unclear as to where the line was to be drawn. It did not identify the provisions that were not civil in nature.[44]

Compounding this confusion was a provision of the law (added at the insistence of the Federation Council) stating that the provisions of a PSA could not conflict with the provisions of the LUR. Because the LUR's administrative approach fundamentally conflicted with the PSA law's civil-contract approach, there was no explicit way to determine how disputes over critical matters such as issuance, suspension, and termination of mineral rights were to be resolved. This ambiguity and the possibility that certain provisions of a PSA could be governed by administrative law created the risk of broader administrative discretion and the nonarbitration of disputes – hence a greater liability exposure for the investors.[45]

A last-minute amendment to the draft PSA Law imposing broad legislative approval requirements also caused concern among foreign investors. Accordingly, exploration and development under a PSA would be permissible only for fields and blocks named in a list that would be approved by the legislature. The draft law also included a second and final legislative approval for any PSA that had been awarded without a tender. Moreover, it stipulated legislative approval for PSAs in fields that were located on the continental shelf and that involved "special state strategic interests." In essence, this meant that after the investor had negotiated a deal with federal and local authorities, the deal could be renegotiated on demand of the Russian legislature as a condition for its approval. Given the thorny legislative journey already set in the PSA law, the requirements of legislative approval for

---

[44] Author's interview with Alexander Levshov.
[45] Hober 1997.

each PSA and its amendments evoked great consternation among investors, for whom the requirement was unprecedented in countries using PSAs.

Another shortcoming of the final draft was the provision that regulated the export of oil production. One of the key benefits provided by the original Duma draft was the unrestricted right to export an investor's share of production in accordance with the terms of the agreement, free of any restrictions such as export quotas, licensing requirements, or the mandatory sale of production through designated organizations. That benefit was weakened in the final version by the addition of the clause permitting export restrictions to be imposed in accordance with the Law on State Regulation of Foreign Trade Activity. This law permitted the introduction of export restrictions or prohibitions based on "national interests," defined to include items such as environmental protection, "the necessity of preventing the depletion of nonrenewable natural resources," and "protection of the external financial situation and support of the balance of payments of the Russian Federation."[46] The uncertainty introduced by the exception could potentially raise the costs of financing a PSA because lenders would demand a higher margin to assume the risk associated with a possible cut-off of project revenue.

Yet another notable concern for the investors was the amendment in the final version of the PSA law that stipulated that PSAs would be governed by Russian law. One benefit provided by the original draft PSA law was the ability to choose foreign law to govern the contractual relationship between the state and the investor – a significant step toward recognition of the realities of cross-border contractual relationships in the energy sector. The use of a foreign law to govern a PSA would reduce political risks because it would prevent the state from obtaining an unfair advantage over the investor through manipulation of its domestic laws. In addition to being neutral, the laws of a foreign country with a more highly developed legal system could be better suited to the specific requirements of multinational oil projects. Hence, given the developing status of Russian law and the possibility of unexpected changes that might affect the interpretation of the liabilities under a PSA, this amendment was considered a very unwelcome term for the investors.

Furthermore, the stabilization provisions of the PSA law were weakened by an amendment introduced by the Federation Council that required revisions on a PSA on the demand of one party in the event of a material change in circumstances in accordance with the Civil Code of

---

[46] Ibid.

the Russian Federation. The Civil Code permitted juridical reformulation of a contract in such circumstances, but the conditions that had to be met in order to grant such a unilateral amendment were very stringent.

Finally, the taxes and accounting provisions that would apply to PSA projects under this law could not be effectively put in place until there was additional legislative action, i.e., amendments to the Tax Code. This conclusion was based on an old Supreme Soviet Decree and the Law on Fundamentals of the Budgetary System and Budgeting Process in the Russian Federation, which stipulated that no changes could be made to the Russian tax system except through the adoption of new tax laws or the amendment of existing tax laws. Taxes could not be introduced or changed by means of nontax laws.[47] Not only was the investor exposed to income taxes that could be as high as 32 percent, but also taxable income would have to be calculated using Russian methods of accounting.

Given these shortcomings in the final version of the core PSA law, except for the three PSAs that had been signed before the adoption of the law and that were grandfathered in when the law took effect, no other PSA project gained any momentum in the 1990s.[48] The investors demanded further amendments to the law, including the elimination or curtailment of the role of the legislature, and resolution of fundamental conflicts with the LUR. Moreover, regulations were needed to delineate detailed rules for taxation, determination of recoverable costs, accounting, and other matters. It had taken almost three years and much difficulty before the basic PSA Law became effective in January 1996. Still ahead lay the tasks of providing the list of fields to be developed under PSAs and devising the amendments and enabling legislation that would allow the basic law to function.

In 1996–97, the government, together with the regional authorities, prepared a number of bills with the lists of fields allowed for PSAs and submitted them to the Duma. The lists accounted for more than 250

---

[47] Sheedy 1997.
[48] Sakhalin II, Sakhalin I, and Kharyaga are the three PSAs that were signed before the passage of the 1995 PSA law. The French company Elf Acquitaine became the first company to sign a PSA with the Russian government, in February 1992, when it contracted to develop fields in the Volgograd and Saratov oblasts. In 1994, Sakhalin Energy (a consortium comprising Marathon, McDermott, Mitsui, Royal Dutch/Shell, and Mitsubishi) signed a similar contract (Sakhalin II) to develop oil and natural gas deposits off Sakhalin Island, and in July 1995, Exxon and the Japanese company Sodeco signed the Sakhalin I contract to develop other fields in the same island (Watson 1996:433). All three have been grandfathered by legislation. A grandfather law for foreign investors creates a shelter against the vicissitudes of Russian legislation. It provides that any new regulations governing the operation of foreign enterprises shall not apply for a period of three years to such business enterprises already in existence at the time the new laws are enacted.

deposits, including 213 deposits of hydrocarbons located in 32 administrative regions of the Russian Federation. After rejecting many drafts of the List Law, the Duma finally approved in July 1997 only seven out of these 250 deposits.[49] However, no contract was signed to develop any of these legally permitted deposits. The basic PSA law was still considered insufficient without the necessary modifications in the existing legislation on tax, customs, foreign investment, as well as in the regulations for the use of underground resources in the offshore zones.

To address these problems, a PSA commission was created in July 1997. A year later, in July 1998, the Duma passed the Amendments Law, which was voted down by the Federation Council on September 4, 1998, on the basis that it imposed unrealistic limits on the share of discovered reserves that would be subject to development under a PSA regime. According to the Duma legislation, PSAs could be used for 10 percent of the reserves – a figure that had already been exceeded. The passage of this bill would hamper future projects under PSAs significantly.

With the help of the parliamentary conciliatory commission, which had been set up to resolve conflicts between the two houses of the parliament, the Duma committee responsible for PSAs drafted a new version of the Amendments Law. After another three years of debate, the Federal Law on the Introduction of Amendments and Additions into the Law on Production-Sharing Agreements was signed on January 14, 1999, and became effective on February 17, 1999.

The PSA Amendments Law, as well as the Enabling Law that followed, resolved many of the legal uncertainties that had been retarding major work on a few existing PSAs and delaying the negotiation and signing of several others. First, the contradictions between the LUR and the PSA Law as to whether PSAs would be treated as civil-law contracts under a special, self-contained PSA regime or would be subject to the general LUR licensing/administrative law regime were settled in favor of PSA contract predominance. This fundamental improvement applied to such issues as the bases for termination of rights, extension of the contract/license terms, and field conservation measures.[50]

Second, the special, stabilized regime of taxes and other payments for PSAs, enacted by Article 13 of the PSA in 1995 but subject to question since then as to its legal validity, has been confirmed through the Enabling Law by specific amendments to the relevant tax laws. As with

[49] DeBeer and Jebrailov 1997.
[50] Hines and Nikiforov 1999.

taxes, exemptions from tariffs also had to appear in the proper legal act to be guaranteed under Russian law. The Amendment to the Customs Tariff Law and the Customs Code provided for import-tariff exemption on goods brought into Russia at the investors' expense for work on a PSA, and export-tariff exemption on goods taken out of Russia under the terms of a PSA.[51] Moreover, PSA investors' right to freely export their share of production was fortified by an addition to the Law on State Regulation on Foreign Trade Activities that stated that any qualitative restrictions on exports introduced by the Russian government must take into account state's free-export obligation to investors under the PSA Law.

Finally, another amendment to the PSA law permitted conclusion of PSAs without the approval of the Duma for projects involving relatively small reserves of oil and gas (up to 25 million tons of oil and/or 250 billion cubic meters of gas). This would give regions a larger role in the PSA process and save certain projects from lengthy parliamentary debates. The reduction of parliament's role in the process was seen as a major accomplishment. In addition, the amendments largely abrogated the previous requirement that investors obtain Duma approval for specific PSAs involving larger deposits. Even though such fields still had to be included on list laws before they could be eligible for a PSA status, the Russian government was now permitted to negotiate and implement PSA terms for individual projects without parliamentary approval (unless the projects involved national security interests, the continental shelf, or an exclusive economic zone of the Russian Federation, in which case the Duma's rubber stamp was needed). Along the same lines, the new legislation did not require Duma approval for conversion of previously existing non-PSA projects into PSAs in cases where the subsoil users had already obtained a license, or for development under PSA terms of unexplored acreage that the Russian government may put up for tender.[52]

Despite these positive steps, the PSA amendments also introduced some new requirements and restrictions that were not welcome by foreign investors. Specifically, the amendments introduced quotas of 30 percent on the reserves that could be subject to PSAs; 70 percent on the value of goods and services that must be purchased from Russian suppliers; and 80 percent as the minimum percentage of the labor-force for Russian nationals. The deputy chairman of the State Duma Economic Policy

[51] Ibid.
[52] Webb 1999b.

Committee, Svetlana Gvozdeva, said of these conditions that Russia was "creating a new iron curtain for investors."[53]

Foreign investors saw the 30 percent quota on the reserves as a major deterrent because the huge old reserves that were on the first field list had already filled up the quota, which meant that the list of new fields would be virtually closed.[54] Investors likened the quota to Lenin's limitation on foreign concessions in Soviet Union to 30 percent of Russian resources. Moreover, the quotas on labor, goods, and services concerned some investors because using Russian goods and technology that were not competitive in respect to reliability, safety, quality, and delivery time could stall major investment projects.

Even though the amendments to the PSA law and the enabling law have been significant steps toward bringing the investment environment to a more favorable and workable position, problems continued to prevent PSA investments. It was two-steps forward, one-step back for oil investors. First, the so-called Normative Acts (detailed government-level regulations to implement the PSA Law), which have been circulating in various draft forms over the past years, remained to be finalized and adopted. These important acts were expected to cover and fill in gray areas and gaps on such fundamental matters as taxation, accounting, cost recovery, and supplemental procedures for tenders and entry into PSAs. Of the Normative Acts, without which there could not be an effective PSA regime, none was put into final form after several years of work on their drafting.

Moreover, by 2000, the PSA tax regime was yet to be incorporated into Chapter 26 of the Tax Code (Part 2) in a way that did not undermine the PSA Law. Part 1 of the new Russian Tax Code, creating a basic general legal framework for taxation, was enacted in July 1998. The need to include PSA tax regime was highlighted by article 18 of the Tax Code, which required that special tax regimes be set forth therein. This legislation was of vital concern to investors in PSAs because, among other things, it would determine the level of the profit tax levied on PSA partners along with non-PSA oil producers.

By 2000, Russia had a PSA law that was seven years in the making but it did not yet have an effective PSA regime. Only 28 fields had been put on the list of PSA projects and none, other than the grandfathered

---

[53] Quote taken from Rutland 1997, 24.
[54] Russia is unique in having a 30 percent quota. This restriction does not exist in any other countries that use PSAs. Author's interview with Sergei Danilkin (Phillips Petroleum), Moscow, April 9, 2001.

three projects, has been in effect.[55] The total investment in PSAs between 1993 and 2000 was only US$1.5 billion.[56] Supporters of PSAs contended that the struggles over the PSA regime conservatively cost the oil industry billions of dollars of capital investments, let alone the lost revenues in tax collections to the country's federal and local coffers and the missed opportunities to create much-needed employment.[57] In 2000, analysts estimated that the state's net revenue from fields already on the PSA List Law and those whose eligibility for development on PSA terms was being considered by the Duma would reach US$100 billion.[58]

Why, then, did the Russian PSA system develop so slowly, showing constant failures to attract the much-needed investment in the oil sector? Why was the investment policy of the Russian state so unstable, inconsistent, and unwelcoming in the 1990s? Next, I discuss the characteristics of the political regime in Russia in the 1990s and the obstacles it created for foreign investors.

Russia's Political Regime

In the 1991–2000 period, Russia was considered a hybrid political regime by many accounts. It had many components of a democracy, such as regular elections and free competition but it failed to approximate an authentic democracy.[59] More specifically, the institutional constraints and competition have been limited in Russia. Democratization produced a number of veto-players in the state, allowing for some competition among different political views and some restraints on the executive but weak political parties and interest groups left pluralism in the state unchecked. A lack

---

[55] Bradshaw (2004) argues that there was a unique set of circumstances surrounding the first generation of Sakhalin projects that enabled them to move on and that is why progress could not be replicated elsewhere in Russia. He lists Sakhalin's distance from Moscow, its oligarch-free qualities, its history in the Soviet Union, and its challenging geology and climate among the many factors that made this region successful in attracting significant amount of FDI.

[56] Amirov 2000.

[57] Gyetvay 2000, 4.

[58] Amirov 2000, 12. Since Sakhalin Energy's contract (the first grandfathered PSA) became effective in 1996, the private sector consortium has paid US$40 million of a US$100 million bonus due over five years to the local Sakhalin Development Fund. It also paid US$45 million in pre-production to the Ministry of Fuel and Energy and Sakhalin governor I.P. Farkhutdinov's administration.

[59] See Fish 2001b, Brown 2001, Shevtsova 2001. More specifically, Fish (2001a) and Shevtsova (2001) called Russia a "low-caliber democracy" and "bureaucratic quasi-authoritarianism," respectively. According to Solnick (1999), Russia during this period was not a democracy but a system with a durable division of power among a fairly stable group of elite actors.

of vertical accountability and accessibility beyond the elections resulted in jurisdictional power struggles among state actors, which then led to policy deadlock and instability in the political environment. The chaos and uncertainty that this hybrid regime produced dramatically affected the terms of the relationship between investors and the host government and consequently the ability to attract much-needed FDI.

Some executive constraints

Despite the 1993 Constitution, which assigned unprecedented powers to the Russian president, in reality Yeltsin was a weak president and the struggle between the legislative and executive branches had a significant impact on the policy environment.[60] Notwithstanding his constitutional powers, Yeltsin did not always rule without regard for the parliament; in fact, he made several compromises on key issues. After the tumultuous relations between the legislative and executive branches during 1991 and 1993, each side refrained from confronting the other too directly and tried to avoid another constitutional crisis like that of 1993.

Although the 1993 Constitution elevated the presidency above parliament, it also reserved sufficient powers for the legislature to complicate presidential rule. For instance, the president could legislate by decree but the decrees were subordinate to statutory law in the Russian hierarchy of legislation. As the principal lawmaker, the Duma could reject or delay draft laws presented by the government. Especially because it was practically constrained in its ability to remove the government (in fear of its own dissolution), the parliament has been less willing to share responsibility for the government's actions and policies.

During most of Yeltsin's presidency, the ideological battle between reformists and antireformists further fuelled the battle over institutional jurisdiction. Opposition parties solidified control over the Duma in 1995 and the Communist Party emerged as the center of an opposition that controlled a working legislative majority. As a result, the Duma's agreement on particular policy issues became extremely difficult for the government and the president. The strategy of the conservative parliamentary majority has been to restrict executive branch freedom of maneuver without assuming governing responsibility. The Duma, which could not influence the government decisions on many major cases, showed its hostility during discussion of laws.[61]

---

[60] Moser 2001.
[61] Author's interview with Alexander Kursky (Advisor to the government), Moscow, April 27, 2001.

In addition to the strength of the lower house of the parliament in challenging the executive branch, the regional administrations also exercised some veto power over government policies. The disintegration of the Soviet Union had resulted in the devolution of considerable political and economic power to eighty-nine regional administrations both in terms of lawmaking and the implementation of laws. In terms of lawmaking, the upper house of the parliament, the Federation Council, played a crucial role. Made up of regional executives and the leaders of regional legislatures, this legislative body was used by Yeltsin as an instrument of legislative control but has developed into a more autonomous lawmaking body that represented the interests of regional elites.[62]

Moreover, in 1996, Yeltsin relinquished his appointive power over regional executives and allowed them to be directly elected. This gave the upper house a greater degree of autonomy. Although it remained less confrontational than the lower house of the parliament, it nevertheless defied Yeltsin and the government on several occasions.[63] It also challenged the Duma and prevented development of federal legislation and regulation. For instance, it has been responsible for the scrutiny and approval of bills prepared and passed by the Duma. As a rule, a bill going through the Russian parliament has to pass through a total of three readings in the Duma, then a fourth by the Federation Council, before being signed into law by the president. In this capacity, the Federation Council became a veto player to be reckoned with. By one account, during the Duma's second term, the upper house vetoed 23 percent of all laws passed by the Duma.[64]

The regional administrations have also been assigned some regulatory and administrative powers to oversee the implementation of laws. Yeltsin's famous statement "take as much independence as you can swallow" to the regional elites in 1990 has been quite instrumental in creating this autonomy. This "parade of sovereignties" was intentionally engineered by Yeltsin in the wake of the breakup of the Soviet Union and the violent showdown between the president and the Supreme Soviet of October 1993. Even though with the 1993 Constitution he later aspired to limit the powers of the regions and centralize state authority,[65] his concessions to the regions with bilateral treaties not only reduced the authority of the

[62] Moser 2001.
[63] Weiss 2001.
[64] Chaisty 2001, 118.
[65] Yeltsin incorporated two articles (71 and 72) enumerating exclusively federal and shared federal and regional areas of jurisdiction in the Constitution, but did not include an article exclusively reserving certain powers for the regions.

federal center but also eroded the legal equality the Constitution assigned to different levels of center-periphery relations. Regional elites won budget privileges, powers of appointment, exemption from various federal requirements, and a tacit understanding that federal officials would look away from violations of the federal Constitution and federal policies.[66] Between 1994 and 1998, forty-six of the eighty-nine subjects of the Federation signed bilateral treaties with the federal executive and many republics and regions adopted their own constitutions and charters. This war of laws produced thousands of laws and constitutional clauses that contradicted the federal Constitution and federal law.[67] The federal government's default on many jurisdictional responsibilities left the regions with empty policy space and a free reign.

Finally, the central bureaucracy, itself, has at times constrained the ability of the government to formulate consistent and effective policies. Especially since the breakup of the Soviet Union, the economic difficulties facing bureaucrats have given them incentives to pursue their self-interest more than the interests of the state. Different government ministries and agencies have been fighting one another to gain as much power and as many financial benefits as possible. In the lawmaking arena, the lack of coherence and hierarchy in the government produced a plethora of government proposals and drafts reflecting different and oftentimes-clashing interests of bureaucratic agencies. In the implementation of the laws, once again this infighting caused confusion and delay in government policies. Once enacted, laws were neglected or distorted at the hands of bureaucratic officials responsible for their implementation.

In addition, the split nature of the executive branch contributed to some pluralism in the state in the 1990s. The president and the government constitute the two major arms of the state that perform executive functions. The 1993 Constitution established them as the two branches of executive power. The president has at his disposal the presidential administration. On the other hand, the government works independently, with only intermittent direction or intervention from the president. This split structure weakened the mechanisms of coherence and responsibility sharing within the bureaucracy in the 1990s. The presence of presidential and governmental teams above the ministries confused lines of authority and encouraged ministries to play the head of state and head of government against

---

[66] Kahn 2001.
[67] Kahn (2001) also reports that in 1996 nineteen of twenty-one republican constitutions violated the federal Constitution.

each other. "All too often, the outcome was confusion and self-destructive competition."[68]

Weakly Institutionalized, Limited Competition

Pluralism within the state is in fact a characteristic of democratic regimes. Separation of powers is crucial for a state to function effectively. And so are the mechanisms of checks and balances. Horizontal accountability among state institutions prevents the tyranny and domination of one over the others. What makes Russia a hybrid regime, however, is the combination of some pluralism in the state with weakly institutionalized, limited competition in society.

Parties are needed to aggregate social interests, construct majority coalitions, and serve as a bridge between the branches of government as well as between national and local politicians. Parties also constrain and discipline their members in parliament but because they aggregate constituent interests, they also provide parliamentary deputies with resources allowing them to act collectively. Without strong political parties, politics becomes very personalistic. Politicians prefer dictating and ruling directly to governing through impersonal, established rules and agencies, and they view institutions as obstacles rather than as necessities.

That Russia had a weak party system throughout the 1990s is a widely agreed observation in the literature.[69] Russian political parties were ineffective in structuring policymaking in ways that furthered the public good. They could not facilitate compromise and cooperation between the legislative and executive branches. The absence of disciplined party blocs endowed parliamentary politics with a fractious fluidity. Fluctuations in the number and size of political groupings complicated the identification of party alliances capable of forming winning majorities. Parties were often divided internally, usually dominated by a single strong personality.[70] Moreover, Russian parties had weak control over policy coordination and legislative strategy across committees. Consequently, deputies enjoyed a high level of personal control over legislative activity in Duma committees, which made for a legislative process that furthered particularistic interests. Finally, Russian parties failed to link state actors to their constituencies. With no vertical accountability, these actors

---

[68] Huskey 2001, 45.
[69] Kitchelt 2000, McFaul 2001, Rose, Munro, and White 2001, Protsyk and Wilson 2003.
[70] Sakwa 2001.

engaged in jurisdictional power struggles over state institutions, furthering the constitutional conflict between the two branches of government.

The absence of well-developed political parties was an obstacle to both stable executive – legislative and center-periphery relations. There were not many national political parties that could perform unifying functions; most had candidates running in the elections to the State Duma who had little institutional presence outside Moscow. The Communist Party of Zyuganov was to a certain extent an exception, but even it was unable to provide a meaningful assistance to local candidates. Many of the communist governors pursued their own agendas, as opposed to their party's interests. Moreover, "most regional assemblies were populated by elected deputies with no party affiliations."[71]

By the same token, weak interest group organizations could not check abuses of office by members of parliament and bureaucracy. For instance, the new trade unions were subject to the factionalism and splits typical of the pseudo-parties. Most of the larger social organizations, including trade unions, tended to be top-down, heavy bureaucratic organizations with weak links to the mass of their memberships.[72] Interest groups played a much less salient role in post-Soviet political life than they did during the perestroika years. Individuals and groups had no organized sphere in which they could articulate and reconcile their interests.

Instead of an open competition, Russia's political life was dominated by key groups, such as finance and raw-materials lobbies. Others, like the agrarians, the manufacturers, and the military-industrial complex, had very little and sporadic influence.[73] Due to financial and organizational constraints, these groups found it hard to mobilize their constituencies. The energy lobby and its banker allies, on the other hand, could pressure the state on various policies, using media outlets and informal personal contacts with government bureaucrats, parliamentary deputies, and regional elites. This oligopolistic grip on the state crippled the institutionalization of different interest groups. It made the lobbying process highly opaque and unbalanced. Rather than providing checks on the executive and mediating among state veto players, it hastened the spread of corruption at all levels of the state.

Given this institutional mix and the enormous stakes involved in controlling oil resources, the PSA issue immediately became what many

[71] Weiss 2001, 124.
[72] Weigle 2000, 335.
[73] Chervyakov and Berezovskii 1996.

observers called a "political football." The hybrid regime that assigned some veto powers to various state actors in the absence of open and institutionalized political competition made it difficult for the proponents of PSAs to ignore or co-opt the opposition to create an attractive investment environment.

Politics of Oil Investment Policy

The passage of the PSA legislation, which potential foreign investors have repeatedly described as key to attracting large-scale investment in the fuel and energy sector, was a source of domestic political debate throughout the 1990s. At the federal level, the executive and legislative branches were locked in a battle for political authority. The government itself had to fight to assert its control over semi-independent administrative agencies. Moreover, the federal government and the regions regularly clashed over resource ownership.

Executive constraints in the absence of strong parties and interest groups that serve integrative and conciliatory functions has eventuated in jurisdictional struggles over oil policy. Unchecked fragmentation in the state hindered the development of a coherent legislative and regulatory framework as well as the implementation of the rules and regulations for the oil industry. In the 1990s, the Russian state produced legislation and regulatory measures at different levels of government that were at odds. The political vacuum made it hard for foreign investors to know who had the authority to strike a deal in Russia.

Struggle between the Executive and Legislative Branches

The initial draft law on PSAs encountered significant opposition in the upper house of the Russian parliament because it would have involved a transfer of regulatory power, away from the legislative branch, which was traditionally responsible for defining license-issuing procedures under the Natural Resources Law, to the executive branch, which would become responsible for negotiating the conditions of production-sharing contracts with investors. This was unacceptable to most Duma members due to their traditional mistrust of government. They assumed that if government officials had the right to sign agreements with foreign investors, the officials would be bought off and the state would be left with nothing. Thus, the reluctance of lawmakers to relinquish the regulatory power, which they enjoyed, was certainly one factor in delaying legal reform.

Especially the Duma's leftist factions had problems with the clauses on the contractual nature of the relations between the investors and the government, international arbitration and the royalty system of payments.[74] Initially, the left-wing factions openly ignored the bill on the grounds that all PSA legislation amounted to "privatization of natural resources." With great difficulty it proved possible, in 1997, to get the first seven deposits eligible for development on PSA terms through the Duma and to clear the first reading of the Law on Amendments toward the final endorsement. The leftist factions agreed to vote for the amendments (upon the third reading) only after the Federation Council approved changes and additions to the PSA law that they demanded and when the president assured them of his signature.

The clash of interests between the two branches was also apparent during the discussions on the List Law prior to deciding which field would be eligible for development under PSA terms. The government, in response to demands from the regions, promised to develop a long list of oil fields under PSA terms. Communist deputies in the Duma, in return, flatly declared that they would never vote for a PSA list exceeding twenty fields. Moreover, they refused to participate in the session organized to adopt the draft law. Even though dissatisfaction with the draft may have been one reason behind the boycott, many argue that it was also a political move. Both Liberal Democrats and Communists were insulted that Yeltsin restructured his cabinet without first consulting them. Moreover, Yeltsin was hoping to cite progress on PSA legislation during a summit with the U.S. president, Bill Clinton, and the leftist factions wanted to avoid any actions that could be interpreted as pro-government or as economically detrimental to regions and workers.[75] For almost a year, neither the legislative nor the executive branch could do anything to advance PSAs.[76] Following months of exhaustive wrangling, the Duma finally approved in principle a draft law on the list of fields eligible under PSA terms.

Passage of the amendments to the 1995 Law on PSAs was also woefully drawn out because of similar conflicts between the government and

[74] One of the opponents of PSAs in the Duma was Sergei Glaziev, leader of the Democratic Party of Russia faction and the chairman of the Duma Committee for Economic Policy. Another key critic has been Gennady Zyuganov, the Communist leader. Neither man had actually ever directly and unequivocally challenged the need for investment in the energy sector and for PSAs; they were really objecting to the terms of these contracts.
[75] "Lurching Forward: Despite Encountering New Setbacks, PSA List Law is Poised to Clear Major Hurdle" *Russian Petroleum Investor* (April 1997), 18–22.
[76] "Something for Everyone: Duma Edges Closer to a Viable Version of PSA List Law, but Foreign Investors Remain Wary" *Russian Petroleum Investor* (March 1997), 19–23.

the leftist majority in the State Duma. By this time, though, the leftist deputies did not want to make either a positive or a negative decision on PSA issues. A vote in favor would have drawn criticism from radicals within its ranks, but voting against the PSA Law would have sparked a falling out with the regions and Russian companies.

Some progress on the PSA regime was finally achieved subsequent to major concessions to parliament. In exchange for its acceptance of some of the government proposals on PSAs, parliament acquired significant veto powers over the PSA process. According to the Article 19 of the Federal Law on Production-Sharing Agreements, for instance, when proposing a draft federal budget law, the government had to submit to the Duma an annual report on the results of work under production-sharing agreements. Moreover, the approval of parliament was needed for each PSA field's initial appearance on the list of fields to be explored. This meant that companies had to present to the Duma a feasibility study before they could even negotiate and prepare contracts with their partners. The approval of the Russian parliament was once again required for specific PSA deals negotiated after a field was included in the PSA zone. The practice dictated that amending a contract would require more than a year.[77] As discussed above, these approval requirements were seen as costly and risky for the investors. They also meant that investors would need to negotiate each contract with, first the Duma and then the government.[78] Essentially, amendments to a commercial contract would be treated like any other federal law. This veto power of the legislative branch over the creation of the PSA law and the approval of each PSA created one of the biggest obstacles for foreign investment in Russia in the 1990s.

Struggle Between the Center and the Subjects of the Federation

The stalemate over the PSA regime has been further exacerbated by the challenge that the subjects of the federation posed for the central government both in terms of making and implementing the laws. Within the

---

[77] Subbotin 2000.
[78] Such a legislative approval is not a very common procedure around the world. In forty-two oil-producing countries that use PSAs, legislative bodies are not involved in the approval of oil contracts. PSAs are approved by the government in Algeria; they require an authorized minister's approval in China; or the president's sanction in Indonesia. On the contrary, in Venezuela and Tunisia, a single joint sitting of the two chambers of the Congress is required to approve an agreement. In Denmark, rights to acreages on the continental shelf (but not the agreements themselves) are approved by the parliament's special committee. In Azerbaijan, as discussed in Chapter 5, the parliament approves agreements but the country does not have a special PSA law. Even in countries with parliamentary approval requirement, the process is very different from Russia's.

legislative branch, the tendency of the Federation Council to challenge the legislative authority of the lower house has significantly contributed to the PSA legislative impasse. The members of the Federation Council on many occasions have utilized their constitutional powers to veto the PSA legislation in fear that it would limit the prerogatives of regional governments and impose financial obligations upon them.

The first challenge came during the adoption of the draft law on PSA in 1995. Even though the Federation Council favored the concept of PSA legislation, it opposed the simplified tax plan contained in the draft.[79] This provision, according to the regional and local government leaders, limited their ability to collect taxes from PSA projects in their territories.[80] Because the law undermined the lengthy tradition of unlimited state control over Russia's natural resources, it faced opposition from several factions within the Federation Council. Moreover, a powerful group of regional senators representing the interests of heavy-equipment manufacturers in their regions also opposed the terms of the PSA draft law. Burdened with a glut of outmoded and financially struggling manufacturers, deputies from those regions fiercely lambasted the current version of the draft law, demanding that the legislation guarantee that domestic enterprises receive as much as 70 percent of the orders for equipment required for use under PSAs.[81] Finally, representatives from agricultural regions had minimal interest in energy-related projects, and saw little benefit from foreign investment in such projects.[82]

Another controversy between the two chambers of the legislature erupted during the discussion of the List Law. Regional representatives in the Federation Council directly accused Duma deputies of disrupting major investment projects whose implementation could markedly improve their regions' economies. Some regions engaged in "revenge politics" and tried to kill the law because their fields had been removed from the list.[83] Although not successful in the end, these regions were at

---

[79] The opposition group in the Council was headed by Krasnodar's newly elected governor, Nikolai Kondratenko, who with Russian Federation Audit Office Chairman and former Council member Yuri Boldyrev, was instrumental in persuading the Council to reject the PSA law in 1995.

[80] "On the Right Track: PSA Legislation Edges Forward" *Russian Petroleum Investor* (April 1995), 18–20.

[81] "Change of Venue: After finally clearing the Duma, PSA legislation meets opposition in parliament's upper chamber" *Russian Petroleum Investor* (September 1995): 17.

[82] "Stalemate: Leftists' New Clout in the Council of Federation Could Endanger Investor-Friendly Legislation" *Russian Petroleum Investor* (February 1997), 13–15.

[83] "Glimpse of the Future: Council of the Federation Chairman Predicts the Future of Foreign Investment in Russia" *Russian Petroleum Investor* (October 1997), 12–14.

least able to prolong the legislation process and delay the PSA projects in the regions approved by the list law.

In addition to the representation of regional interests in the Federation Council, Article 72 of the Russian Constitution invests the regional governments with joint jurisdiction (alongside federal authorities) over their regions' underground resources. Because of this two-key system, which requires that investors negotiate PSA contracts with both the regional governments and the MFE, the regional governments have been pivotal in the signing and implementation of the contracts. For instance, the government of Tatarstan was one of the key proponents of the 1995 Law on PSA during its turbulent passage through the federal parliament. Since adoption of this law, Tatarstan President Shaimiev has continually pushed the federal government to pass the necessary amendments and enabling legislation. Similarly, in Sakhalin, three post-Soviet governors exerted a positive influence on the progress of PSAs. Not only did they support the federal government's efforts to create a PSA regime, they also implemented one of the three PSA projects in Russia today. As a result, after Moscow, the Sakhalin islands became the second-largest FDI recipients in Russia. As some analysts argue, Sakhalin region became the chief laboratory for Russian PSAs.

Although Tatarstan's and Sakhalin's regional administrations have been strong advocates of PSA contracts, others, such as the administration of Nenets Autonomous Okrug, have been opposing PSAs and obstructing attempts by foreign investors to initiate oil-development projects. In April 1997, the governor of Nenets Okrug, Vladimir Butov, excluded several fields of primary interest to Western investors from the list of fields that it was proposing for development under PSA terms. He asserted that he opposed PSAs because they failed to specify time periods for initiation of geological exploration and production. He argued that Western companies' preference for PSA terms was a pretext to reap super profits at the expense of Russia in general and Nenets Okrug in particular. Even when supporting the idea of PSAs, some regions have been passing PSA laws that contradicted or circumvented the federal legislation without openly violating it.[84] An example of this was seen in Khanty-Mansiysk Autonomous District. In 1996, the district passed a law on PSAs that restricted foreign oil company operations substantially.

[84] "More Power to Them: Khanty-Mansiysk's Regional PSA Legislation Could Restrict Investor Rights" *Russian Petroleum Investor* (August 1996), 16.

Moreover, the contest at the subregional level also contributed to the difficulties facing the investors. Autonomous districts (okrugs) in some oblasts were claiming the same rights that oblasts and ethnic republics have based on the ambiguous provisions in the 1993 Constitution. An important example of this institutional feud was seen in the Tyumen oblast. The two okrugs Khanty-Mansiisk and Yamal-Nenets were locked in an increasingly fierce dispute with the Tyumen oblast for control over oil and gas projects and revenues. As a result of the dispute, in February 1999, the Duma decided to exclude three Khanty-Mansiisk oil fields from the proposed Uvat PSA project.[85]

Lastly, even though the 1993 Constitution grants them no rights over underground resources, some municipal governments have used their independent taxation powers (granted to them by a presidential decree) to exact additional revenues from foreign investors. Investors managed at times to win exemptions from such taxation but overall municipal authorities used their control over utilities and their influence with the local population to extort payments from foreign investors.

The significance of the regional dimension is heightened by the fact that Russia's energy resources are heavily concentrated in a handful of its eighty-nine provinces.[86] For instance, Tyumen alone accounts for more than two thirds of Russian oil output. This regional phenomenon has created a tug-of-war between the have and have-not regions. Those regions that are not self sufficient in energy and have experienced frequent energy shortages, as in Russia's far east, have lobbied against some of the terms of the investment relationship with foreign companies. For instance, they opposed the sale of oil abroad and the raising of energy prices, and promoted domestic-content requirements that could help moribund local industry. Those with substantial oil resources, on the other hand, have been more open to foreign investment; generally speaking, they have been inclined to give foreign investors a break on domestic-content requirements, tax burdens, and the like. However, as discussed earlier, the attitudes of the subjects of the federation toward PSAs have not been uniform. Some opposed PSAs in fear that the local governments would have little control over them and be left out.[87] Others welcomed PSAs in principle but delayed the implementation process due to red tape and too much regulation.

[85] Webb 1999a.
[86] According to Rutland (1997), this is partly a result of geography, and partly a result of deliberate decisions in the 1960s to focus development efforts on the West Siberian oblast of Tyumen.
[87] Canzi 1999.

Struggle Within the Bureaucracy

According to some accounts, the real opposition to the PSA regime came from within the government itself. The infamous Russian bureaucracy became the fiercest veto player in the state. There has been covert infighting to control PSAs within the government since 1993 because PSAs directly affect the budgetary revenue on which all parts of the government depend.[88] Proposal after proposal were being drafted and discussed during talks among the Ministries of Fuel and Energy, Finance, Economy, Taxes, and Natural Resources without arriving at a common, constructive approach. Ministers and top civil servants have been regularly reshuffled, making it difficult to consolidate any position.[89] This zigzagging of power at times brought policy deadlock and passivity within the federal government.[90]

Not all bureaucratic entities have been similarly interested in creating an attractive foreign investment climate. The Finance Ministry, the Ministry of Foreign Economic Relations, and the Customs Committee, for instance, viewed PSAs as income flowing into the federal budget. As a result, they imposed, or proposed to impose, heavy tax burdens without taking into consideration the long-term effects of these taxes on foreign investment. It did not help that these bureaucratic organizations also feared the fixed terms of the PSAs, which would potentially reduce their control of oil revenues.[91]

Struggling to maintain their control over the licensing process, geological associations, represented by the State Committee on Underground Resources (Roskomnedra) were equally against PSAs because a contractual regime would bypass the licensing system that these associations so clearly benefited from.[92] On the other hand, government entities responsible for long-term economic development (the MFE,

[88] According to Andrey Krivorotov (Oil and Gas Eurasia) during his interview with the author in Moscow, April 10, 2001, this infighting among Russian bureaucracies was encouraged by Yeltsin on purpose. In order for them not to fight him, he provoked them to fight one another.

[89] "Putin Tells Ministers to End PSA Impasse." *Oil & Capital* V (2000), 8–9. Part of this reason was certainly the legal vacuum that provided no clear guidelines as to how government agencies should act.

[90] Author's interview with Anatoly Averkin (PriceWaterHouseCoopers/advisor to Duma), Moscow, April 13, 2001.

[91] "Everything's Negotiable: Finance Ministry's Opposition Could Slow Approval of PSA Tax Changes" *Russian Petroleum Investor* (May 1996), 30.

[92] "Trench Warfare: PSAs Could Jeopardize Roskomnedra's Control Over Subsoil Use." *Russian Petroleum Investor* (February 1995), 20–21.

the Committee for Foreign Investments, and the Ministry of Economics) tended to be against heavy taxation and in favor of PSAs.[93]

Even though there were understandable ideological differences in terms of priorities among the bureaucratic organizations, the competition for power and money through oil deals became one of the main reasons the enactment and implementation of PSAs have been obstructed by the government for so long. "Instead of explicit laws that clearly delineated the power structure, government officials and agencies preferred a system in which they were more or less free to enter into negotiations with individual clients, ask for kickbacks, and accept bribes in return for particular favors."[94]

The fragmentation within the executive branch and the lack of coordination among federal agencies made the implementation of investment projects extremely difficult. For instance, the Sakhalin II project, one of the three grandfathered PSAs, faced multiple bureaucratic hurdles that at times subverted and delayed its operations. Companies had to obtain more than 600 approvals from various agencies to start only the first phase of their Sakhalin project. They estimated that the number of approvals would be 3,000 for the second phase.[95] Moreover, federal customs officials in Sakhalin were ignoring both the federal Law on PSA and the prime minister's direct order to stop collecting value-added and import taxes on equipment and material imported by both of the Sakhalin projects. By refusing to carry out Russia's obligations, as defined in the Sakhalin PSAs, the State Customs Committee tried to meet its short-term fiscal quotas. This willfulness of bureaucrats who were accustomed to making decisions on matters concerning their departments based less on law than on personal whim was a significant hindrance to foreign investors.[96]

Struggle Among Political Parties and Interest Groups

The main difficulty in creating an attractive investment environment in Russia was not only due to the intense institutional struggle within the state. It was the combination of that partial pluralism in the state with the weakness in interest group lobbying and political party mediation. The

[93] Watson 1996.
[94] Ibid., 440.
[95] Author's interview with Ivan Chernyakhovskiy (Sakhalin Energy), Moscow, April 9, 2001.
[96] "Caught in the Crossfire: Conflicting Agendas Threaten to Stall Russia's Only Active PSAs" *Russian Petroleum Investor* (February 1997), 46–49.

creation of a PSA regime has generated plenty of interest from various groups in Russian society. Even though some of these interests were organized into lobbying the legislators and government officials, they had limited effect on shaping the trajectory of the PSA framework. Chaisty (2007) in his meticulous analysis of the PSA legislative process in Russia finds very little evidence for a systematic linkage between sectoral interests and voting behavior in the Russian parliament.

The main reason for the limited effectiveness of interest group lobbying has been the collective action problems faced by the interest groups. The whole PSA process created winners and losers and there were too many particularistic interests to exert coherent and effective pressure on legislators and government officials. Moreover, because of mostly ideological and jurisdictional concerns, political parties could not facilitate bargaining over PSA legislation by aggregating interests into majority coalitions in the parliament. Oftentimes, they voted as a bloc for or against PSA legislation, but their positions depended more on the institutional balance of power than on the interests of the constituents they represented. Business groups have contributed to political parties and parliamentary factions, but no clear pro-business party organization emerged.[97] Hence, Russian political parties could not provide the representative and integrative functions that are expected of strong parties. The absence of institutionalized political competition left ample room for state actors to get into jurisdictional struggles with one another.

1) **Russian Oil Companies.** Russian oil companies constituted one of the main groups that actively sought influence in the decision-making process through their interest organizations and political connections. The best example of this was Our Home is Russia Party, led by Viktor Chernomyrdin. This party was in fact called "Our Home is Gazprom" Party for it was seen as representing the interests of the energy lobby and the financial corporations associated with it.[98] When Chernomyrdin became the prime minister in December 1992, his government was often called the "government of the energy complex," implying that the industrial background and sympathies of the prime minister gave the oil and gas network unlimited opportunities for interest representation. Chernomyrdin was the founder and head of Gazprom and while holding government positions he obtained important privileges for the oil industry

[97] Rutland 1997.
[98] Ibid.

and Gazprom in particular and promoted their interests. For instance, in terms of the PSA legislation, it is argued that his natural inclination was to go slow to protect domestic oil companies. As a way to stall the process, "he would always find an excuse to leave Moscow whenever there was a discussion of the PSA legislation in the parliament."[99]

The MFE also articulated the interests of the oil industry. The careers of ministers like Vladimir Lopukhin and Yuri Shafranik, for instance, were closely tied to the oil industry, and so they often became active supporters of oil interests in the government. In essence, Russian oil companies had direct access to the government. They strongly affected the appointments of some members of the cabinet. Many midlevel government officials were paid by oil companies to promote company interests.[100] Finally, the oil companies made sure that leaders who were supportive of their interests were elected as governors. This tactic ensured that their interests would be represented in the Federation Council.[101]

Even though the domestic oil lobby has had some success in securing political support for its interests, it lacked the organizational and ideological unity to act as a strong interest group. This had a lot to do with the turbulent ownership struggles and the fierce turf wars within the industry that dominated the 1990s. The collapse of the Soviet Union brought about a major restructuring of the oil and gas industry, which started out in 1991 with a "spontaneous process of privatization" as the central control of the Soviet system disappeared and various parts of the oil industry asserted their autonomy.[102] In order to reaffirm state's control over the industry and put an end to spontaneous privatization, in 1992 the Presidential Decree no. 1403 set out to organize the oil industry into vertically integrated oil companies that would compete in Russian and

---

[99] Author's interview with Glenn Waller (Petroleum Advisory Forum), Moscow, August 28, 2000. It is argued, for instance, that on July 20 and 21, 1995, precisely when the Federation Council was to decide the fate of the Law on PSAs, Chernormyrdin chose to hold a meeting in Tyumen that included the administration heads of Siberian regions, the leadership of local oil companies, and pivotal pro-PSA legislators. Thus, many of the lawmakers supporting the PSA law were forced to miss the reading in the Federation Council. Taking advantage of the absence of many of the bill's supporters, opponents were able to reject the bill.

[100] Author's interview with Alexander Misulin (Head of the Department of Foreign Economic Relations in the Ministry of Energy), Moscow, May 17, 2001.

[101] For instance, such governors included Yevgeny Krasnoyarov of Sakhalin, Yuri Komaravsky of the Nenetsk Autonomous Region; Pavel Balakshin of the Arkhangelsk region; Alexander Filipenko of Khanty Mansiyk.

[102] Lane 1999.

world markets.[103] Surgutneftegaz, Lukoil, and Yukos were created with
government resolutions in 1993; Sidanko, Slavneft, Eastern Oil Company
(VNK), and Onako in 1994; Rosneft, Tyumen Oil Company (TNK) and
Sibneft in 1995.[104] In addition to these vertically integrated companies,
there were also nonintegrated autonomous republic companies such as
KomiTek, Tatneft, Bashneft and Yunko as well as independents like Sibur,
NORSI-Oil, and East Siberian.[105] During the first stage of the mass privatization program, the bulk of the shares of privatized enterprises ended up
in the hands of "red directors" and leaders of local administrations who
bought up shares from the employees and engaged in various transfer pricing and smuggling schemes that earned them enormous rents. Between the
end of 1995 and 1997, the state started to divest most of its shares in oil
companies in the second phase of privatization using a variety of methods,
the most controversial of which was the "loans for shares" scheme.[106] The
objective of the government with this privatization method was to offer
banks and other financial institutions government shares in lucrative companies in exchange for credits to offset the budgetary shortfall. Ownership
and control of the companies once again changed hands with these questionable, uncompetitive insider deals, creating a complex and widely scattered set of industry actors with diverse interests and incentives.

As a result, the Russian oil companies did not have a uniform influence
on investment policies. The most important kind of lobbying has been
informal personal contacts between oil directors and government bureaucrats and deputies in the parliament. The process has been highly opaque,
fragmented, and disorganized. Although there have been some organized
groups, such as the *Union of Oil Industrialists and Entrepreneurs, the
Union of Oil Exporters,* and the *House of Oil,* their influence generally has been weak and sporadic. Because the biggest oil companies produce a significant portion of the GDP but employ very small labor force,
building a broad-based party of oil-business interests has been fairly difficult.[107] Moreover, most other parties and parliamentary factions have

[103] Unlike the oil industry, the gas industry was organized around a single company,
Gazprom, under state ownership and control. According to Lane (1999), the government could not do the same in the oil industry because it faced a large number of conflicting interests.
[104] Sim 2008.
[105] For more information on these companies, see Lane 1999.
[106] For more discussion on the transformation of the ownership structure of the Russian oil
industry, see Fortescue 2006, Barnes 2006, and Sim 2008.
[107] The support for such a party came mostly from regional governors. Despite their lack of
strong representative organizations at the national level, industrialists have been quite

been critical of the interests of the oil and gas industry. Yabloko, a party in the liberal wing of the Duma and a supporter of PSA legislation, for example, supported measures to increase taxes on the Russian oil and gas complex.

Similarly, support for the oil industry in the government has been only conditional. The role of the oil companies in using the Ministry of Energy to express their views depended on the issue and changed over time.[108] The Ministry of Energy also had its own agenda: to maintain its supervisory functions. It has not always been considered the representative of the oil and gas companies. Even with Chernomyrdin, the influence went both ways. In some cases Chernormyrdin was promoting the oil industry's interests; in other cases he used pressure on the oil and gas complex to register its support for certain government policies in return.[109]

The weakness of the oil lobby in pressing its case on the PSA legislation also had to do with Russian oil companies' mixed attitudes toward PSAs. In the first years after the breakup of the Soviet Union, many companies were leery about going into partnerships with foreign companies on an individual basis. Prior to partial privatization, the positions of the heads of large oil production associations, i.e., the "oil generals," were very insecure. They sought to maximize short-term profit and neglected investment. Partnership with a foreign company could generate greater publicity and increased fiscal demands from central and local governments and, as such, was considered more of a hindrance than help.[110] Overall, these companies had no tradition or mentality of partnerships – even with other domestic companies.[111] Moreover, their managers wanted to buy oil companies as cheaply as possible and did not want multibillion-dollar PSAs on the books to drive prices up.[112] They had short-term concerns

successful at coordinating their activities at the regional level. In most regions of Russia, the industrial party in the form of an informal network of local economic elites and their political-bureaucratic allies effectively has been running local politics.

[108] Lane 1999.

[109] Ibid.

[110] Foreign companies, on their part, found it difficult to do business with domestic companies. It was difficult to ascertain who controlled a particular company, what the relations were between the company's component parts and between it and other enterprises.

[111] Author's interviews with Mikhail Subbotin (Advisor to the government), Moscow, April 19, 2001, and with Valeriy Ovcharenko (Conoco), Moscow, April 16, 2001. Ovcharenko further argued that this lack of trust in partnerships was a legacy of the command economy in which companies were competing for funds and equipment but not in selling their product and making a profit from it. If the end goal was profit, these companies could have engaged in a win-win situation by forming partnerships with foreigners.

[112] "Russian Oil: Not a Gusher." *Economist* (October 14, 1995): 78, 79.

and priorities; planning for the long-term performance of the industry was not on their agenda. As the Russian banks gained more control over the oil industry, short-term profits weighed more than attracting investments for the long-term. With access to bank capital, domestic companies did not see a need to attract foreign investors.[113]

Some of the Russian oil companies were trying to limit foreign investment because they feared competition over export capacity as well as the advantages that projects involving foreign investors might enjoy over Russian producers. More importantly, these companies were more interested in "empire building" or exporting their capital offshore than in investing to renew their assets or to restructure their operations.[114] In the beginning, then, most Russian companies were reluctant about PSAs.[115] They were not necessarily always against PSAs but they were not for them either. They lived quite well under the existing system. They knew how to maneuver, how to influence, and whom to influence.[116] They enjoyed being insiders.

Over time, the corporate unity of the Soviet oil elite was weakened by the appearance of outsiders. Increasingly, bankers and financial dealers were recruited to the boards of directors.[117] The change in the management structure made some companies more open to foreign investment.[118] As operations grew and the geographic span widened, some companies became less locally based and more nationwide, with their headquarters located in Moscow. These companies made significant progress in lobbying for the full-scale introduction of PSAs between 1998 and 2000. However, their support was conditional: favoring PSAs when the price of oil dropped, the costs were high, and there was no

[113] The experience of Yukos and Menatep with regard to the Priobskoye project was a good indicator of this trend. The Priobskoye field was supposed to be developed by the Russian oil company Yukos and Amoco (U.S.). However, when Menatep acquired control of Yukos, the Russian partner's negotiating stance changed dramatically. Instead of proceeding with the comprehensive development of the field and waiting eight to ten years to recoup its investment, Menatep insisted on developing the field block by block to get quicker returns.

[114] Gustafson 1999, 226.

[115] Author's interview with Alexander Strugov (director of Center for PSAs in the Ministry of Natural Resources), Moscow, April 18, 2001.

[116] Author's interview with Anders Morland (BP), Moscow, April 3, 2001.

[117] For more information on the configuration of the oil elite and its values and attitudes, see Lane (1999).

[118] For instance, the Russian company TNK was more open than most Russian oil companies to partnership with the West. The company's president at the time, Simon Kukes, was a former Amoco executive with sixteen years of business experience in the United States. This orientation was reinforced in July 1998 when Len Blavatnik, the head of a New York based shareholder in TNK was elected to TNK's board of directors.

alternative financing available; and opposing PSAs when they could finance the projects themselves or through bank loans.[119] Companies that were located in a particular region acted as a monopoly and resisted the liberalization of the investment environment altogether.[120] They either pressured the regional administrations to build barriers against foreign investment or were simply silent regarding the PSA process.

2) Other interest groups. Russian manufacturers of equipment for the oil industry were the other main lobbyists for the PSA legislation. They were especially supportive of the amendments to the 1995 PSA law that guaranteed 70 percent domestic-content requirements of machinery and materials needed for resource exploration and development. Regional authorities, industrial groups and worker unions insisted that these requirements in PSAs could in the long run serve to improve local industries and subsequently bring significant amounts of welfare to the regions. PSAs were especially beneficial to established communities in regions experiencing hard times. These contracts could not only help preserve existing jobs in the old oil towns but could also create new ones in new oil fields.[121]

Even so, these groups had a hard time mobilizing their interests into voting as a bloc to exert influence on state policies regarding PSAs. Similar to the oil lobby, they faced considerable amounts of collective action problems as they realized that not all machine-building firms would be given access to these projects and would profit from foreign investment into the oil sector. The losers of this selection became increasingly threatened by foreign investment and became less enthusiastic about PSAs. This is why, according to Chaisty (2007) some of the bitterest criticisms of PSAs came from the very enterprises that theoretically stood to gain from the legislation. For instance, "Kakha Bendukidze, formerly one of Russia's leading heavy-industry tycoons with major interests in machine-building, was a vocal critic of production sharing; he argued on several occasions that PSAs unfairly penalized enterprises that were excluded from these agreements."[122]

---

[119] Author's interviews with Alexander Levshov (Statoil), Moscow, March 14, 2001, and Dmitri Zhdanovich (Surgutneftegaz), Moscow, April 9, 2001.
[120] "Business: A Dangerous Bear-Dance." *Economist* (August.29, 1998), 57–58.
[121] Typical Russian oil towns that were built next to an oil field and populated by immigrant workers from other provinces are entirely dependent on the viability of oil production in the oil field. In the event that a field closes, Russian authorities face the prospect of mass unemployment and are compelled to evacuate hundreds of residents.
[122] Chaisty 2007, 311.

Importance of Economic Crises and Personalities

Institutional structure can explain the attitudes and policy toward PSAs only to a certain extent. At the end of the 1990s, even though the institutional structure stayed pretty much the same, there had been some progress in the PSA tale. The August 1998 economic crisis[123] and the resulting evaporation of much Western investment forced Russian politicians and businessmen to rethink their traditional opposition to PSAs to attract new sources of Western funding for energy projects. The withdrawal of several Western oil companies raised the alarm that despite the talk, there had been little investment into the oil sector. Falling oil prices highlighted the danger of a sectoral collapse in the absence of significant levels of new investment. Multinational oil companies, under PSAs, were deemed as one of the few reasonable sources of financing for the industry in the short term.

The economic crisis changed the balance of power and negotiation dynamics between the Russian side and the investors. Limited progress in PSA legislation that took place in 1999 was the result of this realization of the immediate need for foreign capital. Criticism of PSAs from communist and nationalist deputies became less vocal. The regional governments that were imposing harsh conditions on PSA projects became more accommodating to foreign investors' interests and increasingly supportive of the PSA regime. And, the Russian oil companies' initial benefits from the ruble devaluation were offset by the decline in the domestic price of crude, from US$67 to US$24 a ton in September.[124] The Russian companies also faced reduced availability of foreign credits owing to a general collapse of investor confidence in Russia. Therefore, the companies that opposed PSAs once started seeing them as worthy of support because they offered the only chance to develop the oil fields.

Some analysts argue that if Russian oil companies had not thrown their full weight behind the PSA legislation, it would not have made much progress during the legislative discussions in 1999. Although initially PSAs were the exclusive goal of foreign investors in Russian oil, especially after the 1998 economic crisis and drop in oil prices, they have also become the goal of most Russian companies. Indeed, many of the

---

[123] The August crisis had two distinctive phases. The first phase was triggered by international developments related to the Asian financial meltdown, the fall in world crude prices, and the "flight to quality" of Western investment capital. The second phase began on August 17 with the Russian government's de facto devaluation of the ruble and default on its short-term debt, and the accompanying collapse of Russia's commercial banking system and key elements of its trade networks.

[124] Eskin and Webb 1999, 11.

fields that the Duma made available for development under PSA terms were exclusively licensed to Russian companies. PSAs secured these companies' operations against unfavorable low oil prices. Companies such as TNK, Lukoil, Surgutneftegaz, Tatneft, and Yukos became the biggest beneficiaries and supporters of PSA legislation.[125] Overall, the harsh realities of the financial crisis of 1998 and the precipitous drop in international oil prices motivated all groups involved to improve the legal environment for Western oil company participation. The obsolescing bargaining power of the Russian side helped to eliminate many of the earlier problems associated with the creation of a PSA regime.

Personalities also played an important role, no doubt. Significant progress on the PSA legislation was not made until Prime Minister Yevgeny Primakov worked directly with the Duma to get the legislation passed. As the former head of foreign intelligence service and deeply respected by the Communists, he was a moderating force. In November 1998, Primakov sent new drafts of enabling legislation and amendments to the 1995 PSA law to the Duma, along with his personal instructions.[126] He personally settled a critical dispute between the MFE and the Ministry of Natural Resources, which ensured that PSAs would take precedence over both the Subsoil Law and the Ministry of Natural Resources' licensing power for exploration and production. He earned the trust of investors by staking his reputation on the PSA laws' passage.[127] His commitment to continued foreign investment was certainly an important factor that pushed this process further. Conversely, the reluctance of Chernomyrdin and the inexperience of Minister of Energy, Alexander Gavrin, contributed to its delay. Some even argue that the fact that Yeltsin was never a "true champion" of PSAs, as was Heidar Aliev in Azerbaijan, for instance, was also influential in the outcome.[128]

The contingency of economic crisis and personalities are certainly important, but by themselves they cannot explain the characteristics of the investment environment in Russia. The institutional structure and power relations within the state and between the state and society outline the constraints and opportunities facing the supporters and opponents of PSAs and the mechanisms at their disposal to overcome conflicts of interests. Interests change

---

[125] "Oil Sector Report" *Troika Dialog* (May 2001), 94.

[126] Szymczak 1999.

[127] *White Paper: Energy Sector Investment in the Russian Federation*, prepared by the Energy Committee of the American Chamber of Commerce in Russia and the Petroleum Advisory Forum (September 1999).

[128] Author's interview with Valery Ovcharenko (Conoco), Moscow, April 16, 2001.

over time due to crises or to initiatives of certain individuals, but they do so within an institutional setting that eventually affects the outcome.

Oil Investment Policy in the 2000s

Early 2000s: Unconstrained Executive and Improved Investment Environment

The relations between foreign investors and the Russian government took another turn in the 2000s. With the change in the leadership from Yeltsin to Putin, came a new political era that replaced the instability and the weakly institutionalized competition of the 1990s with that of stability and "managed" competition. As Putin reigned in the various institutions of the state and restricted political competition, whatever constraints that existed on the executive during the 1990s quickly dissipated. As the theory in this book predicts, the move towards authoritarianism in the beginning of 2000s had the effect of providing a more stable and coherent environment for investment in Russia. There was immediate progress on the issue of PSAs as well as on the general licensing regime with the consequence of increased oil FDI.

Having realized the immediate importance of a PSA regime, Putin took significant measures to deprive certain groups of their rights to oppose and challenge the PSA process. In the beginning of his tenure, he assumed personal control of the PSA process and pledged that the country's PSA legislation would be brought in line with world standards within a year. Addressing the PSA-2000 Conference in Sakhalin, he maintained that PSAs were Russia's "strategic priority" and delaying them would be against the country's interests. Warning against turning PSAs into a "political football," he envisioned several institutional changes. First, to replace the cumbersome and confusing bureaucratic process, he instructed the Ministry of Economic Development and Trade to take charge of PSAs.[129] Under this ministry, the new State Investment Agency was to act as a consulting and support center for PSAs. Second, he structured the state oil company, Rosneft, to realize the income from the state's share of oil production. Rosneft's right to sign agreements on state's behalf was made similar to the role played by Norway's Statoil or Azerbaijan's SOCAR.[130] Hence the

[129] Olenich 2001. Even though the government made its preliminary decision in August, the ministry had to wait for an approval for nearly six months. Some even argue that the statute would have failed to be signed were it not for a direct order from the president.
[130] Creation of a state oil company responsible for PSA projects is seen as an important strategy to overcome the bureaucratic barriers that investors have been facing. A state

new approach to PSAs was based on strengthening the state's regulation and control functions such that PSAs would yield results without further delay. The new PSA negotiation process was designed to reduce approval time for new PSAs to no more than six months, compared with a likelihood of two or three years under the existing legislation. This administrative reform to provide a single-window approach (where the investor deals with one government-authorized agency on all issues) promised to be one of the solutions to the investment conundrum.

As well as streamlining the government bureaucracy, Putin also challenged Duma's involvement in the PSA process by proposing to transfer its approval functions to the federal executive. This proved not to be too difficult, given the new balance of power that emerged between the executive and the Duma since the 1999 parliamentary elections. In the past three election cycles, the Communists have not enjoyed the deciding vote in the Duma. Moreover, the new law on political parties set strict requirements on party formation and on the state financing of parties, which consequently weakened political opposition in the parliament.[131] In addition, the polarization between the executive and legislative branches has waned significantly since the beginning of Putin's presidency, making it easier for the Kremlin to forge alliances between the left and right and to push for reforms. According to some observers, the PSA Law became less of a focal point of political battles in parliament, reflecting the new pragmatism there.[132] For example Alexander Kursky, advisor to the Duma, observed in 2001 that "[B]ills drafted by the government, including lists of PSA-eligible projects, encounter next to no resistance in the Duma and quickly pass the parliamentary hurdles."[133]

In addition to changing the relations between the executive and legislative branches, Putin has also consolidated more power in the state by excluding regional elites from policymaking. In May 2000, he announced a sweeping reorganization that replaced the presidential representatives in most of Russia's regions with seven presidential representatives in seven new administrative districts that are outside the governors' sphere of authority. This decree was also designed to ensure greater presidential control over the thousands of other federal employees who are scattered across the country and who have been subject to control by regional

oil company can save the investor much time and trouble in terms of reducing the number of gatekeepers.

[131] Fish 2001.

[132] Mescherin 2000.

[133] Author's interview with Alexander Kursky (advisor to the government), Moscow, April 27, 2001.

authorities. The decree removed all such federal employees from the direct jurisdiction of the governors.[134] In an even more direct challenge to the governors' authority, Putin also introduced legislation that would remove governors from the Federation Council and empower him to dismiss governors and disband regional legislatures on legal grounds.

Finally, Putin's tax reform aimed at centralizing collection and distribution of the tax revenues left to governors. The 2001 tax law took about 60 percent for the federal budget as opposed to the previous 52 percent.[135] As such, Putin succeeded in significantly rolling back powers seized by the regions during the 1990s. The creation of a new layer of lawmakers – not elected, but appointed – led to unrepresentative legislative action.[136] The move was interpreted as a clear breach of the principle of the separation of executive and legislative powers but a measure that improved the capacity of the federal government to deal with foreign investors unhindered.[137]

As Putin centralized political power in Russia, foreign investors started to utilize the opportunity offered by this country's huge natural resource potential. For instance, Anglo-Dutch Shell and Germany's Wintershall almost simultaneously announced major increases in their involvement in Russian oil projects off Sakhalin and in the Barents Sea.[138] Other companies speeded up their projects and readied themselves to invest in the Russian oil and gas industry.[139] In 2003, BP agreed to pay US$6.75 billion to form a new Russian oil company, a deal considered to be the largest single investment in post-Soviet Russia. This BP investment in a new Russian oil company underscored the fact that foreign investors were increasingly feeling more secure with the terms the Putin regime was providing and were more comfortable operating in Russia even without the guarantees provided by a stable PSA regime.[140] A strong and stable centralized power was increasingly cited by foreign companies as the reason why they were feeling more comfortable investing in Russia.[141] Announcing the deal to form TNK-BP JV in February 2003,

[134] Webb 2000a.
[135] "Federation Council Passes Tax Overhaul." *The Moscow Times* (July 27, 2000).
[136] Latynina 2000.
[137] Zhaeikhin 2000.
[138] "The Put-In Effect: Major Foreign Investors Signal Confidence in Putin's Policies, Hike Investments" *Russian Petroleum Investor* (August 2000), 9–12.
[139] Author's interview with Yuri Mikhailovih Ten (Duma deputy), Moscow, May 23, 2001.
[140] "BP Completes Big Oil Deal with Russians" *The New York Times* (February 12, 2003).
[141] Author's interview with Peter Henshaw (BP), Moscow, April 11, 2001.

Mikhail Fridman, head of TNK-BP shareholder Alfa Group called the deal "a reflection of the political change that has taken place in Russia over the past three years." He argued that Russia stopped being associated with instability and nontranparency.[142] The Russian daily, Izvestia called it the "deal of the century" and that "foreigners have now accepted that the investment climate in Russia has improved significantly and are willing to sink billions of dollars into the economy."[143]

Mid 2000s: High Oil Prices, Energy Statism and Energy Nationalism

The 2000s, however, have not been completely a honeymoon period for foreign investors and the Russian government. In addition to the political regime, the dynamics of the international oil industry were changing as well. As oil prices started their dramatic climb in mid 2000s, the balance of power, once again, started to shift in favor of host governments. There were now more incentives to invest in large, untapped oil reserves around the world. In order to be able to make substantial profits, foreign companies became much more accommodating to the demands of host governments. Contrary to the 1990s, the Russian government was not an exception this time. High oil prices had filled Russia's coffers, making it less dependent on immediate production growth. In line with the expectations of the obsolescing bargain theory, high oil prices gave the Russian government room to play hardball with foreign investors.[144] Putin's administration immediately started to enjoy and utilize its advantageous position in relation to the investors. Not surprisingly, starting with 2003 the Russian state became more and more assertive in its energy investment policies.

What is interesting about the Russian case is that the state reasserted control over the oil industry by taking over private Russian company assets first as opposed to targeting foreign companies – as is usually the case in most nationalizing oil-rich countries.[145] In essence, energy statism preceded energy nationalism in Russia. It is commonly argued that the most blatant and controversial sign of the shift towards greater state control was the arrest of Mikhail Khodorkovsky, the CEO of the largest

[142] Elder 2008.
[143] "BP investment sounds unprecedented trust in Russian economy," *Johnson's Russia List* (February 12, 2003).
[144] Hoyos 2006.
[145] This anomaly is due to the fact that prior to 2003, Russia was the only major oil exporter in the world that had a significant private oil industry.

Russian oil company and the richest man in Russia, at gunpoint on charges
of tax evasion, fraud and embezzlement in October 2003. The now infa-
mously known "Yukos affair" was significant not only for the sad fate of
a politically-minded oligarch and the changing oligarchy- state relations
that captured the political and popular imagination in Russia for so long
but also for the dismantling and expropriation of the company assets by
the government and its consequences for investor confidence in Russia.[146]
First, Yukos assets were frozen by the courts. Then, the company was
forced into bankruptcy through demands of back taxes, and its prize assets
were captured by the state in rigged, noncompetitive auctions. The main
Yukos production unit, Yuganskneftegaz, was sold to state-owned Rosneft
through an intermediary in December 2004. Yukos' two other subsidiaries,
Samaraneftegaz and Tomskneft were also sold to Rosneft by May 2007.

The process of state acquisition that started with the Yukos affair gained
full steam in the second half of 2000s.[147] Until 2005, the share of state-
owned companies' production in the Russian upstream and downstream
sector was negligible. After Rosneft's takeover of Yuganskneftegaz in 2004
and Gazprom's purchase of Sibneft (the fifth largest oil company in Russia)
in 2005, the share rose to slightly over a quarter of the total crude output
and 16 percent of total refining capacity. According to Tompson (2008), the
state's share of the total crude output exceeded 40 percent by early 2007.
In 2006, the Kremlin was dominating the Russian oil and gas industry
through two state-controlled enterprises, Rosneft and Gazprom.[148] With
Putin's close allies in the chairmanship positions, the Kremlin also began
to keep close tabs on the management of both companies. For example,
in July 2004 Putin's deputy chief of staff Igor Sechin replaced Economic
Development and Trade Minister German Gref as chairman of Rosneft.[149]

The move towards energy statism in Russia in the mid to late 2000s
was followed by an energy nationalism as clearly reflected in the changing

---

[146] For more information on the Yukos affair and its costs to Russia, see Hanson (2005) and
Tompson (2005a).

[147] The increasing involvement of the state was not only experienced in the oil and gas
sector. Since 2004, there has been a clear and unmistakable expansion of the direct role
of the state in other strategic sectors of the economy as well, such as aviation, finance
and power-generation machines. For example, the state's share of the equity market
capitalization rose from 20 percent in mid-2003 to 35 percent in early 2007 (Tompson,
2008:3). The increase in state control of the oil industry is perhaps not surprising considering that Russia's economic growth is largely driven by hydrocarbon export and production. This sector represents over 25 percent of the GDP and a 10 percent change in
international oil prices allows an increase of 2.2 percent in GDP (Locatelli 2006:1080).

[148] Cavenagh 2006.

[149] Rutland 2008.

investment terms for foreign companies. In 2005, the Natural Resources Ministry announced that foreign companies would be banned from bidding for large strategic oil and metal deposits. According to this regulation, foreign participation would be permitted only for ventures in which a Russian partner holds at least 51 percent of its shares.[150] The 2008 law on foreign investment sets further limits on foreign investment in strategic sectors.[151] Under the new rules, foreign investment in fields with reserves of at least 500 million barrels of oil or 50 billion cubic meters of gas will be limited to just a 10 percent stake and any purchase of more than 10 percent will require government approval.[152] Aside from the concern with encroaching state control, many investors worry that this law in practice will add to the formidable bureaucracy in Russia, slowing down investment projects significantly.

Moreover, since 2006, the Kremlin has been renegotiating the terms of the only PSA projects in Russia to force foreign oil majors to give up part of their advantageous contract terms (negotiated when oil prices were lower) to Russian state monopolies like Rosneft and Gazprom. On December 21, 2006, Gazprom acquired a stake of 50 percent plus one share in the US$20 billion Sakhalin-2 gas project from Shell, Mitsui, and Mitsubishi.[153] This project was signed in 1994 and was the first PSA project in Russia with an estimated cost of US$20 billion to Shell and its Japanese partners.[154] Before the Gazprom takeover, the Russian Federal Service for the Oversight of Natural Resources (Rosprirodnadzor) threatened to block the continuation of the project on the basis of its concerns over ecological damage and cost overruns.

In addition, ExxonMobil and the Russian government have been at odds over rights to newly discovered reserves adjacent to the Sakhalin-1 project. Ministry of Natural Resources auctioned it to the only applicant, Rosneft. The Ministry has also been reviewing Total's PSA for the Kharyaginsk oil project. Furthermore, the government has been backing Gazprom's attempts at wresting control of some of the most valuable assets of TNK-BP. As mentioned above, in February 2003, BP bought 50 percent into TNK, creating a new company, TNK-BP. At the time, it was

[150] For more detail, see Lavelle (2005) and "Russia Risk: Alert –Foreigners Held Back." *Economist Intelligence Unit* (February 2005).

[151] The law lists around 40 sectors of the economy that are defined as strategic. These sectors include defense, aerospace, nuclear power, biotechnology, extraction of mineral resources, mass media and others.

[152] Hanson 2009.

[153] *RFE/RL Newsline* 10:236 Part I (22 December 2006).

[154] Aron 2007.

considered the largest foreign investment in Russia since the collapse of the Soviet Union. By 2006, the company had become Russia's second-largest oil/condensate producer next to Lukoil. Similar to the beginning of the Yukos debacle, government pressure started with back-tax claims in 2006. Then, BP executives were harassed by the Russian authorities, the latest of which was a ban by a Moscow court for TNK-BP's American CEO from working in Russia for two years.[155] Finally, in 2007, the government succeeded in forcing the company to sell a majority share in the Kovykta giant gas field in Eastern Siberia to Gazprom. BP was developing the field through TNK-BP, which owned 62 percent of Russia Petroleum, the field's operator. Russian regulator threatened to withdraw the license citing a failure to hit production goals in the field.

A final example of the toughening terms for investment and a resurgence of Russian state interests is seen in the Caspian Pipeline Consortium (CPC) expansion negotiations. In 1994, Russia signed on to the CPC that was initially conceived by Kazakhstan and Oman in 1992 to build a pipeline connecting Caspian oil to Russia's Black Sea port of Novorossyisk. It was significant because it was the only oil export pipeline to be built on Russian territory that was not under the control of the state company, Transneft, at the time. Foreign investors were invited in 1996 once Russia, Kazakhstan, and Oman acknowledged that they were unable to finance the project themselves. CPC's shareholding structure was split 50–50 between three states and private oil companies such as ChevronTexaco (leading with 15 percent), ExxonMobil, BP, Shell, and Agip. Given the complex and fragile balance of power in its ownership and management structure, CPC soon came to be "seen by the international investment community as a bellwether of Russia's investment climate."[156] The pipeline, which was completed in November 2001, became very successful until it was time to negotiate the terms of the expansion of the pipeline to meet increasing production from the Caspian. When Putin took office, he immediately began to emphasize the strategic importance of the pipeline for Russia and signaled that Russia would pay more attention to it. True to his word, during the expansion discussions, Putin's administration stalled progress and insisted that its demands be met before it could agree to any expansion. The demands, taken altogether, amounted to a serious change in the structure of investor interests and would basically mean a complete overhaul of the original contract.[157] In December 2006, the

[155] "A New Start for TNK-BP". *Business Week* (September 4, 2008).
[156] Heslin 1998.
[157] See Dellecker 2008 for a more detailed analysis of Russian demands.

head of the Federal Energy Agency explicitly threatened to nationalize the pipeline. In April 2007, Russia's 24 percent stake in the CPC, which was originally held by the Federal Property Management Agency, was transferred to Transneft by a presidential decree. And finally, when some of the shareholders voted against Transeft's tariff demands in July 2007, "Russia's Federal Tax Service came up with back-tax claims of 290 million US dollars for the 2004–2005 period."[158]

These recent maneuvers by the Russian state in abrogating on its contractual obligations are seen by many as a sign that Russia does not respect the rule of law and will no longer tolerate foreigners' strategic assets or interests in oil and gas projects. Especially after the Yukos affair, the initial fear was that foreign investment would significantly dwindle. Contrariwise, however FDI has increased since this incident and reached a record level in 2004, surpassing 2003's achievement and promoting Russia to the top division of emerging-market FDI recipients.[159] Russia recorded FDI inflows of US$27.8 billion in 2007 up from US$6.8 billion in 2003. Per capita FDI rose almost sevenfold to US$369, far higher than other emerging economies.[160] In 2007 alone, fixed capital investment rose by a record 21 percent. According to one survey conducted among foreign firms in Russia, 82 percent were broadly satisfied with the investment climate in 2007.[161]

Furthermore, a spate of new deals, worth billions of dollars, in the energy sector has been announced in the immediate aftermath of the Yukos affair and continues to be signed. For instance, the French oil major Total announced that it would buy a 25 percent blocking stake in Novatek, Russia's second-largest natural gas producer, for an estimated US$1 billion. Shell approved a US$1 billion investment into the Salym oil field in Western Siberia, where it operates a venture with Russian

---

[158] Ibid., 18.
[159] "Getting Past Yukos" *Business Week* (September 13, 2004); "Russian Economy: Yukos Crisis? What Crisis?" *Economist Intelligence Unit* (October 19, 2004). According to these articles, one explanation for this seemingly ironic situation is that many foreign investors see the conflict between the government and Yukos as merely an isolated criminal case and thus a domestic matter for Russia. It seems that if the oligarchs were to steer clear of politics, Putin would allow them to keep the lucrative assets they amassed during the chaotic rule of Yeltsin. Putin himself had said many times that the results of the privatization would not be revisited in Russia. There is also a sense among foreign investors that the Kremlin may even prefer to deal with large foreign multinationals rather than the most powerful domestic oligarchs because the former are seen as less likely to pose a political threat to the state. Finally, the greater political stability that Putin has created (as discussed above), as well as the robust and ongoing economic recovery in the recent years, may explain the fact that the Yukos affair did not have the expected reverse effect on FDI.
[160] World Bank 2008.
[161] "Russia's Eoonomy: Smoke and Mirrors," *The Economist* (February 28, 2009).

independent Evikhon. Also announced in September 2004 was US$3.5 billions-worth of the South Korean investment in Russian oil projects.[162] In addition, the U.S. oil major ConocoPhillips paid nearly US$2 billion in September 2004 for a 7.59 percent stake in Russia's second-largest oil company, Lukoil.[163] By the end of 2006, it further increased its stake in Lukoil to 20 percent and entered a JV with Lukoil to develop oil in Timon-Pechora province.[164] Moreover, in 2007 Chevron and Gazprom's oil unit, Gazprom Neft, formed a JV to develop oil fields in Yamal-Nenets autonomous district.[165] Finally, in February 2008, the French company Total and Norwegian company StatoilHydro signed a shareholder agreement with Gazprom for the creation of Shtokman Development AG to develop the massive Arctic oil and gas field, Shtokman.[166]

This surge in FDI in Russia points out to the fact that despite concerns, foreign investors now have a place at the table. This is because, if Russia wants to continue and increase oil production, it still very much needs foreign investment. According to the International Energy Association (2003), the total investment that the Russian oil industry needs until 2030 is at US$328 billion.[167] Otherwise, as many analysts point out, Russian oil production will soon face a steep decline because far too little has been done to develop new fields.[168] The bulk of current production comes from fields in the middle to late stages of their production lives and domestic companies are able to exploit these old fields without much foreign involvement. However, the next generation of oil deposits will require substantial foreign investment to develop because they are generally offshore or in hard-to-reach areas without sufficient infrastructure. The PSAs in Sakhalin have all now entered the production phase. Altogether investment in the first three PSAs is estimated at over US$16 billion as of the beginning of 2006. The companies involved in the Sakhalin PSAs estimate that their projects will ultimately generate US$85 billion for Russia in the form of oil revenues, taxes, and royalties.[169] Apart from offshore

---

[162] "Getting Past Yukos" *Business Week* (September 13, 2004).

[163] "ConocoPhillips buys Lukoil stake" BBC News online (September 30, 2004).

[164] "ConocoPhillips increased stake in Lukoil to 20 percent," *The European Weekly: New Europe* (January 12, 2007). Available at http://www.neurope.eu.

[165] "Chevron and Gazprom JV to tap oil in West Siberia," *Reuters* (January 11, 2007) and "Chevron Teams up with Gazprom," *Moscow Times* (January 12, 2007).

[166] "Gazprom, Total and StatoilHydro create Shtokman Company," *StatoilHydro* (February 21, 2008). Available at http://www.statoilhydro.com.

[167] International Energy Association 2003, 144.

[168] Dienes 2004, Gaddy 2004.

[169] Webb 2006.

Sakhalin however, the East Siberian and Far Eastern provinces remain untapped and barely explored. According to the director of the Russian company, TNK, the US$10,000 million invested annually by the Russian oil companies will not be sufficient to develop any of these projects.[170]

Aside from the obvious need for Western finance and managerial and technological expertise, Putin also realizes that in order to be treated as a global player and a member of the Western club, Russia has to have an open economy- or at least the appearance of one. Russia's bid for WTO membership, dependence on energy consumers in Europe, and the efforts of the Russian oil and gas companies to invest abroad, all necessitate a welcoming approach to foreign investment. Moreover, as some analysts rightly point out, Putin wants the political cover that he hopes would come with Western corporate involvement.[171]

The new criterion for investment is that foreign investment – to the extent that it is allowed – will have to be on Russian terms. Foreign investors are welcome as long as they accept the operating control of the Russian state. Investors understand that only investments with the direct blessing of the Kremlin have any hope of success.[172] This new investment attitude of the Russian state reflects Putin's own ideas as outlined in the dissertation that he wrote when he was at St. Petersburg's State Mining Institute. In it, Putin explored the ways in which to introduce western management-style into Russia's oil and gas sector while protecting the best interests of the Russian state. He clearly supported the idea of state-sponsored foreign investment in Russia's extractive industries. He argued that the state needs to provide the necessary guarantees and incentives for foreign investors but that foreign investment should be made in a manner consistent with the Russian state's ability to exert guardianship over the country's oil and gas assets.[173]

Therefore, instead of ruling out foreign investment completely, the Russian state will most likely allow it selectively. The big foreign companies that will be welcomed will be those that buy minority shares on public offers from Rosneft and Gazprom because the presence of those kinds of

---

[170] Locatelli 2006, 1077. For instance, between 2000 and 2002, Yukos spent less than 2 percent of its investment resources on exploration, while Sibneft and TNK spent less than 2 and 5 percent, respectively (Dienes 2004).

[171] Rutland (2008) argues that the most blatant example of this thinking was the appointment of the former German Chancellor Gerhart Schroeder to chair the North European Gas Pipeline project and the invitation to the former US Commerce Secretary Donald Evans to chair the Rosneft board in 2005.

[172] "Foreigners Flocking to Yukos Carve-up? *Business Week* (February 28, 2007).

[173] Olcott 2004.

investors will help the state-owned giants secure access to international capital markets without any threat to the giants' control.[174] Moreover, according to some analysts, there will be a fair amount of activity in the middle-to-small end of the Russian oil and gas market – for assets (corporate or otherwise) in the US$100–500 million range that fall below the radar screens of the state-owned companies.[175] Foreign equipment and technology will remain crucial to the success of the more challenging offshore projects. So far, nearly all of the Russian companies' offshore projects involve partnerships with foreign companies or use of key foreign technological components or both.[176] The recent Shtokman deal between Gazprom and two foreign companies is a good example of this trend. Instead of giving ownership rights and decision-making powers to Total and StatoilHydro, the Russian government offered them a position that is slightly better than a service provider, in which they receive long-term profits rather than merely payments for work performed.

It is important to note that despite the changing attitude of the Russian state toward foreign investment as well as the continuing bureaucratic foot-dragging to some extent, the PSA regime continues to be relevant, thanks to the enthusiastic support of an increasing number of Russian oil companies – among which are the state-owned companies. As discussed before, these companies have increased their interaction with global equity and financial markets over time and have become commercially more sophisticated. They have also increased their participation in PSA projects outside Russia and intensified lobbying for PSA terms for some of the more demanding Russian projects.[177] PSAs, then, will continue to have a place in the Russian oil industry, albeit on a selective, case-by-case basis.

Finally, it would be insufficient and unrealistic to explain the changes in government-investor relations since the mid 2000s solely as the return of the obsolescing bargain. In addition to the changing international oil market dynamics, the improved bargaining position of the state is closely linked to the evolution of its political regime. Putin created a large number of new state-owned companies and adopted a host of distributive policies to extend further the potential patronage resources that could be used to solidify United Russia's hegemony. In exchange for these patronage

---

[174] For instance, ConocoPhillips bought an 8 percent share in Lukoil in 2004, which was raised to 17 percent by 2008.

[175] Cavenagh 2006.

[176] Webb 2006.

[177] Ibid.

opportunities, the Russian parliament entered into a grand bargain with the president and delegated him wide autocratic powers.[178] The recent trends in the Russian investment environment confirm the main argument of this book; that is political institutions matter. They do not dictate policy choices but they mediate the effects of external factors and shape the opportunities and constraints that decision-makers face.

Implications of Oil FDI on Development

Whether or not Russia should be treated as one of the many oil-rich countries that have succumbed to the resource curse is a complicated question that does not generate an easy and simple answer. So does the question about the role of foreign investment in the Russian economic and political development. One can argue that some of the conditions that made foreign investment difficult – if not impossible – in Russia in the 1990s were ironically the same conditions that prevented it from contracting the oil curse during that period. Ironically, as the investment environment improved for investors in mid-2000s- due to changes in the political regime as well as the price of oil- so did the odds of catching this infamous disease.

Most analysts agree that today Russia is a resource-based economy. Russia's economic growth in the 2000s has been driven primarily by energy. The oil sector comprised roughly 45 percent of the growth of industrial production between 2001 and 2004.[179] According to the recent US Energy Informational Administration report, the oil sector accounts for about 20.5 percent of GDP and together with the gas sector, generates more than 60 percent of Russia's export revenues.[180] Thanks to oil, government revenues have increased from US$40 billion in 2000 to $153 billion in 2005.[181]

Russia-an Outlier?

As demonstrated in more detail in Chapter 4, resource-dependent economies are typically prone to an over-valued exchange rate and slower economic growth in non-oil sectors, also known as the Dutch disease. While there is some evidence that Russia is contracting this disease, with the value of the ruble appreciating since 1999 and the manufacturing and agricultural

---

[178] Tompson 2008.
[179] Ahrend 2005.
[180] USEIA 2008.
[181] Rutland 2008.

sectors becoming fairly uncompetitive, the Russian economy is still fairly diversified when compared to single-commodity economies that are based in the Middle East or Africa. For example, the manufacturing sector still accounts for a high percentage in GDP. It expanded by 7.4 percent in 2007, up from 2.9 percent in 2006.[182]

When it comes to spending-inducing effects of oil dependence, Russia has also seemed to have mostly escaped the resource curse. The Russian state has been fairly disciplined in its fiscal and monetary policies. By general standards of petro-states, state spending as a share of the GDP has been low floating at around 32 percent. Thanks to the dramatic increase in oil prices and the restraint from extreme government spending, Russia has been able to accumulate a substantial fiscal surplus of 7.5 percent of GDP in 2005.[183] Most of this excess revenue has been spent on paying off state's foreign debt rather than squandering it on wasteful infrastructural projects – also known as white elephant projects – as would typically be expected in a petro-state.[184] Moreover, in order to sterilize the oil windfall and reduce the vulnerability of the state budget, the Russian government has followed the example of many oil-rich countries and created an Oil Stabilization Fund in 2004. With this fund, the Russian government has been able to put aside the excess taxes from oil exports beyond a certain price ($27 since 2006).[185] By 2008, the revenues in this Fund reached US$168 billion, a dramatic increase from US$4 billion and $50 billion in 2004 and 2006, respectively.[186]

Finally, the relationship between oil and authoritarianism that is found in most petro-states is not easily observable in Russia. As discussed in Chapter 4, typically, it is argued that oil dependence distorts political institutions via three mechanisms.[187] The first is the rentier effect, whereby oil rents allow rulers to escape accountability and to co-opt opposition by reducing the

---

[182] World Bank 2008. Oomes and Kalcheva (2007) find evidence for slower growth in the manufacturing sector since 2001 than in other sectors but argue that this relative de-industrialization could not be regarded as evidence of Dutch disease because it may have occurred for other, transition-related reasons. After controlling for the transition effect, they do not find a significantly negative effect of oil prices on manufacturing growth.

[183] Rutland 2008.

[184] Ahrend 2005.

[185] Rutland 2008. The fund collects revenues from a portion of the export duty on crude oil and a portion of the mineral resources extraction tax on oil.

[186] In February 2008, the fund has been split into the Reserve Fund and the National Welfare Fund. With the Reserve Fund, government plans to insure the Russian budget against a steep fall in oil prices. It will hold US$125 billion and be maintained at roughly 10 percent of Russia's GDP. The National Welfare Fund, on the other hand, has $32 billion and is intended to support the pension system (Kramer 2008).

[187] Ross 2001.

incentives to tax and spend prudently. Steven Fish (2005) relies on two indicators of rentierism – the ratio of nontax revenues as a percentage of central government revenues and the ratio of tax revenues to government expenditures – to prove that Russia does not fit this aspect of rentier states. He shows that 14 percent of Russia's revenues comes from nontax sources, even though this number is quite high for some oil-based economies like Kuwait (90 percent) and Oman (71 percent). Fish also finds that central government's tax revenue as a percentage of overall government expenditure is quite high with 72 percent, clearly demonstrating the fact that the Russian government relies overwhelmingly on taxes to be able to spend. Similarly, Tompson (2005b) demonstrates that Russian fiscal institutions prior to the new tax code under Putin paid little attention to imposing high taxes on the fuel sector and capturing resource rents. He argues that the total effective tax burden on the fuel sector was considerably less than the nonfuel sectors and that "export duties and resource taxes accounted for only about 20 percent of revenues in 2003, far less than either social taxes (22.2 percent) or taxes on consumption (29.5 percent)."[188]

The argument that oil rents make governments reluctant or lazy to push for reforms also does not seem to hold in Russia. Since he came to power, Putin pursued an ambitious program of structural reforms. Budgetary and tax reforms reduced the number of taxes and the overall tax burden. The tax system was designed to capture a larger share of the windfall profits from high oil prices. According to a World Bank report, the government improved tax collection and customs administration, eliminated noncash budgetary settlements, created more stable revenue and expenditure assignments among different layers of government and even began to improve judicial efficiency and independence.[189]

Fish (2005) further argues that the repressive effects of oil rents that are commonly found in resource-rich states are not easily observable in Russia. He demonstrates that even though the amount of the government budget that goes to the military is relatively high and that oil rents help sustain the armed forces, it is not clear how much the real agent of repression – the internal security apparatus (FSB) – is dependent on oil revenues to finance its operations. Finally, he also rejects the assumption that oil retards and/or delays modernization in Russia on the basis that Russia by many socioeconomic indicators already approximates the European norm, rather than the norm in most oil-rich societies.[190]

[188] Tompson 2005b, 5.
[189] World Bank 2008.
[190] Fish 2005, 138.

There may be several reasons why Russia seems to have escaped the full extent of the resource curse so far. First of all, Russia was very different from other resource-rich economies in the 1990s in the ownership structure of its oil industry and the general complexity of its economy. While oil production is commonly controlled by state oil companies in the majority of oil producers, Russia had a predominantly private oil industry prior to 2003.[191] Aslund (2005) states that by 2003 Russia was closer to the Anglo-American model of resource management with its private ownership of oil companies, a competitive domestic market and a reasonable openness to the world market than the resource curse model.[192]

In the aftermath of the Soviet collapse, the former Soviet oil ministry was split into thirteen vertically integrated private companies as well as a number of small companies that were not entirely integrated.[193] Many experts treat the pluralistic ownership of the Russian oil industry as a positive exception to the rule.[194] Accordingly, ownership matters because state and private ownership generate different incentive structures when it comes to managing the resource wealth. State's direct control of resource rents creates disincentives for supplying institutions that would limit the governments' fiscal independence or discretionary decision-making power. Alternatively, privatization leads to the development of societal actors that may become powerful enough to challenge the state and demand strong fiscal and regulatory institutions that can better manage the resource wealth.

In Russia, the pluralism within the oil industry led to intense political bargaining, both vertically between the federal government and oil-rich regions as well as horizontally among rival companies.[195] These new actors were able to pressure the government to support greater liberalization within the energy sector as well as develop institutions outside the energy sector to promote greater transparency and fiscal stability.[196] Furthermore, because Russia's resource endowment is not limited to only oil, the equally important natural gas and metals industries have added to the plurality and complexity of the Russian political economy, diluting the damaging effects of dependence on a single commodity.[197]

---

[191] Aslund 2005.
[192] Ibid., 616.
[193] Lane 1999.
[194] See for instance Tompson 2005b, Ahrend 2005, Weinthal and Luong 2006, Rutland 2008. It is important to note that in contrast to the oil sector, the gas sector in Russia remained a state-controlled vertically integrated monopoly.
[195] Rutland 2008.
[196] Weinthal and Luong 2006.
[197] Rutland 2008.

Another reason why Russia did not become a full-fledged petro state in the 1990s has to do with its political regime at the time. As discussed earlier, Russia was neither a democracy nor an autocracy in the decade that it gained its independence. While political competition and the institutionalization of political parties and interest groups were limited, the government was constrained to some extent in its ability to rule as it saw fit. As discussed above, the two branches of the parliament, regional governments as well as various bureaucratic agencies exerted significant veto powers in the system. This partially pluralistic structure of the political system prevented the government from taking complete control over the oil rents and having an unfettered authority to spend the windfall. In fact, one can argue that the hybrid political regime that made it difficult for the Russian government to create an attractive investment environment ironically allowed Russia to escape the resource curse in the 1990s.

Finally, the negative regime effects of foreign investment that were felt in the neighboring Azerbaijan were missing in Russia. As discussed earlier in this chapter, unlike in Azerbaijan, foreign investors in Russia in the 1990s did not have an easy access to and an alliance with those in power. Consequently, their economic and political effects were negligible; there were no opportunities for multinational oil companies to help endorse and legitimize an oil dictatorship that they themselves could feed on.

Russia becoming the Norm

Just as many agree that Russia has so far escaped the oil curse for the most part, many are also concerned that the recent trends do not fare well for the future of Russian economic and political development. While still not a full-fledged petro state in the conventional sense, Russia is beginning to show signs of many of the problems associated with the resource curse. For instance, since 2002, the ruble has appreciated much more rapidly, 43 percent by the end of 2007.[198] In recent years, the government has not been able to prevent the inflationary pressures caused by the oil windfall. Consumer price index inflation accelerated to 11.9 percent in 2007 from 9 percent in 2006.[199] As a result of the appreciating ruble, real GDP growth has shifted toward nontradables sectors like construction and retailing. In line with a Dutch disease scenario, construction grew at 14.5 percent a year in 2003–07, and retail trade at 13 percent, outpacing the rest of the economy.[200] In addition, Russia has not been investing in industries that could diversify

[198] Cooper 2008.
[199] World Bank 2008.
[200] Ibid.

its economic base. The bulk of the investments have remained in resource industries and in transportation and communication services.

Moreover, since 2006, Russia's budget has become more dependent on oil revenues. According to the International Monetary Fund, while the Russian federal budget enjoyed a fiscal surplus equivalent to 7.4 percent of GDP, if oil-related revenues were excluded, the budget would have been in a deficit equivalent to 3.8 percent of GDP.[201] The fact that 10 percent increase in international oil prices allows an increase of 2.2 percent in Russian GDP provides enough proof that Russian economy is becoming extremely vulnerable to oil shocks.[202] A significant drop in the price of oil could easily tip Russia into deficit spending.

Furthermore, since the end of 2007, government's fiscal stance has become much more relaxed. There has been growing political pressure to spend a larger share of oil windfalls as prices remained high. Public spending increased from 31.5 percent in 2005 to 34.1 percent in 2007.[203] For instance, spending on domestic security went from US$4 billion in 2000 to $39 billion in 2008.[204] The general government surplus declined to 6.1 percent of GDP in 2007 from more than 8 percent in 2005–2006.[205] There are also increasing signs that the state is using more and more oil windfalls to increase wages and pensions to appease social protest.

Dependency on oil is also increasing the rent-seeking behavior, corruption, and inequality in Russia. Russia is by all measures a very corrupt country today. Even though corruption is not new to Russia, many organizations that measure corruption cross-nationally generally agree that corruption has increased in recent years. For instance, according to Transparency International (TI), an organization that ranks countries from least to most corrupt on a scale of 0 (highly corrupt) to 10 (highly clean), Russia earned a score of 2.1 in 2008, compared to 2.5 in 1996 and 2.8 in 2004.[206] In 2007, TI ranked Russia 143rd out of 180 countries on corruption perceptions index, putting it on par with Gambia

---

[201] Cooper 2008, 29.
[202] Locatelli 2006, 1980.
[203] World Bank 2008.
[204] Rutland 2008.
[205] Ibid.
[206] Transparency International corruption perceptions indices (1996–2008). Available at http://www.transparency.org. This range is certainly not too wide, indicating that there was pervasive corruption during Yeltsin years as well. However, the numbers show that while there has been a slight improvement in the early years of Putin's presidency, corruption started to increase once again since 2006.

and Indonesia.[207] According to INDEM Center for Applied Political Studies, businesses paid US$319 billion in bribes in 2005, surpassing the budget revenues that the government collected that year by 2.6 times.[208] In a December 2006 policy memo, the Program on New Approaches to Russian Security (PONARS) noted that while the overall number of bribes have shrunk (bribe tax going from 1.4 percent of revenue to 1.1 percent), the size of the bribes has been growing as much as 50 percent in recent years.[209]

One of the consequences of high-level corruption has been the widening inequality in Russian society. Incomes of the top 10 percent of earners in 2007 were reported to be 15 times higher than those of the lowest 10 percent of earners. In the first quarter of 2007, 16.3 percent of the population lived below the minimum subsistence level and about 75 percent of the population in December 2006 had no savings.[210] A recent study has shown that between 2000 and 2005, regions rich in oil were characterized by a higher level of income inequality than regions without oil.[211] Corruption has also been affecting the quality of public services. For instance, despite its oil wealth, Russia faces huge health care problems. Medical care in Russia is among the worst in the industrialized world. World Health Organization report ranked Russia's health system 130th out of 191 countries, on par with such nations as Peru and Honduras.[212]

Certainly corruption is nothing new in Russia. Neither is it limited to one sector of the economy. Its growth since the late 1980s is a result of many factors, among which are the breakdown of the bureaucratic controls of Soviet system, and the haphazardly carried out privatization program of the 1990s. Russia has always provided a very rent-rich environment. Even without the oil endowments, one would still find high levels of corruption in Russia (like the many former soviet republics that do not have significant natural resources).[213] However, there is also no doubt that the higher oil prices starting with 2002 and the ensuing oil windfall have increased the incentives and stakes for rent seeking and intensified the struggle over the control of resources.

---

[207] Transparency International 2007.
[208] Myers 2005.
[209] Orttung 2006.
[210] US-Russia Business Council 2007.
[211] Buccellato and Mickiewicz 2009.
[212] Danilova 2007.
[213] Tompson 2005b.

Finally, even though oil is not the main cause of authoritarianism in Russia, increasing oil windfalls are making it very difficult – if not impossible – to reverse the authoritarian trend and establish a decent level of democracy. As discussed above, in order to capture a bigger share of the oil windfall, Putin is reorganizing the oil industry to more forcefully reflect state interests. After contentious acquisitions of various private companies, the state's share of the total crude output exceeded 40 percent by early 2007.[214] Many experts are concerned that the state's domination of the oil industry allows it too much discretion in its fiscal decisions. Greater state control will most likely lead to more financial opacity, less efficiency, more rent-seeking and slower growth in the very sectors that have been driving the Russian economic expansion in recent years. It is also argued that the increase in state control over the economy is causing a sharp decline in the pace of economic restructuring and reforms that occurred during Putin's first term.[215] Furthermore, concentration of huge rents in the state is giving the ruling elites ample incentives to continue to restrict participation and competition in the political system. Fish (2005) finds ample evidence that links resource abundance in Russia to corruption in the state as well as to economic statism, both of which in turn have been further undermining elite support for open politics in recent years.

Conclusion

The study of the investment environment in the Russian oil industry illustrates the importance of political institutions in understanding FDI patterns. International economic theories of business cycles and obsolescing bargaining fall short of adequately explaining what went wrong in Russia in the 1990s. Even though foreign investors were clearly interested in Russia's vast energy resources and had the upper hand vis-à-vis the government in terms of international market conditions, they did not get the investment environment they asked for. This was not because the Russian side did not need or want foreign investment. On the contrary, the Russian oil companies themselves could not or would not provide the necessary investment capital and expertise to develop the technologically challenging new deposits. Understanding the implications of this for oil production, various groups in the state – including the president – adamantly pushed for the liberalization of the investment regime. Despite these favorable

[214] Tompson 2008.
[215] Cooper 2008.

conditions and some genuine attempts, it was not possible for the government to create a stable and attractive investment environment. In this chapter, I argue and demonstrate that the government's failure was a result of the institutional structure it operated in. Some strong veto players in the state and a lack of strong interest aggregation and mediation by interest groups and political parties made it extremely difficult to reach a consensus on the investment policy. The legislation and regulations necessary for foreign companies to operate securely in the Russian economy could not be developed in the course of a decade.

The PSA saga illustrates clearly the political struggles that took place over investment policy. The PSA legislation became an indicator of Russia's investment climate, an acid test as to whether the investment crisis can be overcome, how radical the reforms in the economy can become, and whether there is hope for permanent economic growth. The legislation has arguably been one of the most contentious to be passed by the parliament since the collapse of the Soviet Union. Investment conditions in Russia have made PSA legislation and regulations a necessary precondition for the huge amounts of FDI that have been identified and in some cases contingently committed. The law was meant to unleash billions of dollars of investment in oil projects and help Russia reverse a dramatic decrease in production, especially at a time of low international oil prices in the 1990s.

As I demonstrate in this chapter, things have changed since the beginning of 2000s. First of all, the political regime moved towards authoritarianism and increasing authoritarianism correlated with increased FDI. Putin's authoritarian style did not necessarily produce the equivalent of an open arms policy toward foreign investors. After all, in contemporary Russia, Putin cannot institute a "sultanistic," completely unconstrained authoritarian regime like Azerbaijan's. Putin is still constrained "by the need to win elections; to maintain a loyal majority in parliament; and to avoid popular protest by non-violent means".[216] Nevertheless, Putin's administration streamlined the decision-making process, made it clear who was in charge, weakened oppositional pressures, and established clear rules of conduct for investors.

The 2000s was also a period during which the bargaining position of the state improved significantly. Thanks to high oil prices and strengthened state capacity, Putin was able and flexible enough to pursue Russian state interests more aggressively. Today, the Russian government has a welcoming attitude toward foreign investors to the extent that investors

[216] Rutland 2006.

accept a larger and more controlling role for the Russian state. Essentially, investors have little choice but to accept these new terms. Russia's hydro-carbon reserves and economic potential make it far too large for inter-national investors to ignore, particularly in an era of high prices and concern for future energy supplies.

In this chapter I also draw attention to the effects that foreign invest-ment and the ensuing oil rents have had on the economic and political development in Russia. Evidence suggests that so far Russia has escaped many of the economic and institutional malaise that is associated with dependence on oil. This is partly because of the ownership structure in the 1990s and partly because of the hybrid political regime that dominated this period. I argue that ironically the very institutional structure that made it difficult for foreign investors in the 1990s also slowed down or circumvented some of the negative effects of an oil addiction. What this also means is that as political power gets more and more centralized to make the investment environment more attractive, the oil curse becomes more likely. Russia in recent years is certainly moving in that direction. The more authoritarian it becomes, the more it wants to own and control the oil industry and the rents that are generated by it. It remains to be seen how increasing FDI will affect the chances of catching the oil disease and whether Russia will eventually follow the path of Azerbaijan and the likes and get trapped in the vicious cycle of corruption, inequality and authoritarianism. Russia certainly has another option. It can instead create an institutional structure that is both welcoming to foreign invest-ment and equipped to manage the different domestic interests over its oil policy. The case of Norway offers that alternative.

7

Norway: Icon of Stability

Oil came as a surprise to Norway. In 1962, when Phillips Petroleum Company announced its intentions to explore the Norwegian coastal waters, many were skeptical about the venture even to the extent that a geologist, in disbelief, said that he would drink oil if it were found.[1] With no prior experience and expertise, the country in less than a decade established a broad national competence in oil with significant contributions from foreign companies in terms of capital, expertise, and technology. Most of the major multinationals have been involved in the development of Norwegian oil, among them BP, ExxonMobil, Royal Dutch/Shell, TotalFinaElf, Phillips Petroleum Company, and Conoco. U.S. Department of Energy described the development of the Norwegian oil industry as a "grand-scale clubbing together" of the Norwegian state and the world's largest oil companies.[2]

According to one account, between 1971 and 1996, a total of US$200 billion was invested in exploration, construction, and operations on the Norwegian continental shelf.[3] In the first offshore licensing round in 1965, the foreign share of the oil fields was 91 percent. Over time,

---

[1] Author's interview with Bjarne Moe (director general of the Norwegian Ministry of Petroleum and Energy), Oslo, January 15, 2001. Moe also stated that Trygve Lie – the former secretary general of the United Nations and then the representative of the Norwegian Department of Industry – when approached by a delegation from the Phillips Petroleum Company, said that the company was mistaken and that there was no oil or gas in Norway.

[2] USEIA 2001c.

[3] International Trade Administration 2001. This figure includes both international and domestic investments. The exact and systematic data on oil FDI levels going all the way back to the 1970s is missing. According to author's rough calculations, based on

however, with the maturing of the national industry, the balance between Norwegian-owned and foreign companies changed significantly. In 2001, for example, the foreign companies operated roughly 20 percent of the oil resources in producing fields.[4]

In terms of the inward Foreign Direct Investment (FDI) performance index, of approximately 140 countries, Norway ranked 59th highest during 1988–1990 and 60th highest during 1998–2000.[5] Even though Norway needed less FDI over time – thanks to its increasing national competence – it has consistently encouraged the participation of foreign oil companies in the exploration and development of the Norwegian continental shelf. Not surprisingly perhaps, the world investment report ranked Norway among the top five "potential" destinations for foreign investment in 2006.[6]

The existing and potential oil reserves of the Norwegian continental shelf are certainly what made investing in Norway attractive in the first place. With 0.8 percent of world's total proven oil reserves, the country is the sixteenth-largest oil province in the world.[7] Trends in the international oil market also contributed to Norway's attractiveness. High oil prices and problems of supply on a global scale during the 1970s explain why foreign companies found it strategically compelling to invest in Norway. Oil embargos imposed by Organization of the Petroleum Exporting Countries (OPEC) forced multinational oil companies to secure access to new oil resources and thereby reduce their dependency on the Middle East. On top of this, Norway's proximity to major European markets and consumers made it geographically suitable for investment. Also, its merchant marine was traditionally a thriving domestic industry that augmented Norway's competitiveness among other oil-producing countries. Norway has been and still is heavily engaged in tanker trade transporting oil for multinational oil companies.

Although Norway's reserve potential, proximity to markets, and strong domestic industries ensured the initial interest of foreign companies, harsh weather conditions, the difficulty of drilling in the North Sea's deep offshore waters, strong state tradition, and high taxes dramatically increased the costs of oil development for investors.[8] It is interesting in

UNCTAD (2002b), USEIA country reports, and BP (2001), Norway received 92 cents of foreign investment per barrel of its proven oil reserves between 1994 and 2001.
[4] USEIA 2001c.
[5] UNCTAD 2002a.
[6] UNCTAD 2006. In terms of FDI potential, Norway has been ranked second since 2001.
[7] BP 2006.
[8] Water depths and weather conditions make development of offshore oil resources in the North Sea very difficult and risky. The Gulf of Mexico and Middle East are considered

this connection that despite these commercial risks, foreign companies continued to invest significant amounts of capital in the industry. This chapter addresses the puzzle of why foreign oil companies persisted against the physical and fiscal challenges of operating in Norway. I argue that the obsolescing bargaining theory cannot adequately explain why despite the country's increasing market and bargaining power in the 1970s and 1980s, the Norwegian government did not create significant political risks for foreign investors. In addition to market conditions, we need to look at the stability, predictability, and transparency that its political regime has generated over time in order to understand Norway's continuing ability to draw foreign investors.

In the first part of this chapter, I discuss the evolution and characteristics of the investment relationship between foreign investors and the Norwegian state. Then, I focus on the highly competitive and institutionalized democratic regime to explain the attractiveness of the investment environment. Lastly, I reverse the causal relationship to address the role foreign investments and oil revenues have played in the consolidation of the democratic welfare state, as well as the elevation of a small country to the status of important player on the world stage.

History of Relations between Investors and the Norwegian Government

The Initial Phase: The 1960s

In the mid-1960s, Norway basked in its strong economic growth and full employment. It ranked seventh in gross domestic product per capita among the Organization of Economic Cooperation and Development (OECD) countries.[9] High living standards prevailed; poverty had been virtually abolished. With no pressing need for oil revenues, the Norwegian government could initially afford not to give in to all the demands of foreign investors.

In addition to this economic flexibility, a cautious policy toward the multinationals resulted from the traditional sensitivity of Norwegian society to the question of sovereignty. Having been dominated by the Danes and the Swedes for four centuries, Norwegians had become

---

less risky places to produce oil. According to USEIA (2001c), the cost of oil production is about US$12 to US$14 per barrel in Norway; while it is US$3 to US$4 in the Middle East.

[9] Galenson 1986.

averse to "exploitation" by foreigners. Moreover, their experiences with
hydropower production in the beginning of the twentieth century had
taught Norwegians important lessons about doing business with outsiders.
Hence, from the outset of oil development, they believed that it was crucial to set up a broad framework to regulate foreign-company operations
closely and provide a base for state control and capture of oil rents.

In 1962, the Norwegian government received the first application for
permission to explore oil and gas on its continental shelf but could not
process it because of the legal issues of dividing the continental shelf. By
1963, the Norwegian government declared its sovereignty over the continental shelf and approached the exploration and exploitation of natural
resources as a matter of national jurisdiction.[10] In 1964–1965 a group
of professionals, led by Jens Evensen, formulated the first comprehensive
regime for North Sea exploration and production.[11] A royal decree was
passed and the first production licenses were awarded based on the concessionary model.[12] In 1965 the Labor government granted seventy-eight
licenses to nine groups of foreign companies.[13] Each license provided an
oil company or group of companies with exclusive rights to exploration,
drilling, and production within geographically defined areas.

The concessions were much more restrictive than the "traditional concessions" at the beginning of the century in terms of geographical area
and duration of permitted operations. Moreover, they were granted by a
means of administrative procedure: the state used discretion in selecting
companies that met certain criteria.[14] In the first licensing round in 1965,

[10] Noreng 1980.
[11] Andersen 1993. Jens Evensen, then director general of the Ministry of Foreign Affairs,
was the principal architect of the Norwegian offshore strategy. In this early period, politicization of oil issues was limited and the top civil servants had a huge role in formulating
the oil development framework.
[12] For specifics on this model, refer to Chapter 2. The concessionary licensing regime was
firmly rooted in the nation's long tradition of regulating foreign investment in hydropower production. Beginning in 1906, the Norwegian parliament passed a series of laws
that was eventually named the Concession Act of 1917. National control was a sensitive
issue; hence the state introduced strict concession terms to control the activities of the
foreign companies.
[13] In September 1965, the Labor government was defeated by a liberal-conservative coalition. Both the oil policy and the administration of oil were left unchanged. The only
change was in the criteria for license allocation, which now included provisions for state
participation. In 1969, the government granted fourteen new licenses that provided for
state participation in the form of "net profit sharing" and "carried interest" (Noreng
1980:43).
[14] In this discretionary method of allocating licensing, the applicants were not allowed
to form license groups on their own but were chosen by the authorities on the basis

despite its strong control over entry, the state had limited say over operational matters and was not in a position to demand much from the companies. This is because it neither had the expertise nor the capacity to control operations.[15] Without prior experience and technological edge, the government initially had to rely on foreign oil companies and provide them with incentives to invest.[16] As a well-known Norwegian analyst put it, the period until the early 1970s was one of "wait-and-see."[17]

The "Norwegianization" of Oil: The 1970s

In 1969, the discovery of a major Norwegian field, Ekofisk, changed the dynamics of the relationship between the state and the multinationals.[18] When it became evident that the Norwegian part of the North Sea was an area with potentially huge oil reserves, the government adopted a new strategy of "Norwegianization" of the oil industry, which entailed gradual increases in state control, participation, and revenues. The increased bargaining power of host governments around the world during the 1970s was used as a pretext to impose new demands on the multinationals.

State participation in the second licensing round between 1969 and 1971 was the first manifestation of the new strategy. The oil companies had to accept a minor degree of state involvement, either as an agreed percentage of net profit or as an option to participate directly if commercial discoveries were made.[19] Another indication of Norwegianization was the three *White Papers* that the government presented to the Norwegian parliament (Storting) between 1968 and 1971. In 1971, based on these proposed principles of oil exploration and production, the Storting's Committee on Industry issued the "Ten Oil Commandments," which spelled out the goals and nature of national control; development of a Norwegian industry that would pay attention to existing businesses and to the environment; and the creation of a state-owned oil company.[20]

---

of specific criteria. The state used its authority to form groups with the desired mix of companies and with regard to nationality, size, state ownership, track record, and so on. According to Andersen (1993), this system increased inter-company competition and allowed built-in checks and balances for the government.

[15] Andersen and Arnestad 1990.
[16] The competition with the British for companies willing to explore in the North Sea was another reason that led the Norwegians to offer easier terms to the investors.
[17] Andersen 1993, 61.
[18] Before 1969, as a result of some unsuccessful drills on the Norwegian shelf, some companies were contemplating pulling out their investments (Andersen 1993).
[19] Berrefjord and Heum 1990.
[20] Ibid.

During the 1970s it became a priority to encourage Norwegian-based competence in offshore oil activities, and "over the long run reduce the role of the foreign oil companies to that of consultants, developers, and minority partners."[21]

Pursuing its objectives, the Norwegian government gradually began to assert managerial, operational, fiscal, and ownership control over the industry. For the management of oil operations, as mentioned earlier, the government used administrative licensing rather than the auctioning of fields to the highest bidder. In this way, bureaucratic discretion took precedence over obtaining a maximum share of economic rent. As a result, the Ministry of Industry (predecessor of the Ministry of Petroleum and Energy) was able to encourage the exploration of less attractive areas by smaller companies and to insist that foreign companies use Norwegian goods and services as a condition for license approvals.[22] The government also restricted leasing policies to accelerate oil extraction. It divided offshore areas into smaller blocs to speed up exploration. In 1972, it also cut concession periods for licenses to thirty-six years from the traditional ninety years to encourage timely development of resources. Furthermore, it increased its managerial control through a depletion policy, which determined the rate at which oil resources were extracted. In 1973, it imposed an annual production ceiling of 90 million tons of oil.[23] The goal was to establish a moderate and conservative pace that lessened the relative influence of foreign oil companies over production policy. In this way, the Norwegian oil companies and offshore suppliers would have time to develop sufficient capacity to play a major role in oil development.

As for regulatory control, shortly after drilling activities began, a set of national safety regulations was issued by the Royal Decree of August 27, 1967. It addressed safety issues related to seismic explorations, drilling, and the use of floating rings.[24] In addition, the Petroleum Directorate was set up to be responsible for enforcing safety and environmental regulations. These regulations demonstrated the determination of Norwegian authorities not to blindly give in to the demands of foreign oil companies – even when they provided the expertise on exploration and production of oil. Citing their expertise in maritime activities, the Norwegian Directorate of Shipping and Navigation came to exert a dominant influence on the promulgation of regulations, many of which at times

---

[21] Andersen and Arnestad 1990, 55.
[22] Klapp 1987.
[23] Ibid., 77.
[24] Ryggvik 2000.

encroached upon the normal working practices and procedures of the oil companies.

In terms of revenue control, the government was able to carve out a significant share of public oil revenues for itself through taxation. In the beginning, due to the uncertainties about its actual oil reserves, the government hesitated to discourage companies from investing by taxing them too heavily. Between 1965 and 1972, the government collected royalties, area fees, and taxes on the posted prices that OPEC had established above market prices to assure minimum revenues for producer governments. The initial taxation rate for oil based net profits was 10 percent in 1965 and was changed to a sliding scale of 8 to 16 percent by 1972.[25]

After 1973, the government became more interested in getting its fair share of profits as a result of OPEC price increases. In 1974 and 1975, it reached an agreement with the companies whereby the latter would be taxed at a substantially higher rate of 70 percent. In 1975, the government also created a new excess profits tax of 25 percent – the Special Tax – on residual profits after income taxes and royalties.[26]

At the same time that it was increasing its tax revenues, the Norwegian state was also growing unsatisfied about having revenue control only by means of taxation policies. Royalties and taxes provided the government with only a 20 percent share of total returns from oil production. In order to increase state revenues, government control was carried a step further, to ownership. First, the government took a 51 percent controlling interest in a domestic oil company, Norsk Hydro. In 1969, it also introduced state profit-sharing participation in leases to foreign oil companies. The participation percentage was based on the net profits of foreign oil companies; for instance, state participation increased from 5 percent in the Frigg field in 1969 to 40 percent in the Heimdal field in 1971.[27]

State's involvement in the oil industry reached its peak in 1972 when Norway created a state oil company, Statoil.[28] In addition to the fees, royalties, and taxes paid by foreign oil companies, now the government would also receive the direct income from its operations. A state-owned

---

[25] Klapp 1987, 77–79.
[26] Ibid., 77–79.
[27] Ibid.
[28] Policy makers generally agreed on the need to establish a state-owned company, but there was some dispute over the form it would take. Many on the political right thought that Norsk Hydro, Norway's largest and most powerful manufacturing company, was already well situated to take on the role. Yet others proposed to create a government holding company that would service smaller state companies in joint ventures with foreign

company would also give the government a lot of political control over the oil industry and allow it to shape oil activities according to its political priorities and interests. As some pointed out, in this arrangement the government would be an entrepreneur and the Ministry of Industry would essentially function as Statoil's general assembly.[29]

These organizational arrangements established in the 1970s reflected a strong political wish to "Norwegianize" the petroleum industry. Concession rules were changed by the parliament to give Statoil a minimum 50 percent share in all licenses. In addition to Statoil, the two other Norwegian oil companies, Norsk Hydro (51 percent state owned) and Saga (privately owned), were also given licenses of highly promising operations. After 1973, Norwegian ownership interests in all licenses would be more than 60 percent on average, compared to some 10 percent in the pre-1973 period.[30]

To develop Statoil as a fully functioning oil company, the state required that the foreign companies bear all the exploration expenses in the licensed fields. The companies agreed to a sliding scale scheme, in which Statoil's shares could be increased up to 75 percent if major discoveries were made.[31] Furthermore, the state wanted the companies to contribute to the development of Norwegian industry through industrial and technology agreements and to give preference to Norwegian suppliers of goods and services if these were competitive.[32] Foreign companies were also strongly encouraged to develop relations with Norwegian businesses by informing them of future activities and by entering into joint projects with them. To monitor compliance, the ministry established a system of reporting that opened the bidding process to government scrutiny. These measures broke the traditional supply patterns of the foreign companies and raised the Norwegian share of the offshore business (oil and oil-related) from 28 percent in 1975 to 62 percent in 1978.[33]

As some aptly put it, the beginning of the 1980s was "harvest time" for the Norwegian government.[34] With increased national competence the government depended less on multinational corporations. Statoil had morphed into a vertically integrated oil company and almost achieved

companies. It was believed that there was greater flexibility and economic efficiency in a small holding company.

[29] Berrefjord and Heum 1990.
[30] Ibid.
[31] Ibid., 37–39.
[32] Andersen 1993.
[33] Nelsen 1991, 70–72.
[34] Andersen 1993.

the capabilities of a multinational oil corporation. However, during this period, the Norwegian economy had become increasingly dependent on oil revenues and government had become heavily indebted due to the investment requirements and inflationary effects of oil.[35] To get itself out of debt and improve the economy, the government speeded up oil activities. It offered seventy offshore blocks for development between 1980 and 1985, as opposed to the thirty-one that had been offered during the period 1973–1979. This consequent increase in production coincided with the price hikes in 1978–1979, almost tripling the amount of revenues the government received from the oil industry. The 1980 increase in the special tax from 25 to 35 percent further augmented government revenues, bringing the oil sector's share of GNP from 9.4 percent in 1979 to 19.1 percent in 1984.[36]

The Late 1980s

By the mid 1980s, the relative power of host governments vis-à-vis multinationals had changed once again. Oil prices started to drop and then collapsed in 1986. OPEC was losing its grip on the international oil market. Demand for oil had been subsiding because OPEC's high prices in the previous decade had stimulated production in non-OPEC countries. This advantaged consumer countries at the expense of producing countries with high costs.

Norway as a high cost producer was no exception. By this time, its economy had deteriorated significantly. Because of the great importance of the oil sector as a source of government revenues and as a stimulus for the national economy, Norway was among the first to feel the oil price collapse in 1986. Government revenues from oil and gas production fell dramatically. Economic growth fell 2 percent from 1986 to 1987. In the subsequent years, Norway was hit by the strongest recession since the 1930s. GNP decreased while unemployment more than doubled: from 2.0 percent to 4.5 percent. The balance of trade went from record surpluses during the first half of the 1980s to record deficits. The oil and gas share of Norwegian exports dropped from 38 percent to 29 percent.[37]

---

[35] After 1973, some of the Norwegian industries became less competitive because of oil-induced inflation and currency appreciation. Companies were near bankruptcy and industries were in decline in shipbuilding, fishing, farming, and textiles. Committed to full employment, the government heavily subsidized these industrial sectors: US$14 billion between 1973 and 1980 (Andersen 1993:144).

[36] Andersen 1993, 142–144.

[37] Ibid., 148–150.

Due to these economic hardships, the government recognized the need for multinationals to bear a larger share of the financial risk, contribute to lower production costs through technological innovation, and help secure market outlets. It was believed that foreign companies were pivotal in the negotiation of large-scale gas contracts with gas-importing countries given their close links to decision makers in those countries. The relationship between foreign companies and the government was no longer dominated by the latter. As Andersen and Arnestad put it, it turned into more of a "reluctant common-sense partnership."[38]

To further reduce the financial burden for companies, a new tax regime was put in place in 1986 by the Labor government. Under it, foreign companies no longer had to bear the government's and Statoil's shares of exploration costs. Moreover, the ban on year-round drilling in the Far North, originally imposed for environmental reasons, was lifted. These measures were aimed at encouraging exploration, especially in the risky northern area. Another tax reform in 1990–1991 was based not on changes in the oil sector but on improving the general investment climate. The ordinary tax rate was reduced from 50.8 percent to 28 percent, and the Special Tax rate increased from 30 percent to 50 percent.[39] Moreover, the royalties on oil and gas production (8 percent to 16 percent of gross production value) were phased out, starting in 1999.[40]

Beginning in 2000s, the government introduced further changes in licensing and taxation to encourage new and, in some cases, smaller foreign companies to enter the Norwegian continental shelf. For instance, to lessen the financial risk to a company that fails to find exploitable resources in the license area, it is now allowed to reclaim its exploration expenses up to the level of the petroleum tax (78 percent). This encourages new entry into the industry by removing the risk of facing all the exploration costs in the case of unsuccessful drilling activity. Other changes include further risk-reduction measures such as reimbursement of deficits at termination of activity for new companies that are unsuccessful.[41]

Overall Characteristics of the Investment Environment

In the 1970s and 1980s, Norway offered an investment environment very different from those offered by other major oil-producing countries.

---

[38] Andersen and Arnestad 1990, 56.
[39] Andersen 1993, 152–154.
[40] International Energy Agency (IEA) 2001.
[41] International Energy Agency (IEA) 2005.

Given its strong state tradition, the government was actively concerned with resource policy and determined to intervene directly in the industry.[42] As discussed above, this meant increasing state participation, regulation, and revenues from the oil sector as the state gained experience. It also meant modest rates of return for the oil companies, whose revenue shares and operational controls in licenses often changed – sometimes for the worse during these decades.

All this is certainly in line with the rise of the relative market and bargaining power of the Norwegian government, as predicted by the obsolescing bargaining theory. Yet contrary to the assumptions of the theory, investors in the Norwegian oil industry did not face any major political risks due to three important characteristics of the investment environment.

First, Norwegian demands on the companies were considered relatively modest and predictable, especially at a time when major oil-producing countries around the world were nationalizing their oil industries or imposing harsh terms on foreign investors. The Norwegian government almost always ensured that investors had enough after-tax profits to make it worthwhile for them to continue. Fluctuations in government demands were in line with the fluctuations in oil prices.[43] The government raised taxes only when the oil prices rose, and reduced taxes when the prices went down. Political considerations were adaptive to market changes, caught between high and low oil prices. Moreover, the government did not aggressively change its tax regime to accumulate huge rents. Instead it used it to maintain an equitable distribution of income in society. Further, the tax regime was not discriminatory against foreign companies. It was applied equally to domestic companies.

The government was also able to give significant incentives to lessen the tax burden of the companies. For instance, the companies were allowed to deduct most of their oil-related expenditures anywhere on the Norwegian continental shelf over a six-year period.[44] Thus, they could reduce or eliminate their tax bill on revenues generated from

---

[42] In the United States, companies had experienced tough antitrust regulation but no direct government intervention. In the Third World countries, governments were generally weak, and companies had privileged positions and were often exempted from national law.

[43] Author's interview with Oystein Noreng (professor and oil analyst in the Norwegian Business School), Oslo, January 22, 2001.

[44] This is a system where government takes most of the risk so the foreign investor can deduct all expenses for exploration. As Gunnar Gjerde, deputy director general of the

producing fields by investing in exploration or development work in other parts of the Norwegian North Sea.[45] Moreover, the rules governing the calculation of the Special Tax provided for a deduction called an "uplift." The uplift provision allowed companies to deduct 10 percent of the purchase value of all installations and equipment taken into use over the preceding fifteen years, thus permitting companies to deduct a total of 150 percent of their capital expenditures from their Special Tax bills over a fifteen-year period. This introduced a progressive element into the system by exempting companies with high capital investment, and low North Sea income from the Special Tax.[46] This flexibility in adjusting to the market and offering incentives ensured a decent return for investors. As two experts on the industry put it, "[T]here was enough fat to keep them happy."[47]

The second attractive feature of the investment environment has been the stability of the organizational framework of the oil industry despite major fluctuations in the international oil market during the 1970s and 1980s, and despite some subsequent changes in the economic terms of the investment relationship between the government and the companies. Bureaucratic competence in oil has been achieved as a result of the vertical differentiation and specialized organization of the oil administration, as well as the clear delineation of rights and responsibilities among bureaucratic agencies.[48] The Ministry of Petroleum and Energy has been exclusively devoted to policy functions but control functions belonged to the Petroleum Directorate, which was an independent body that was immune to political pressures. In addition, the Finance Ministry, the Central Tax Board, the Ministry of Environment, the Ministry of Social Affairs, and the Ministry of Communal Affairs constituted the secondary structure in the vertical administration of oil. Finally, the tertiary government structure consisted of permanent or ad hoc public bodies and committees with advisory or consultative functions, such as the Special Committees on Petroleum Taxation, and the Petroleum Council.[49] This basic institutional arrangement, established in the 1970s, has remained pretty much intact throughout Norway's oil development. No major changes were made in

Ministry of Petroleum and Energy, stated during an interview with the author in Oslo, January 24, 2001, "If there are no profits, there are no taxes for investors."
[45] Author's interview with Willy Olsen (Statoil), Oslo, January 20, 2001.
[46] Leif 1987.
[47] Andersen and Arnestad 1990, 71.
[48] Noreng 1980, Andersen 1993.
[49] Noreng 1980.

the principal rights and obligations of public authorities and companies even when the government changed hands.[50] The clarity, consistency, and stability of the administrative and regulatory environment quickly became an argument for oil companies to accept the investment terms, even when they became less favorable commercially. As one oil expert put it, "Every company knew that it was going to be heavily taxed. What companies really cared about was whether or not they could predict when they were going to be taxed and by how much."[51]

Finally, the transparency of the decision-making process made investing in Norway attractive. Foreign companies always faced a level playing field in the oil industry. The process of continuous consultation and debate on oil issues has provided a regular flow of information between bureaucrats and business groups, and has created coherence on policy issues. For instance, when civil servants led by Jens Evensen were formulating the concessionary regime in 1965, they worked very closely with foreigners to create a system that was attractive to them.[52] Even though oil policy became more contested in the 1970s and nationalist slogans abounded, the bureaucracy continued to hold periodic consultations with foreign companies.[53] It was able to continue with entrepreneurial policies despite instances of parliamentary opposition. The clear apportionment of responsibilities among state institutions; open channels of negotiation; regular consultations with the government and interest groups; and reliable conflict-resolution mechanisms have given oil companies the means to influence policy and thus ensure the security and profitability of their projects in the long run. In many cases, foreign companies pressed for favorable decisions in a manner indistinguishable from that of the domestic groups. In the decisions involving the profitability and sustainability of their projects, they always had a "seat at the table" to make their case.[54]

In order to understand the conditions under which such predictability, flexibility, and transparency in the investment environment were

---

[50] Berrefjord and Heum 1990, 32–34.

[51] Author's interview with Olsen.

[52] Author's interview with Helge Ryggvik (researcher at the University of Oslo), Oslo, January 22, 2001.

[53] These consultations became even more institutionalized in 1997 with the creation of INTSOK- Norwegian Oil and Gas Partners. The Norwegian Ministry of Petroleum and Energy helped create this entity comprising 160 companies to promote the internationalization of the Norwegian oil and oil-related industries (Norwegian Ministry of Petroleum and Energy and Petroleum Directorate 2007).

[54] Author's interview with Noreng.

created, we need to examine the interests and preferences of the winners and losers from foreign investment as well as the institutional structure within which these groups interacted and reached policy outcomes. A discussion of the Norwegian political regime and its ability to generate pro-investment policies follows.

Norwegian Political Regime

Constrained Executive

Norway has a stable democratic tradition going back to the early nineteenth century. It is a consolidated democracy with strong veto players and competitive political parties and interest groups. To start, the Norwegian parliament, the Storting, is a prominent veto player in Norwegian politics.[55] It is called a "working" parliament because it does not rubberstamp government proposals but gives the opposition a chance to criticize and present alternative proposals. Parliamentary committees and party groups actively participate in reworking government proposals to meet objections of the parliamentary majority. Between 1945 and 1970, the Labor Party's majority government ruled in the face of an opposition divided among four small parties. Since the 1970s successive minority and coalition governments have enabled Storting veto power to have greater control over oil policies. Although the government presents legislative proposals to the Storting and keeps it informed on oil-related issues, it is the Storting that makes the final decisions as to which areas are to be opened for drilling, and how the fields that are discovered should be developed. Production cannot start until the Storting has sanctioned the plans.

In addition to the Storting, the regional and local governments have also been able to constrain central government policies. Norway is a unitary state, but local governments – consisting of municipal and county levels – have a long and healthy tradition of participating in policy making.[56] Opposition to the center, or what some people call

[55] The Storting consists of two chambers; a division used only when the parliament debates new laws. This semi bicameralism does not have many implications other than making the minimal time to adopt a law three days.
[56] There are geographical and historical reasons for this de facto decentralization of power in Norway. Geographically, the small population of Norway is thinly scattered and urban concentration is a relatively late phenomenon for Norway. Historically, center-periphery relations have been crucial to the political landscape. Local autonomy within the unitary state was legally secured in 1837 and the later constitutional battles and the secessionist issue had a strong geographical aspect (Osterud and Selle 2006:25–27).

the Oslo elites, has been crucial in the shaping of government policies. Municipalities are led by elected councils and headed by boards composed in proportion to the local parties' electoral strength. County councils are popularly elected but do not enjoy the same grassroots support and interest as the municipal councils. The municipal level provides many of the most important welfare services and local governments have traditionally held the power to tailor welfare programs to local conditions.[57] Most income is collected locally, and the municipal authorities can take over state responsibilities unless the constitution defines them as belonging to the central government. Known as "local democracy" or "community democracy," this aspect of Norway's political structure contributes greatly to political competition. Moreover, the number of representatives in the Storting from peripheral districts is disproportionately great. Because constituency size is not adjusted, the "one person, one vote" principle is violated, which gives peripheral interests heightened weight in decision making.[58]

Finally, the Norwegian bureaucracy serves as an important veto player in the state. In many scholarly accounts, the Norwegian bureaucracy is given credit for being extremely professional and autonomous. As in the Weberian ideal bureaucracy, recruitment has been based solely on merit and civil servants have been the best-educated elite group in society.[59] Moreover, bureaucrats have been insulated from group pressures and, thus, from corruption. They have been able to pursue state goals independently and with utmost efficiency. The behavior of civil servants in Norway has been predictably cautious and incrementalist and based on expertise and strong organizational routines.[60]

This high degree of pluralism in the state has often produced significant constraints on the decision makers, especially in the area of oil policy. For instance, since the 1970s the fight for new jobs in the periphery strongly affected decisions on the location of new supply bases for the oil industry and on the oil depletion policy. The government has also on many occasions been pressured by the parliament to change its tax and regulatory policies regarding oil activities.

---

[57] Osterud and Selle 2006. According to these authors, more than 60 percent of all public expenditure is channeled through the municipalities, and 75 percent of municipal expenditure is spent on health, social services, and education.

[58] Author's interview with Trygve Gulbrandsen (researcher, Institute for Social Science), Oslo, January 22, 2001.

[59] For the characteristics of civil service in Norway, see Higley et al. (1975) and Olsen (1983).

[60] Karl 1997, 215–217.

Institutionalized, Open Competition

Horizontal accountability in the state, however, coexists with strong vertical accessibility and accountability. Conflict among veto players in the state is regulated and contained by the presence of strong societal institutions such as strong political parties and interest-group organizations. These institutions aggregate interests, build policy coalitions, and pressure the government to be accountable and responsive to different demands. Decision makers are able to defuse potentially divisive political issues by co-opting veto players into government policies by intense negotiation and compromise. The resulting balance of forces moderates political divisions and promotes consensus and stability.[61] As such, Norway's institutional setting reduces the potential for political risks that foreign companies might otherwise encounter in their investments.

Political parties are the traditional instruments of mobilization and participation in Norwegian politics. They offer the voters political alternatives at elections, recruit state political personnel, and control the commanding heights of executive power.[62] Individual politicians either rise through the parties or with the help of parties, and they depend almost entirely on the party system to further their political careers. Politics in Norway is by and large party politics.[63]

Even though most parties are political coalitions in the sense that they encompass more than one cleavage, the left-right cleavage has always been the most important in defining the Norwegian political battleground. In broad terms, the Labor and the Socialist Left parties have been on the left; the Center, the Christian, and Liberal Parties have been in the middle; and the Conservative and Progress parties have been on the right. From 1945 to 1968, Labor was the dominant party, defining the broad contours of state policies, including oil policy. Since 1968, however, there has been a two-bloc competition for power. Although party membership has been in decline in recent years, political legitimacy within most parties has rested with the party organizations. Especially since the 1970s, professionalism in party organizations has been on the rise. Public subsidies have provided parties with a financial basis to employ party members and party sympathizers with organizational and media qualifications.[64]

---

[61] Elder et al. 1988.
[62] Heidar 2001.
[63] Katzenstein (1985) argues that partisan politics in small countries like Norway play the crucial role of narrowing differences among interest groups.
[64] Heidar 2001.

Despite the importance of political parties, many believe that interest groups are more central to the Norwegian democracy. Political scientist Stein Rokkan (1966) argued that crucial economic decisions were seldom made by the parties or by parliament but occurred instead at the bargaining table, where public authorities met directly with trade union leaders, farmers, fishermen, and the Employers' Association. Considering the volume of interest-group activity, this assertion may not be far from the truth. During "the early 1990s, roughly 2,400 national organizations claimed 17 million members (in a country of 4 million inhabitants). More than half of the population is a member of at least one national organization, and about half of these organizations operate within the field of industry."[65] Moreover, these organizations operate at the regional and local levels. According to surveys in 1975, about half the voters had taken part at least once in a political action group. Later studies show that the proportion having signed at least one political action petition was 56 percent in 1981 and 61 percent in 1990.[66]

Political participation by interest groups in Norway has been in the form of societal corporatism (or corporate pluralism).[67] Under this configuration, interest organizations within a free, pluralist private sector bargain with public authorities and with one another in order to influence public policies. The public authorities, in turn, consider private organizations both useful and legitimate partners and feel accountable to them. To accommodate the interest groups, decision makers use institutional strategies such as co-optation into advisory committees or study commissions, or they consult extensively when preparing legislation (the "remiss" system).[68] In this corporatist structure, a centralized and concentrated core of interest groups and informal, voluntary bargaining partners forge consensus among interest groups, the state bureaucracy, and the political parties. Civil society organizations become an integral part of the state machinery and as a result the members of the organizations exercise a fair amount of indirect control over the central government decision-making process.[69]

In the case of oil policy, one of the reasons for this synergy – especially between the bureaucracy and business groups – has been the composition and mobility of the staff serving in various state bureaucracies

[65] Ibid., 76.
[66] Ibid., 76–78.
[67] For a distinction between societal and state corporatism, see Schmitter (1974).
[68] Lehmbruch 1982.
[69] Osterud and Selle 2006.

and companies. Studies show that almost 60 percent of the staff in the Ministry of Energy moved into jobs in the private sector, more than half of those into the oil industry in 1984. A similar situation prevailed in the Petroleum Directorate: more than 80 percent of those who left the directorate in the 1980s found employment with companies in the petroleum sector. This movement from the public sector to oil companies led to the transfer of bureaucratic values to the oil industrial complex and created a mutual understanding, a "cognitive coalition" that made for smooth functioning of the industry.[70] High bureaucratic capacity has been complemented by Norway's open and participatory democracy. As Karl (1997) puts it, the existence of non-oil-based vested interests that were able to present their concerns in a democratic context "prevented Weber's dictatorship of the bureaucrats."[71]

I turn now to a discussion of the political competition over three oil policy arenas: the role of the state oil company, the rate of oil production, and oil taxation. All three issues were important for foreign investors because they were issues that determined the extent of their operational involvement in oil projects and the profits they would accrue as a result. They are illustrative of the way conflicts among different veto players have been contained and resolved in Norway's mature democratic setting.

Politics of Oil Investment Policy

Historically, there has been a tradition of strong state involvement and regulation in the Norwegian economy. Industrialization came late to Norway, which was at the time one of the poorest countries in Western Europe with a weak capitalist class. Hence, an active government role was deemed necessary to speed industrialization. Moreover, except for four years between 1968 and 1972, Labor Party coalitions governed Norway from 1945 to 1981 and their ideological goals of full employment and economic growth without sharp price rises could be achieved only with heavy state involvement in the economy.[72]

Despite this state tradition, over time the role of the state in the oil industry became increasingly disputed. After 1973, the 50-percent share requirement for Statoil meant that Statoil was in a position to considerably shape the licenses on the Norwegian shelf.[73] Moreover, as discussed above,

---

[70] Berrefjord and Heum 1990.
[71] Karl 1997, 217.
[72] Klapp 1987.
[73] Berrefjord and Heum 1990.

other companies – especially the foreign companies – were obligated to finance Statoil's share of exploration and production. The increase in Statoil's power was attributed to the political ambitions of the Labor Party and Labor governments. Statoil had always been considered the "Labor Party's baby" in the sense that the government used it to assert national and public control of domestic oil production but also to serve its partisan interests in keeping Conservative Party oil interests at bay politically.[74]

As oil prices rose during the 1970s, the opposition parties became increasingly concerned that Statoil was becoming too powerful economically with its ability to control huge sums of cash. Especially, the conservatives were worried that instead of using Statoil in line with the national oil policy, politicians were becoming conduits of company interests.[75] As a result, a split arose between the Labor government and Statoil, on the one hand, and the Conservative Party and the Petroleum Directorate on the other, with the Ministry of Petroleum and Energy caught in the middle. "The major issue was control over foreign companies (a Labor Party priority) versus democratic accountability; that is, making sure that no one Norwegian actor got too big (a Conservative Party priority)."[76]

Domestic and foreign business groups were equally suspicious of Statoil's role in the industry. Foreign companies did not want to lose their relative shares to the state. They were also worried that Statoil could veto any major proposal in every license granted after 1973.[77] Similarly, various domestic business groups were unwilling to give up oil-related contracts and industrial opportunities so the public sector could make gains in oil. Concerned with the growing role of Statoil in the 1970s, many Norwegian industrialists, especially in the shipping industry, aggressively sought a larger share of oil profits.

As one of the biggest beneficiaries of foreign exchange in the country, the shipping companies were in an advantageous position. Shortages in the world tanker market brought major tanker profits in 1970 and 1971 and gave Norwegian ship owners enough financial clout to challenge government policies. Fifty shipping companies and forty companies in other industries combined their capital to form their own oil company, Saga Petroleum, in 1972.[78] Meanwhile, Norway's corporate giant, Norsk Hydro, also began to counter the preeminence of Statoil by organizing

[74] Klapp 1987.
[75] Berrefjord and Heum 1990.
[76] Andersen 1993, 148.
[77] Berrefjord and Heum 1990.
[78] Klapp 1987, 80–82.

an independent advisory body known as the "Oslo Group" to offer the government advice on petroleum policy.[79] Composed of business leaders and politicians from a variety of parties, including Labor, the Oslo Group aggressively criticized Statoil.[80]

In addition to Statoil's proposals to invest in shipping, its advantageous position of controlling at least 50 percent of all the fields, in comparison to Saga's 8 percent, caused these industrialists to join ranks with foreign companies and mobilize in the Storting against government policies. Using their influence with the Conservative and Liberal Parties, shipowners created a stalemate for Statoil. Because the Storting controlled the company's budget, the parliamentary coalition cut Statoil's 1976 request for capital to finance its Statfjord development by 14 percent.[81] The government was also forced to concede to private shipping interests control over domestic subcontracting operations, such as supply boats and drilling rigs related to oil production. Moreover, it had to promise Norwegian ship owners that state companies would no longer invest in shipping-related operations.[82]

The government again made a compromise in 1984 by creating the State's Direct Financial Interest (SDFI) so that the state could be directly involved financially in oil projects at the expense of Statoil. The financial base of Statoil was reduced and its share of licenses was weakened by changing the voting rules.[83] A clearer distinction was made between Statoil and the state. Statoil was not to collect royalties on behalf of the government. The government was to finance its own investment out of the state budget.[84] With the state directly financing oil activities, the government exempted the other two Norwegian-owned oil companies from the obligation to finance Statoil's exploration expenses. The obligation was abolished for the foreign investors as well in 1986.[85]

The conflict over the proper role of Statoil and over its impact on the activities of other business groups, including foreign entities, was resolved through compromises among the government, the major parties in the Storting, and the business groups. Organized interests in the Storting were able to act as veto players and pressure the government to reduce the power of Statoil. In exchange, the government created the

---

[79] Statoil's rapid growth brought it into conflict with Norsk Hydro as it tried to expand into some of the latter's traditional domains.
[80] Nelsen 1991.
[81] Huger 1976.
[82] Klapp 1987.
[83] Berrefjord and Heum 1990.
[84] Andersen 1993.
[85] Berrefjord and Heum 1990.

SDFI, which ensured that the state would still be the major investor in oil production. Overall, strong interest representation and clear mechanisms of accountability in Norway produced these compromises among veto groups and ultimately helped protect the interests of foreign companies against the state.

The democratic regime also created an institutional setting for foreign companies to represent their interests and challenge the state by forming alliances with domestic companies and interest groups. For instance, industrialists such as ship owners, who depended on open access to foreign markets, supported foreign companies in their efforts to challenge the government's offshore-goods-and-services policy of Norwegianization. Fearing foreign retaliation against them, the Norwegian Ship Owners Association charged that the policy fostered inefficiency in Norwegian industry and raised costs on the continental shelf far above those in other areas of the world. The association staunchly defended the rights of foreign companies against the Norwegian Engineering Industries and the Norwegian Iron and Metalworkers Union, which rejected free trade in offshore supplies.[86]

Another major political debate concerning the oil investors was the depletion policy, which determined the rate of oil extraction. The policy was crucial in shaping the bargaining position of the government in relation to the foreign companies.[87] The Labor Party returned to power in 1973, and in 1974 it presented two White Papers to the parliament regarding a new concession policy and the need to control production volumes.[88] The parliamentary report titled "Petroleum Industry in Norwegian Society" recommended a moderate rate of oil depletion which was regarded as an annual level of production of approximately 90 million tons of oil equivalents. In the parliamentary debate of 1974 concerns were expressed about inflationary pressures and structural changes from too much oil revenue. The implication was that controlling production volume was essential for avoiding the "Dutch Disease" in Norway.[89] Moreover, there were worries that necessary adjustments in sectoral and regional distribution of employment would threaten the Norwegian way of life.[90] Even though the parliamentary report assigned a role to foreign

---

[86] Nelsen 1991, 100–103.
[87] The logic is that a government opting for a high rate of production can be more exposed to the demands and needs of foreign companies controlling the technology than a government opting for a low rate of production.
[88] Andersen 1993.
[89] Ibid.
[90] Dam 1976.

oil companies, it recommended an increasing and progressive system of state participation in oil production.

The depletion policy met opposition from several quarters. Interests that might have profited from a higher rate of production and a greater role for private enterprises felt cheated. These included private banks, private oil companies – both domestic and foreign – and, again, the private ship owners who had invested heavily in drilling rigs. The Norwegian Ship Owners Association accused the government of politicizing the oil issue by using the oil revenues for its socialist agenda and undermining confidence in private industry.[91]

The government was also subjected to counter pressure from a wide range of interests fearing a rapid pace of oil development. These interests included fishing, agriculture, small enterprises, labor-intensive industries, and many wage earners who saw inflation, high costs, and a more unequal distribution of income with a rapid depletion.[92] Many of these interest groups argued that the announced level of production was too high. The Socialist Electoral Alliance, for instance, asserted that a lower rate would be more environmentally responsible, cause fewer disruptions in Norwegian society, and preserve Norway's sovereignty over its resources by not tying the country too closely to the West.[93]

Another interest group that felt it would be adversely affected by high oil production was the fishing industry. By 1970, 40 percent of the Norwegian fish harvest was coming from the North Sea. Meanwhile, about half of the Norwegian shelf south of the sixty-second parallel was in various stages of oil and gas exploration, causing many operational problems for the fishing industry. Nets were being damaged and navigation was being significantly impeded by oil activities.[94] By 1975 and 1976, southern fishermen responded by organizing politically. To allay the opposition of these domestic groups to oil development projects by foreign and domestic companies, the government began granting compensation for gear damage through the Directories of Fisheries. The total amount granted by August 1977 was US$1.67 million.[95] The institutional strength of these interest groups made the government responsive

[91] Noreng 1980.
[92] Ibid.
[93] Nelsen 1991.
[94] Klapp 1987. According to Noreng (1980), experiments indicate that oil has a fairly lethal effect upon plankton, fish eggs, larvae, and shellfish. Because oil is lighter than water, it spreads over a large area rather quickly and can be taken by currents toward the large fishing areas off northern Norway.
[95] Klapp 1987, 80–85.

to their interests. To enlist the support of both sides in the depletion policy, the government co-opted them through various compromises.

The debate over depletion policy did not end there. In 1971, the government had established the north of the sixty-second parallel as the northernmost limit for oil licensing because Norway, the United Kingdom, and USSR at the time were disagreeing on how to divide rights north of that line. In the mid 1970s, however, domestic and foreign oil companies, backed by the Conservative Party, a coalition of construction and ship-building industries, and southern labor union groups pressed for northern licensing. Soon, the coastal counties of Nordland, Troms, and Finnmark joined them. These regions stood to gain from oil-production activity off their shores and argued that more drilling would increase the rate of oil production, spur economic growth, and provide much-needed jobs.

This time, the northern fishermen reacted by organizing politically. They opposed oil production above the sixty-second parallel, and pressured the Ministry of Fisheries to protect their interests. Soon they were joined by environmentalists and liberals who lobbied in the parliament to prevent future northern oil operations. The movement, which came to be known as the "Green Opposition," called attention to oil spills, damage to the fishing industry, and negative changes in the economy and lifestyles of the region.[96]

Once again, a compromise was reached due to the institutional veto power of the regions and the strength of organized interests. The "northern fishing industry had pivotal political clout because fishing communities in the North controlled two seats critical to the Labor Party's parliamentary majority. These fishing interests threatened to shift the Socialist votes of northern fishermen if the Labor government, which was supported by the Socialists in the Parliament, allowed drilling north of the sixty-second parallel."[97] The debate in the Storting in the early summer of 1974 showed that the government was ready to strike a balance between opposing groups. It required the oil companies to develop oil-related support and service industries onshore. Moreover, it demanded that oil companies finance the cleanup of the seabed. In fact, Norway became the first North Sea country to introduce requirements for oil companies to avoid pollution and damage to marine life. In turn, the labor organizations of two northern fishing counties, Troms and Finnmark, decided to support northern drilling but at a much slower rate.[98]

[96] Ibid.
[97] Ibid.
[98] Ibid.

One complicating factor for further oil development in the North was the blowout that occurred on the Bravo platform of the Ekofisk field in 1977. Despite its rather small proportions, the blowout had a direct effect on the depletion policy.[99] Due to criticism from environmentalists, the government added to the safety regulations it imposed on the oil companies and postponed the opening of new areas for exploratory drilling in the northern waters until the 1980s. The blowout, slower licensing, and hence delays in the development of new areas combined to reduce the level of oil activity in the Norwegian sector of the North Sea. The government ensured oil production in the South by compensating fishermen and in the North, fishing and environmentalist interests triumphed. Eventually by early 1981, some drilling was under way in northern waters.

Taxation policy was another area where the democratic regime ensured compromises that eventually benefited foreign investors. Even so, conflicts of interest arose among bureaucratic organizations and between the government and foreign companies. The Ministry of Finance, the protector of government revenues, almost always pushed for higher taxes imposed on profitable fields to enable it to pay for the state's welfare services. The Ministry of Energy, ship owners and domestic oil companies, on the other hand, regularly pressured the authorities to use tax concessions to maintain activity on the continental shelf. The Industry Association for Oil Companies (NIFO) and the Ship Owners Association lobbied the government on behalf of foreign oil companies.

Foreign companies were also able to participate directly in oil tax policy. For example, during tax policy discussions in November 1974, a specially appointed Petroleum Revenues Committee presented a plan to the companies that served as the basis for discussions between the oil industry and the Ministry of Finance. The committee's central proposal was a tax of 40 percent to be levied on top of the corporate income tax of 50.8 percent. The companies, as well as the domestic groups mentioned above, strongly objected to the proposal. As a result, the government rewrote the plan after extensive consultations with the companies.[100] It finally established a new excess profits tax – the special tax – at 25 percent in 1975.[101]

To sum up, after the discovery of the Ekofisk field in 1969, Norway's oil policy became very politicized. Political parties, many interest groups,

[99] The blowout lasted eight days and poured 22,500 tons of oil into the ocean. A more serious accident (which received much less attention) was the 1980 Alexender L. Kielland disaster in which a total of 123 lives were lost (Ryggvik 2000).

[100] Nelsen 1991.

[101] Noreng 1980.

local authorities, and government agencies became involved in one way or another in the formulation and implementation of policies that affected the attractiveness of the investment environment for foreign companies. Despite the high degree of political competition among many interest groups, the policy environment stayed stable and posed very little political risk for foreign investors, thanks to the checks and balances available in the political system.

The institutionalized competition among various interest groups provided incentives for political elites to build policy coalitions and reach consensus through compromises. The outcome was a balanced attitude toward foreign investment that did not infringe on the rights of the investors to make a profit. Parliamentary Report number 25 in 1972 ensured the rights of democratically elected institutions to exercise full control over all aspects of oil policy. All the major policy changes were prepared in consultation with every relevant state institution and interest group that had a stake in oil policy. The system of periodic parliamentary reports on the oil industry kept the general public well informed of the various issues.[102]

The stability, predictability, and transparency of the system also provided foreign companies with access to decision making. By allying themselves with certain interest groups and political parties in the Norwegian society, foreign companies ensured that their interests were adequately represented in policy decisions. They were directly consulted by the government on a regular basis, and their consent was required to make any major change to the oil policy. The checks and balances among the institutions of the state and the resulting rule of law ensured that the rights of foreign companies would not be compromised even when their economic interests were.

Implication of Oil FDI on Development

FDI made it possible for Norway to realize its oil potential. The oil industry is Norway's largest industry today. Norway ranks as the world's fifth-largest oil exporter and the tenth-largest oil producer. In 2006, the industry accounted for 25 percent of GDP; 36 percent of state revenues; and 51 percent of total exports. After more than three decades of oil production, the sector has generated great revenues to the state as a result of direct and indirect taxes, and direct ownership.[103] It is estimated by some

[102] Lind and Mackay 1979.
[103] Norwegian Ministry of Petroleum and Energy and Petroleum Directorate 2007.

that the Norwegian state has managed to absorb about 80 percent of the resource rent since 1980.[104]

Abundance of oil and the rents that have been generated by the oil industry could have created huge risks for the economic and political development of Norway, as have been the case in many oil-rich states including Azerbaijan and to some extent Russia. Defying the conventional wisdom, however, Norway turned out to be a success story in the way it managed and used its resources. Not only did it avoid the infamous resource curse, Dutch disease, rentierism, and corruption, but it in fact managed to turn oil into a blessing for its people. Oil contributed to economic growth, helped diversify the economy through spillover effects, increased the capacity of the state to provide more services to its citizens, gave legitimacy to the regime, and made Norway an influential player in the international scene. While there are many reasons for this success, the quality of democracy in Norway played a crucial role in overcoming particularistic pressures and distributional conflicts and in creating a transparent, professional, equitable and fair system of resource management.

The Norwegian Exceptionalism

Since the discovery of oil fields in 1969, Norway has experienced significant economic growth. Larsen (2005) shows how relative to its highly similar Scandinavian neighbors, Norway's GDP per capita accelerated after it started selling oil. By many accounts, Norway also avoided the Dutch disease by ensuring the long-term competitiveness of the non-oil tradeable sectors. Maintaining a diverse economy quickly became a clear and consistent goal of the Norwegian government. Even though the ratio of manufacturing exports to GDP has been stagnant since the mid 1970s[105] and there has been some contraction of manufacturing activity in recent years, the non-oil industry continues to command a significant size of the workforce and the value created in the economy.

The Norwegian state has also managed to escape the rent-seeking behavior and myopic policy making that have afflicted many other oil-rich states. In order to reign in the urge to spend the huge oil rents and shield the economy from overheating and waste, the Norwegian government established a Petroleum Fund in 1990 and invested most of the

[104] Gylfason 2004.
[105] According to Gylfason (2004), the share of manufacturing in total exports fell from 60 percent in 1974 to 22 percent in 2002.

oil revenue in foreign securities.[106] The government institutionalized the spending rule whereby public spending was limited to financial returns on the fund's positions. To further distance the fund from political interference, the government also transferred the management of the fund from the Ministry of Finance to the independent Central Bank of Norway in 1999. In a sign of far-sightedness, Norwegian government has been saving a significant portion of the revenues in the fund as a safeguard for future generations.

Norway has also been exceptional in the way it used its natural wealth for the betterment of its people. Abundance of oil has not made the Norwegian government more reluctant or slow to reform. In fact, the influx of oil rents permitted Norway to expand an already extensive system of social services, including education, medical care, and child and elder care. For example, the total public social expenditure as a percentage of GDP increased from 16.9 percent in 1980 to 22.6 percent in 1990 and 25.1 percent in 2003, ranking well above the OECD average.[107] More specifically, the public expenditure on education as a percentage of GDP was also the highest among OECD countries in 1995 with 6.8 percent, and second-highest in 2003 with 6.5 percent. In terms of public per capita expenditure on health, Norway was the sixth-highest among OECD countries with US$1,153 in 1990, second-highest in 2000 and 2004, with US$2,541 and US$3,311, respectively.[108] The United Nations – based on its human development index – has been considering Norway as one of the best places to live in the world. For instance, it was ranked number one in 2000.[109]

Moreover, the government was able to use these resources for the benefit of the current and future generations without unreasonably expanding the size of the central government during the oil booms. Gylfason (2004) reports that even though the local governments have expanded in terms of expenditure and manpower in recent years, Norway continues to have a smaller central government than its Scandinavian neighbors, which do not have oil.

Furthermore, contrary to the experiences of many oil-rich countries, Norway did not have to sacrifice its democracy as it discovered and

[106] The need for a Fund became obvious only in the early 1990s because the earlier revenues were spent on debt repayment. According to Larsen (2005), as Norway shifted from net debtor to a net creditor, the spending effect came into focus.

[107] OECD 2007a.

[108] Ibid.

[109] United Nations 2002. The index combines indicators of gross domestic product per capita, life expectancy, and education into a single index.

developed its resources. FDI played two critical roles in this juncture between oil and democracy. First of all, the success of attracting FDI has had a direct effect of legitimizing, reinforcing and thus perpetuating the democratic regime that was already in place. The fact that foreign companies came to Norway and never left during its nearly four decades of oil development has given a substantial boost to the regime and in people's trust in the regime. But perhaps more so indirectly, FDI has strengthened the democratic regime in Norway as it helped build the national oil industry, which in a short span of time contributed significantly to economic growth and to the financing of the Norwegian welfare state.

The aggregate revenues have contributed to the stability, political peace, and democracy in Norwegian society in significant ways. For one, they allowed governing elites to "co-opt" domestic groups that opposed the pace and form of oil development. As discussed earlier, there have been major disagreements over oil policy. However, the availability of resources reduced the intensity of conflict and provided the government with enough resources to make compromises to reach policy outcomes that were acceptable to all. For instance, during the international recession of 1974–1977, the government raised real incomes by 25 percent even though it meant compromising to some extent the competitiveness of non-oil sectors. The government also used oil revenues to subsidize declining public industries and Statoil bought off opposition from within private Norwegian shipping by informally promising ship owners dominant shares of oil-related drilling and shipping operations.[110] In this respect, foreign capital indirectly greased an already smoothly functioning political system. Foreign investment and the ensuing oil revenues have also increased the legitimacy of and the satisfaction with the democratic regime in Norway by making possible the strengthening of welfare programs. The transparent, honest and equitable distribution of rents helped to shore up confidence and trust in the political system.

Finally, foreign investment and the ensuing oil revenues have allowed Norway to become a significant player in the international arena. In 2006, Norway ranked fourth among the world's twenty-one richest countries for its efforts in seven policy areas that are important to developing countries: aid, trade, investment, migration, environment, security, and technology.[111] More specifically, Norway is now one of the few countries that donate millions more in foreign aid than the United Nations' target

[110] Klapp 1987, 138–140.
[111] Center for Global Development 2006.

of 0.7 percent of a nation's GDP.[112] Nearly 1 percent of its GDP is spent each year on foreign economic assistance. According to the commitment to development index report, of the world's twenty-one richest countries, Norway ranks first in net aid volume as a share of the economy.[113] One-third of Norwegian aid is routed via the United Nations, which Norway considers an essential partner in the struggle for peace, human rights, and democracy. Poverty alleviation and equal rights for men and women are other key targets for aid and are directed mainly to the poorest nations. Sub-Saharan Africa, for instance, receives 48 percent of total Norwegian bilateral official development assistance.[114] Norway was also one of the first non-G7 creditor nations to offer total debt forgiveness to the least-developed countries.[115]

To a significant extent thanks to oil, a small country like Norway was able to project its economic power onto the international diplomatic and peacekeeping scene, proving that Norwegians are more humanitarians than they are oil barons. Norway has been active as a peace mediator not only in the Middle East (most prominent example, the Oslo peace talks between Israel and Palestine) but also in Sri Lanka, Colombia, the Sudan, and North Korea. It has played a central role in pushing a United Nations treaty banning land mines.[116] In terms of financial and personnel contributions to internationally sanctioned peacekeeping and humanitarian interventions over the past ten years by share of GDP, Norway ranked first. Moreover, Norway ranked seventh among rich countries for bearing a large share of the burden of refugees during humanitarian crises.[117]

In addition to development aid and diplomatic engagement, Norway also takes the lead in spreading good governance and ethical management strategies around the world. For instance, its Oil Fund (now called the Pension Fund), which is considered the world's largest retirement fund today, uses strict ethical guidelines in its investment decisions. To date, it has screened out many companies, including those involved in the production and distribution of weapons; those that cause severe environmental damage; and those that have serious human rights violations.[118]

---

[112] Williams 2001.
[113] Center for Global Development 2006.
[114] OECD 2004.
[115] Ibid.
[116] Landler 2007.
[117] Center for Global Development 2006.
[118] For instance, Wal-Mart was excluded because of its violation of labor rights, as was Boeing for its connection to weapons (Landler 2007).

Finally, drawing on its experience, Norway provides assistance to the oil sectors of developing countries. For instance, in 2005 it launched the Norwegian Oil for Development initiative to support countries in their efforts to overcome the "resource curse." As of 2006, Norway cooperates with more than twenty countries, covering capacity building in areas such as legal frameworks, administration, and supervision mechanisms, licensing and tendering processes, organization of public-private interfaces, local content and industrial development, environmental challenges and revenue-management issues, including taxation and petroleum funds.[119] It displays leadership in encouraging developing countries to join the Extractive Industries Transparency Initiative (EITI) in order to prevent corruption in the management of oil revenues. It is one of the four contributors to the World Bank Special Trust Fund to assist in its implementation.[120]

Overall, Norway's highly idealistic international engagement and altruistic foreign and domestic programs were all partly made possible by the injection of foreign investment into the oil industry, which over time increased oil production and generated a significant amount of windfall. Its highly democratic regime has not only ensured the flow of investment but also guaranteed a sound resource management mechanism that in turn helped immunize the Norwegian society from the oil curse, perpetuate the already-existing democratic regime and elevate Norway to a global-player status.

All this is not to suggest that oil wealth has never threatened the Norwegian society. In fact, Norway experienced some economic dislocations and a milder version of the resource curse in the late 1970s. As discussed earlier, oil production initially crowded out some of the non-oil sectors, endangering to some extent the competitiveness of the manufacturing industry. Moreover, the government redistributed national income in the direction of wages and salaries and away from profits. The overwhelming temptation to use easy money for short-term purposes was apparent between the years 1974 and 1977. By the end of 1977, Norway had accumulated a foreign debt corresponding to about 50 percent of GNP. In the first half of the 1980s expansionary fiscal and monetary policies resulted in an overheated economy with surging inflation and further loss of competitiveness in the non-oil tradeable sectors. The currency was devalued and the government called for an economic emergency, freezing incomes and prices.[121]

---

[119] Norwegian Agency for Development Cooperation 2006.
[120] Center for Global Development 2006.
[121] Noreng 1986.

The debt crisis, however, forced the political system to change course. It was a warning call and the system recovered quickly, creating one of the most successful models of resource management in the world. This was achieved through a complex set of preventive economic policies that was possible because the resources were publicly owned and democratically managed.[122] High levels of institutional constraints and competition that allowed the Norwegian government to attract foreign investment also helped it with balancing the competing claims for oil revenues with the long-term objectives and stabilization goals of the state. The government put together a commission with representatives of all political parties, labor, business groups, economic experts and public officials to formulate new policies. In addition, transparent and accountable state institutions, a functioning legal and judiciary system, strong media scrutiny have all helped to prevent the corruption and rent-seeking behavior that cripple so many oil-rich countries in their management of their resources. Despite periods of excessive spending and growth in aggregate demand like other oil exporters, imbalances have been brief and excesses relatively modest. More importantly, the Norwegian democratic system made it possible to learn from mistakes in a timely manner and reach consensus to prevent the recurrence of bad management.[123]

The professional management and oversight of the Oil Fund in Norway provides a good example of how a mature democracy manages the oil windfall successfully. A separation of powers in overseeing the Fund allows various institutions of government to keep one another in check. The day-to-day management of the fund is delegated to the Central Bank, which is independent in its investment decisions but operates within the guidelines and risks set by the Ministry of Finance. The Central Bank regularly submits reports to the ministry, which then makes them available to the public. The parliament, on the other hand, has the discretion to decide how much it will deposit or withdraw from the fund and the government regularly consults with the parliament and keeps it informed of developments concerning the fund.[124]

Today, many analysts are warning once again against the potential for increased spending that comes with easy money. Norwegians' rising expectations of benefits from oil fortune are creating some pressures on the government to spend the oil wealth instead of save it for the

---

[122] For further details on Norwegian policies to overcome the resource curse, see Larsen (2005).

[123] Eifert et al. 2002.

[124] For more information on the management of the fund, see Bagirov et al. (2003).

future.[125] There is a perception that there are no limits to the Norwegian wealth and that the government should increase public spending to tackle many challenges facing the Norwegian society. While Norway's record of managing its oil wealth has generally been highly successful, this recent turn has created some concern for the long-term sustainability of Norway's fiscal policies.[126] Only time will tell whether or not the Norwegian democracy will be able to withstand this rising discomfort and dissatisfaction among its citizens and continue to avoid a full-blown resource curse.

Conclusion

Despite its potential resources, Norway in the 1970s and 1980s was not an easy place in which to do business. Compared to most of the oil producers at the time, Norway offered a very different political context with an experienced civil service, long traditions of democratic government and active state involvement in the economy. The 1970s were also a time when relations between investors and host governments changed worldwide, posing many challenges to the former. In line with the rise of their relative market and bargaining power, Norwegian governments increased taxation and imposed state participation as well as tougher regulations on foreign investors. As the industry became more politicized, the terms of the investment relationship became more demanding. These policy changes affected the economic attractiveness of the Norwegian investment environment but not the level of political risks facing the investors. Despite the predictions of the obsolescing bargaining theory, investors found the investment environment acceptable in Norway and stayed.

In this chapter, I argued that continued FDI was due to the stability, predictability, and transparency that the Norwegian democratic regime offered to investors.[127] I demonstrated how strong state veto players and institutionalized competitive interests gave governing elites the incentives and the structure to mediate among different stakeholders and reach compromises as a result. High levels of accountability ensured responsiveness to different interests and prevented any arbitrariness in or overuse of

---

[125] Listhaug 2004, Larsen 2005.

[126] Eifert et al. 2002.

[127] Noreng (1980.24) argues that the mature democratic context in Norway could be only seen as a disadvantage to the oil industry in a narrow sense. In the long run, this context proved to be an advantage by offering security and continuity.

executive power. Foreign investors could make use of this institutional environment by either allying themselves with certain domestic groups or behaving like one and pressuring the government directly. All throughout their presence in Norway, the investors were included in the political debate, had institutional means to influence policies, and were supported in their interests by various domestic groups. They were regarded as partners and given enough incentives to stay. The political regime successfully balanced the need to serve the welfare of the society with the need for foreign capital to develop the Norwegian oil resources. The consolidated democracy of Norway proved to be compatible with the expectations of the global economy.

The success of the Norwegian state can be attributed to its ability to attract foreign investors and pursue oil projects as partners. It can also be attributed to the ability of the state to resist the overwhelming impact of the oil bonanza that had become a curse for many other oil-producing countries. The Norwegian state, unlike states in most other oil-rich countries, was able to resist the temptation to spend oil revenues on corruption and white-elephant projects. The state warded off the insidious rentier behavior that has accompanied booms elsewhere. Moreover, unlike other states, it managed to sustain its domestic tax base and protect its non-oil fiscal capacity. Norway put much of its oil revenues into a petroleum fund to store wealth for the time when oil starts to run out. Highly institutionalized networks of organized interests and significant opportunities for public debate prevented the symptoms of "Dutch Disease" from turning into an oil curse. As Johan P. Olsen (1983) rightly argued, Norway's institutions managed to turn petroleum into "just another raw material."[128]

---

[128] Quotation in Karl 1997, 221.

8

Beyond Three Cases and Oil

A comparative analysis of the experiences of three oil-rich states with foreign companies helps us observe the causal dynamics of the relationship between political institutions and Foreign Direct Investment (FDI) and generate testable hypotheses. It is important, however, to test whether or not these hypotheses apply to other oil-rich countries and for foreign investment into sectors other than oil. To that end, in this chapter I first provide a brief analysis of another major oil producer, Kazakhstan.

Similar to Azerbaijan and Russia, in the beginning of the 1990s Kazakhstan also had considerable hydrocarbon reserves that received significant attention from foreign investors. After Russia, Kazakhstan has the largest proven oil and gas reserves in the post-Soviet region. According to some estimates, its proven oil and gas reserves are currently 39.8 billion barrels of oil and 105.9 trillion cubic feet of natural gas – roughly constituting 3.3 percent and 1.7 percent of the world's total proven reserves (comparable to Nigeria and Libya).[1] Kazakhstan has a significantly higher share of estimated global reserves than of its current production, which suggests that its importance in global oil supply is likely to increase in the near future.[2] Given its rising significance, it is worth noting the similarities and differences between this case and the others discussed in this book regarding their performance in attracting FDI.

Next, I conduct a series of statistical tests on 132 countries over three decades to test whether or not there is any relationship between political institutions and the ability to attract FDI. Both the analysis of

---

[1] BP Statistical Review 2007.
[2] Ahrend and Tompson 2007, 164.

Kazakhstan's investment regime and the findings of the large-n study confirm the nonlinear relationship between democratization and FDI procurement. The brief discussion on Kazakhstan demonstrates that Kazakhstan's political structure in many ways were similar to that of Russia's in the beginning of 1990s. The existence of some veto players in the immediate aftermath of independence made it extremely difficult for the government to create a stable and attractive environment for investors. Realizing the problems with that institutional setting, President Nazarbayev soon curtailed any political competition that existed, stripping veto players of their powers. As he consolidated his control over the country and the oil industry, he brought the regime closer to the authoritarian model of Azerbaijan. Reflecting that change in the political structure, the Kazakh government was able to create a much more stable and attractive investment regime and soon became one of the largest recipients of FDI in the region. Furthermore, the statistical tests find a significant relationship between the two institutional variables – the level of executive constraints and political competition – and FDI levels. The findings lead to the conclusion that both authoritarian regimes and consolidated democracies are successful at attracting FDI and that more democratization is not always a guarantee of more FDI.

The Case of Kazakhstan: How it fits in with the theory

Kazakhstan's Oil Investment Policy

Even though Kazakhstan's hydrocarbon resources were well known, they remained largely underdeveloped during the Soviet times when compared to other regions of the Union.[3] This was mostly due to the fact that the oil and gas deposits in this region required much more technically challenging offshore drilling. The significant drop in oil prices in the second half of the 1980s shifted the attention of Soviet leaders from exploring and developing new fields to increasing production from the existing Siberian fields. Nevertheless, in the beginning of 1990s, Kazakh oil production from the onshore areas on the Mangyshlak and Buzachi peninsulas constituted about 5–6 percent of the former Soviet total.[4]

---

[3] For instance, the most important discoveries took place in 1979 with two gigantic oil and gas fields: Tengiz and Karachaganak. Another important breakthrough came in 1981 with the discovery of Kumkol oil field.

[4] Sagers 1994, 271.

Foreign Investment and Political Regimes

Given the underdeveloped state of the deposits, the technical challenges posed by offshore drilling and the desire to reduce their country's dependence on Russia, the Kazakh leaders began courting foreign investors immediately after independence.[5] The Oil Ministry of the Soviet Union and Chevron Corporation had already signed an agreement in 1988 to develop the Tengiz oil field in the northwestern part of the country. After gaining independence, the Kazakh leadership cancelled all previous agreements and negotiated and signed new ones. The first one was signed in 1992 with Chevron to form the TengizChevrOil joint venture. Another major contract was signed with British Gas and Agip to develop the Karachagank gas fields. The success of these agreements opened the door for more foreign investment into the Kazakh energy sector. By 1998, Kazakhstan received the largest FDI in per capita income in the CIS region.[6] During 2001–2005, net FDI inflows averaged around 10 percent of the gross domestic product, as compared with levels of 1.5 to 2.5 percent in Russia.[7]

By the end of the 1990s, just like Azerbaijan, Kazakhstan had become an attractive and stable destination for foreign investors. Like Azerbaijan (and unlike Russia), Kazakhstan chose to rely heavily on tax and regulatory packages tailored to meet the needs of investors in large projects, whether in the context of PSAs, joint ventures, or concessions.[8] Today, about 60–70 percent of Kazakh production is governed under royalty/tax contracts, including Tengiz and most of the older, smaller, onshore fields. Karachaganak, Kashagan, and offshore contracts in the Caspian, on the other hand, are written under a production sharing contract framework.[9] Unlike Azerbaijan's case by case approach, however, Kazakhstan designed a body of law applicable to all projects. Similar to Azerbaijan, the key factor in the attractiveness of the Kazakh investment regime was the readiness of the leadership to protect the sanctity and stability of the contracts. The tax and regulatory stability was ensured for the life of the contracts.

Another difference between Azerbaijan and Kazakhstan has been in the organization of the oil industry. Unlike Azerbaijan, Kazakhstan privatized most of its existing oil and gas enterprises – mainly to foreigners and to locals that had close connections to the government. Prime Minister Akezhan Kazhegeldin was tasked to carry out the privatization campaign in a very short amount of time between 1996 and 1997. In an attempt

[5] Luong and Weinthal 2001, Ahrend and Tompson 2007.
[6] Luong and Weinthal 2001.
[7] Ahrend and Tompson 2007, 171.
[8] Ibid.
[9] Kaiser and Pulsipher 2007, 1306.

to generate revenues as quickly as possible, the Kazakh government also prioritized the sale of its most promising and lucrative oil and gas fields.[10] Meanwhile, by 1997, the Kazakh authorities created the national oil and gas company, Kazakhoil, to manage the state's remaining control over energy enterprises and its interest in PSAs, which had until then been carried out by the Ministry of Energy and Mineral Resources.[11] Kazakhoil was also seen as an important instrument to ease cooperation with the foreign oil companies. State assets were further consolidated in 2002 by the merging of Kazakhoil and the state oil and gas transportation company, Transneftegaz. The creation of this new state company, Kazmunaigaz, produced a more united and coherent state policy and a one-stop shopping for foreign investors.

Politics and Oil FDI in Kazakhstan

The relationship between politics and FDI in Kazakhstan has been a lot more complicated than it has been in Azerbaijan. In fact, up until the mid 1990s, the political environment has not been very conducive foreign investment. It would be plausible to argue that the Kazakh political structure in the beginning of the 1990s resembled the one in Russia more than the one in Azerbaijan. Just like Yeltsin in Russia, Nazarbayev in the beginning tried to establish a quasi-pluralistic political system in Kazakhstan.[12] This was partly because the demographic parity between the Kazakhs and the Russians in Kazakhstan had the potential of politicizing many issues along ethnic and geographic lines.[13] In order to hold this new country together, Nazarbayev realized that he had to concede to different interests. Within the oil industry, he used a corporatist approach to accommodate the different interests of the Kazakh indigenous oil men. This structure of the oil industry allowed Nazarbayev to appease oilmen in the peripheries,

---

[10] Luong and Weinthal 2001.
[11] Ahrend and Tompson 2007.
[12] Olcott 2002, Cummings 2005.
[13] Ethnic Kazakhs were primarily located in the southern and western rural parts of the country. Russians, on the other hand, were located in major cities and in the north along the Russian border. These ethnic divisions were well represented by social movements and political parties throughout the country and exerted significant pressure on the Kazakh government. "Some Russian nationalist parties and movements, for example, called for the annexation of Kazakhstan's northern and eastern oblasts to Russia, or demanded outright secession from Kazakhstan. Meanwhile Kazakh nationalist parties and movements called for greater linguistic and institutional privileges for Kazakhs, such as elevating the status of the Kazakh language over Russian and filling governmental posts with Kazakhs" (Luong and Weinthal 2001: 19).

which were at times unhappy with his politics. The problem, however, was that this political landscape in the immediate aftermath of the independence produced too many veto players and temporarily hampered the development of an investment environment that would be attractive and stable for foreign investors. For one, the local administrations – especially in oil-rich areas – wrestled too much power from the central government and began signing licenses and contracts for oil and gas development without coordinating with the responsible federal bureaucracies. In other cases, regional leaders and oil men challenged the contracts negotiated by central authorities only to set up their own companies and sign similar contracts for the same area. "This situation spun out of control to such extent that by 1995, no one knew how many signed contracts existed in the country, much less what their terms might be."[14]

The Kazakh parliament was another veto player that constrained the investment policies of Nazarbayev in the early years of independence. The parliament consisted mostly of communist legislators who challenged the government's plans to privatize the oil industry and open it up for foreign investment. Parliamentarians questioned the speed, direction and objectives of the privatization and hampered the development of a legal framework that would specify the rules for privatization in the oil sector as well as the engagement of foreign capital in it. Within two years after drafting the basic petroleum legislation in 1992, the law was revisited a staggering 18 times, and created significant confusion. "By late 1993, about fifty laws had been passed governing foreign investments, which were seen as moves in the right direction, but still insufficient."[15]

In addition to the parliament, the divisions within the bureaucracy also constrained the government's ability to create an attractive investment environment in the early years of 1990. In 1992, Kazakhstan had created three bureaucratic bodies in the oil industry that were controlled by competing interests and that had overlapping jurisdictions over various areas. The national oil company, Kazakhstanmunaigaz, was tasked with carrying out exploration, development, production, transportation and refining activities throughout the country. The Ministry of Energy and Fuel Resources, on the other hand, was held responsible for regulating oil and gas production and refining. Finally, the Ministry of Geology and Protection of Mineral Resources was set up to regulate the development of Kazakhstan's mineral resources.[16] Especially during the discussions over

[14] Ostrowski 2007, 73.
[15] Ibid., 76.
[16] Ibid., 62.

the partial privatization of Kazakhstanmunaigaz in 1993, the struggle between these bodies became very disruptive.[17]

This chaotic industry structure resembled that of Russia's rather than Azerbaijan's. As discussed in chapter five, in Azerbaijan the national state oil company, SOCAR, had the undisputed control over the direction of the industry throughout the 1990s and was able to avoid any bureaucratic challenges from outside the company. In Russia, on the other hand, the jurisdictional overlap between bureaucratic organizations in charge of the industry created a lot of confusion and led to a significant delay in the formulation and implementation of investment rules and policies throughout the 1990s.

Different from Yeltsin, Nazarbaev was able to reign in on the political system by mid 1990s to get back the control of the country as well as the oil industry. Nazarbayev consolidated his power by dissolving the parliament in March 1995, calling for a referendum to extend his presidential term until 2000, and drafting a new constitution. Compared to the 1993 constitution, this new constitution of 1995 expanded the powers of the executive branch and subordinated all other branches of government – both at the national and local level – to the executive branch. The president now had the power to rule by decree, disband parliament and appoint and remove key state officers. In spring 1998, Nazarbayev further consolidated his grip on power when he merged a number of regions and changed the patterns of governor (*akim*) appointments. Rather than home-grown governors, Nazarbayev began appointing more and more people who were loyal to him and were too weak to challenge him.[18]

Alarmed by the internal struggles and chaos within the bureaucracy and the growing concerns of foreign investors, Nazarbayev also took steps to streamline the bureaucracy and consolidate his control over the oil industry. First in October 1994, he appointed a new cabinet and a new prime minister, Akezhan Kazhegeldin, with the specific task of privatizing the oil industry and attracting FDI. The new cabinet concluded work on the Law on Oil in a speedy fashion and defined the procedures for licenses and contracts. Moreover, Nazarbayev created a new entity called, the State Investment Committee (SIC) with the exclusive right to deal with foreign investors. This "one-stop shop" for investors allowed them to bypass Kazakhstan's bureaucratic maze in their dealings with the government.[19]

[17] For more detail on these disputes, see Ostrowski 2007.
[18] Cummings 2000, 43.
[19] Ostrowski 2007, 84.

Concerned with the growing power of Prime Minister Kazhageldin, Nazarbayev decided to take charge of the oil sector himself by 1997. With the decree that he signed in March 1997, he dissolved the Ministry of Geology and Subsoil Protection, the Ministry of the Oil and Gas Industry, the State Tax Committee, the State Pricing Committee, and the State Property Management Committee and established in their place the KazakhOil National Oil and Gas Company. This company was charged with the control and management of government's interests in all oil and gas enterprises, including joint ventures and production sharing projects with foreign investors. The creation of this company gave Nazarbayev the leverage to shift control over the oil industry firmly within the presidential apparatus and away from the jurisdiction of the prime minister.[20] Soon Kazhegeldin was forced to resign and thereafter was banned and exiled from political life due to his growing opposition to the president. Just like in Azerbaijan, Nazarbayev started installing members of his family to the highest positions in the country and in the oil industry.[21] He surrounded himself with a core loyal elite and "skillfully facilitated the transition of potential opponents to the private sector (generally private oil enterprises), politics, local and state administration, and Kulibayev's controlled KazakhOil and as special advisers to various foreign oil companies."[22] By the end of 1990s, essentially an authoritarian regime was created in Kazakhstan and any resemblance of checks and balances was eliminated.

As I argue in this book, this turn towards more authoritarianism made Kazakhstan a more attractive destination for foreign investors. As Nazarbayev reigned in the veto players and limited political competition, he was able to provide a licensing and contracting regime that protected the interests of the foreign investors and ensured them a stable return on their investments. That is why despite a couple of contracts signed in early 1990s, the majority of sales to foreign investors and contracts signed with foreign oil companies took place in the late 1990s and into the 2000s. In essence, Kazakhstan provides an interesting case between Azerbaijan and Russia as it borrows elements from each and confirms the hypothesis that moving away from a partial democracy towards a more closed authoritarian system increases the attractiveness of an investment regime and thus

[20] Ibid., 89.
[21] For instance, his son-in-law, Timur Kulibayev, became financial director and Vice president of KazakhOil.
[22] Ostrowski 2007, 93.

the likelihood of more FDI in a country. Nazarbayev's policies in the post 1995 term resemble more closely the Putin policies since 2000s.

It is important to note here that Kazakhstan's investment regime in the past couple of years has taken a different turn. The government's attitude towards foreign investors has grown tougher. State's greater involvement and control over the energy sector has raised tensions between the government and investors. Generally three controversial legislative changes have caused concerns among investors. The first is the state's preemptive right clause that was added to the law on December 1, 2004. This clause "grants the government a pre-emptive right to acquire any subsoil use right and/or equity interest that a subsoil user wishes to transfer."[23] It was initiated after British Gas announced its intention to sell its share in Kashagan offshore project. According to the original contract, the consortium members had a right of first refusal to the stake but the government insisted that the right of first refusal was its and that the transfer for stakes should be made to the state oil company, Kazmunaigaz. Even though after two years a compromise was reached, little progress was made on the development of the field during this time and an important turning point was reached in terms of investor-government relations. This was the first time the authorities had openly violated the sanctity of the contracts, and not just the new ones but also the ones that have already been signed. Contract provisions were no longer protected from subsequent changes in national legislation.

Another issue of contention has been over local content requirements. In order to reinvigorate the economy and improve local capabilities, the government amended the Subsoil Law to increase local content of works, goods and services and require investors to commit to infrastructure and other socioeconomic development projects in the country. In case investors did not comply with these obligations, litigation channels were opened to any potential supplier of the good.

Finally, the power of the state oil company was significantly increased in 2000s. KazMunaiGas, which was created in 2002, is an investor in several joint ventures, monopoly operator of the domestic oil and gas pipeline network and the regulator of the industry. In 2004, the government introduced legislation to further increase the company's participation in new projects. "KazMunaiGas has been given the right to first tender on all new blocks with minimum 50 percent ownership."[24] Furthermore,

---

[23] Kaiser and Pulsipher 2007, 1310.
[24] Ibid., 1311.

some dramatic changes have taken place in the field of taxation. On new projects, a sliding scale tax has been imposed on all crude oil exported from the country and the stability of tax treatment on new concessionary contracts has been revoked so that investors are no longer protected from future changes in tax legislation.[25]

These recent developments in the Kazakh investment environment are neither unique nor surprising. As discussed in Chapter 2, the obsolescing bargain theory assumes changes in the terms provided for investors as the balance of power between them and the host government changes. Low oil prices and Kazakhstan's initial need to attract large scale investment gave the oil companies in the 1990s significant leverage over taxation, regulation and ownership. However, once the investments were made and experience gained, it became possible for Kazakhstan to revise the terms of their interaction with investors. As its bargaining position strengthened into the 2000s, it was only natural for the state to assert itself and insist on tougher terms. As discussed in Chapter 7, one can identify similar patterns in Norway during the 1970s and 80s as the Norwegian government adamantly protected its interests against foreign investors or in Russia in the 2000s as Putin reconsolidated state's role in the oil industry.

Finally, despite the increasing assertiveness of the state in the oil industry, the investment environment in Kazakhstan is still regarded as acceptable to foreign investors. "With the exception of the state's exercise of preemption rights to the British Gas Kashagan stake, the authorities have so far resisted the temptation to revise unilaterally the contracts concluded with investors though they have sometimes pushed questions of contract interpretation as far as they could."[26] As for local content requirements, investors for the most part were willing to make some concessions to allow the Kazakh regime to save face. There was a tacit understanding between the two parties: "the foreign oil companies were willing to partly accept the regime's demands to take greater responsibility for the social and economic development of the oil-rich regions, while the regime on its part largely left the companies to carry on with their business as usual."[27] Finally, the toughening tax regime was also somewhat acceptable to foreign investors since it corresponded to the increases in international oil prices as well as to the government's justifiable concern with the "Dutch disease" syndrome that could be "caught" with an aggressive depletion

[25] Ibid.
[26] Ahrend and Tompson 2007, 175.
[27] Ostrowski 2007, 195.

of the resources. Overall, even though there have been some complaints about government policies, no major player has left Kazakhstan yet. Today, foreign investors continue to have a significant role in the development of energy resources in Kazakhstan and in the creation of a new energy super power in Asia.

Beyond Case Studies and Oil

In order to analyze the role of political institutions in attracting FDI across a larger number of cases and for all industries, I employ a dataset that utilizes economic data from the World Bank's World Development Indicators and political data from the POLITY IV.[28] Together, they provide relevant information on 132 countries from 1970 through 2004. This time-series cross-sectional dataset allows for analyses of changes within countries over time as well as among countries at any given time.

The dependent variable is FDI net inflows measured in billions of current U.S. Dollars. FDI is defined as lasting managerial acquisitions of at least 10 percent of voting stocks in an enterprise operating outside of the country of the investor. Because the net inflows include any divestments, the value may be negative or positive. This variable construction is the same as that found in other studies that examine global patterns of FDI in all sectors of the economy.[29]

The primary explanatory variable is Polarized Constraints and Competition (PCC). The variable captures the nonlinear effects of executive constraints and political competition analyzed hitherto in this study. Low as well as high levels of constraints and competition tend to create relatively attractive investment environments; intermediate levels tend to create relatively unattractive investment environments. To accommodate this, I create a single variable that ranges from intermediate levels of constraints and competition to either lower or higher levels of constraints and competition: thus, the polarized nature.

Specifically, PCC is based on two variables from the POLITY IV dataset: XCONST and POLCOMP. XCONST is defined by POLITY IV as the extent of institutional constraints on the decision-making powers of the chief executive, whether an individual or a collective executive. The POLITY IV study suggests that this variable is similar to the notion of "horizontal accountability" and includes the constraints imposed by the

---

[28] World Bank 2006, Marshall and Jaggers 2004.
[29] See Chan and Mason 1992, O'Neal 1994, Li and Resnick 2003, Jensen 2003, 2006.

legislative and judicial branches of government. As such, it approximates the executive constraints that I focus on in this study. Its values range from 1 (unlimited executive authority) to 7 (executive parity or subordination), with higher values indicating a greater degree of executive constraints.

POLCOMP variable, on the other hand, considers two dimensions of political competition: the degree of institutionalization or regulation of political competition, and the extent of government restriction on political competition. The competitiveness of political participation refers to the extent to which alternative preferences for policy formation and leadership roles can be pursued in the political arena. This variable is a good approximation for the strength of political parties and interest groups. The political competition variable values range from 1 (suppressed) to 10 (institutional electoral), with higher values indicating a greater degree of political competition.

In terms of investment environment, then, the effects of these variables essentially range from a flexible institutional environment to a stable institutional environment. Institutional configurations in between the two end values provide neither. To model the nonlinear nature of institutional constraints and competition in a single variable, I use the following equation.

$$PCC = [\, | \, (35 - (XCONST * POLCOMP)) \, | \,] + 1$$

This formula creates a single variable with values that range from 1 to 36. The higher the value, the more attractive is the country's investment environment. Thus, I expect PCC to be positively correlated with FDI net inflows.

I also control for many potential economic factors that are commonly thought to influence the pattern of FDI inflows. First is the variable Market Size. It is measured as the gross domestic product, in current U.S. Dollars, of each nation. Larger markets tend to attract more foreign capital because of the possibility of greater returns; China is the classic example. Second, the Economic Growth of a country is also typically thought to be a good indicator of investment potential. It is measured as the annual growth rate of the nation's GDP. Economies that are growing relatively quickly also offer relatively greater potential returns. Third, I control for the volume of Global FDI, which is measured by the total volume of FDI for the whole world for each year, measured in trillion of current U.S. Dollars. The more capital in international markets, the more FDI each country should receive. As such, I expect Market Size, Economic Growth, and Global FDI to be positively correlated with FDI net inflows.

I also include controls for inflation and three sectors of the economy for each country. The variable Inflation is the annual growth rate of the GDP implicit deflator, expressed in decimal form (i.e., 1 percent = 0.01). The sectoral variables measure the value added, in current U.S. Dollars, in the agricultural, manufacturing, and service sectors in each country and each year as a percent of the country's GDP. In general, these four variables measure different aspects of the economic environment. Investors likely differ on their assessment of each based on the particular industry that they represent.

The final two economic control variables focus on trade. First, a country that has a relatively high volume of trade may signal to investors that the country is well established in the global marketplace and that it has a vibrant economy. The variable Trade, then, is the sum of a country's exports and imports of goods and services measured as a percent of GDP. To test whether oil plays a special role in the global economy, another control variable is labeled Oil Exports. It is the value of all mineral fuels exported by a country expressed as a percent of the country's GDP.[30]

Lastly, I include a set of regional control variables. Each country is coded as being part of one of eight regions of the world: East Asia and Pacific, East Europe and Central Asia, Latin America and Caribbean, Mideast and North Africa, North American, South Asia, Sub-Saharan Africa, or Western Europe. Seven of these eight binary variables (Sub-Saharan Africa is omitted) are included in all of the regressions; however, for ease of presentation, the results are suppressed in the tables. Regional variables are commonly used because countries within these regions tend to have similar levels of historical and social development, as well as incidence of war or other forms of instability. As such, these variables are meant to provide a broad control for such effects.

Model and Results

To test the theory, I examine FDI net inflows and the institutional environment for policy-making for 132 countries over 34 years. Because the dependent variables can be compared among nations and over years, a

---

[30] The World Bank's World Development Indicators only report the broadest category for this sector (SITC 3, mineral fuels) and not the specific data for crude oil or petroleum products. These latter products, however, generally comprise the vast majority of the broader category. For example, in 2006 the SITC 3 value for exports was US$779 trillion; petroleum products contributed US$618 trillion to that figure.

time-series cross-sectional random effects general least squared regression is used. In addition, the residuals may not be independently distributed; therefore, a Huber and White estimator is used to produce robust standard errors.

Table 8.1 reports the results. The first column of numbers (labeled World) reports the coefficient estimates from the regression with all countries in the dataset included in the analysis. The second column of numbers (labeled Oil Exporters) focuses the analysis only on countries whose fuel exports are greater than 10 percent of their overall GDP. Over the 34 years of this study, 44 countries reach that threshold at least once. The third column of numbers (labeled Non-OECD) focuses the analysis on just the countries that do not belong to the Organization of Economic Co-operation and Development (OECD). If a country joined the OECD midway through the dataset, such as Mexico, the country is included up until the year in which it joined. The non OECD countries, then, represent the developing world. Finally, the fourth column of numbers (labeled ARN) focuses the regression analysis solely on Azerbaijan, Russia and Norway – the countries of the preceding case studies. The regression certainly suffers from a small n, and thus we should be quite cautious in interpreting the results and drop it from some of the subsequent analyses.

The coefficients for PCC are positive and statistically significant in each of the four models. This indicates that while controlling for regional variations and the economic factors that are commonly expected to influence foreign investors' decisions, a country with either low or high constraints on the executive and political competition tend to be relatively more successful in attracting FDI than a country that is situated towards the middle of this institutional spectrum. As the theory predicts, an executive who has the flexibility to make deals with foreign investors can provide a relatively attractive investment environment; an executive who is fully constrained by democratic competitive institutions can provide the stability that is also attractive to many foreign investors. However, executives that have neither the flexibility of autocrats nor the predictability of democrats tend to attract less FDI.

In the model that includes all of the countries of the world for which there is data, the coefficient indicates that a country that moves one point up the scale can expect to attract US$68 million more in FDI.[31] Although

---

[31] This result actually underrepresents the potential impact. Because of data limitations, FDI is measured in current U.S. Dollars and thus typically deflates the real value of past investments.

TABLE 8.1. *Polarizing Constraints and Competition (PCC) and FDI Net Inflows, Random-Effects GLS*

	World	Oil Exporters	Non-OECD	ARN
PCC	0.068	0.016	0.013	0.634
	(0.016)***	(0.009)*	(0.004)***	(0.197)***
Market Size	0.015	0.018	0.029	0.037
	(0.004)***	(0.005)***	(0.002)***	(0.004)***
Economic Growth	0.057	0.019	−0.002	0.132
	(0.019)***	(0.008)**	(0.006)	(0.143)
Global FDI	2.216	0.128	0.020	0.647
	(0.466)***	(0.133)	(0.041)	(0.480)
Inflation	0.027	0.004	−0.003	15.116
	(0.013)**	(0.001)***	(0.004)	(10.007)
Agriculture	12.279	1.670	2.638	−79.776
	(4.490)***	(1.733)	(0.663)***	(30.348)***
Manufacturing	−2.771	−4.693	−5.194	−25.235
	(4.524)	(2.720)*	(1.473)***	(25.542)
Services	0.127	1.556	−0.489	−35.113
	(2.860)	(1.123)	(0.718)	(12.843)***
Trade	0.034	0.020	0.013	0.045
	(0.012)***	(0.006)***	(0.003)***	(0.040)
Oil Exports	−0.021	–	−0.009	−0.434
	(0.013)		(0.003)***	(0.135)***
Constant	−9.570	−2.623	−1.334	−0.737
	(2.631)***	(1.095)**	(0.579)**	−10.335
Number of observations	2278	485	1868	39
Number of countries	132	44	109	3
R-squared (overall)	0.49	0.76	0.76	0.90
Random Effects GLS Regression				
Robust standard errors in parentheses				

* significant at 10%; ** significant at 5%; *** significant at 1%.
Coefficients for the regional variables have been suppressed.

the magnitude is not as strong among Oil Exporters and all non-OECD countries – presumably because there are fewer consolidated democracies within these groups to contribute to the higher end of the spectrum – the relationship between a country's political institutions and its ability to attract FDI is still positively correlated and statistically significant.

Most of the economic variables perform as expected as well. The coefficient for the variable Market Size is positive and significant in each of the four regression models. These results indicate, as expected, that

countries with larger economies tend to attract more FDI. The rate at
which the economy is growing is also significantly and positively related
to the FDI net inflows for all countries in the world and for oil exporting
countries. The relationship is not statistically significant for the remaining two.

The Global FDI variable measures the total amount of FDI invested
around the world in a given year. The coefficient is positive in each of
the four models, as expected, but is statistically significant only when all
countries in the world are examined. This is likely a sign that developed
countries capture much of the FDI inflows. FDI is unevenly distributed
around the world.

In the first two models, the coefficient for the Inflation variable is
also positive and significant. This indicates that – at least, presumably,
within a moderate range – investors may view higher levels of inflation
as relatively attractive: it may be a sign for a certain amount of economic
growth potential, or it may signal bargain investments.

The three sectoral measures – Agriculture, Manufacturing, and
Services – produce a mixed set of results. Among all countries as well as
among all non-OECD countries, a higher percentage of the agricultural
sector in the GDP is significantly and positively correlated with higher
levels of FDI net inflows. Manufacturing, on the other hand, is significantly and negatively correlated with FDI among non-OECD countries.
And, Services in the domestic economy is not statistically significant in
any of the first three models.

The Trade variable is – not surprisingly – statistically significant and
positively correlated with higher levels of FDI flows. The more that a
country is involved in the global market place – through the exporting
and importing of goods and services, the more likely it is that foreign
investors will invest their capital in that host country. Higher levels of
trade, in other words, seem to provide a sign to investors about the potential for a relatively strong return on their investments.

Finally, in the model for all of the countries of the world, the amount
of oil that a country exports is not significantly related to the amount of
FDI net inflows that the country receives. For the Non-OECD and ARN
models, however, the coefficients are significant but negative, meaning
that the more a country exports oil, the less it receives FDI. This finding is not too surprising given the obsolescing bargaining model. As the
oil industry of a developing country grows, its exports increase and it
becomes more self-sufficient. In other words, as the national oil industry
matures, there is less need for FDI.

Robustness Checks

I also conduct three additional analyses to check the robustness of the above results. First, instead of the random-effects model, Table 8.2 reports the results from a fixed-effects model. This allows us to concentrate on within-country variations over time. All of the regional variables are dropped from the regression, though, because they are invariant; the analysis on just Azerbaijan, Russia, and Norway is also dropped due to a lack of within-country observations.

In each of the three analyses reported in Table 8.2, PCC is again, as expected, positive and significant. As before, this indicates that either

TABLE 8.2. *Polarizing Constraints and Competition (PCC) and FDI Net Inflows, Fixed-Effects GLS*

	World	Oil Exporters	Non-OECD
PCC	0.078	0.029	0.012
	(0.017)***	(0.011)***	(0.004)***
Market Size	0.021	0.024	0.030
	(0.006)***	(0.004)***	(0.002)***
Economic Growth	0.054	0.016	−0.003
	(0.020)***	(0.008)**	(0.006)
Global FDI	2.271	0.161	0.042
	(0.548)***	(0.143)	(0.040)
Inflation	0.022	0.003	−0.004
	(0.012)*	(0.001)**	(0.004)
Agriculture	13.871	3.388	2.309
	(4.509)***	(1.931)*	(0.856)***
Manufacturing	1.479	−5.858	−6.924
	(6.624)	(2.873)**	(1.501)***
Services	−3.844	−0.257	−1.814
	(3.876)	(1.024)	(0.681)***
Trade	0.011	0.013	0.009
	(0.010)	(0.005)***	(0.002)***
Oil Exports	−0.036	–	−0.011
	(0.013)***		(0.004)***
Constant	−6.229	−1.719	0.154
	(1.886)***	(0.716)**	−0.516
Number of observations	2278	485	1868
Number of countries	132	44	109
R-squared (within)	0.23	0.15	0.66

Fixed-Effects GLS Regression
Robust standard errors in parentheses

* significant at 10%; ** significant at 5%; *** significant at 1%.

low or high levels of institutional constraints and competition attract relatively more FDI net inflows, while levels that fall in between these extreme points do not seem as successful in producing enough guarantees and incentives to attract FDI. Most of the other results are substantively similar to those discussed for Table 8.1.

Finally, I substitute a different independent variable for PCC to capture the broader relationship between regime type and FDI. The following regressions instead use Polarized Regime Type (PRT) variable to test whether the effects we see with institutional constraints and competition are generalizable to political regimes. The POLITY IV dataset provides a variable, Polity, that measures all countries on a regime spectrum, which ranges from the most autocratic (-10) to the most democratic (10). Similar to the construction of PCC, I simply take the absolute value of Polity. This creates PRT, with values that range from 0 (hybrid regimes) to 10 (the most autocratic or the most democratic regimes). I expect that PRT is also positively correlated with FDI net inflows.

Table 8.3 reports the results from the regressions that substitute PRT with PCC in the same random effects generalized least squares regression with robust coefficients used in Table 8.1. Most of the economic controls have similar effects as discussed earlier. The coefficient for the PRT is, as expected, positive and significant when all the countries of the world for which there is data are included. The coefficient is positive, but not statistically significant, when either oil exporters or non-OECD countries are examined alone.[32] A postregression analysis of the variable inflation factors (VIF), though, indicates considerable multicollinearity between manufacturing and PRT. When the former is dropped from the regression of all non-OECD countries, PRT remains positive and again becomes statistically significant.[33]

The last step of these robustness checks is to test whether PRT maintains its direction and significance in a fixed-effects model. Table 8.4 reports the results. The model on just Azerbaijan, Russia, and Norway is dropped for lack of within-country observations. Again, PRT is a strong,

---

[32] In my opinion, this demonstrates that the finer institutional distinctions among oil exporters provide a better measure in explaining FDI levels than simple regime type differences. This is why I do not exclusively rely on generic regime labels but instead use more specific institutional variables to explain the relationship between politics and FDI. The simpler regime type analyses are included to empirically demonstrate this point as well as to provide a comparable analysis to other studies that use this type of variable construction.

[33] Polarized Regime Type: coefficient = 0.033, standard error = 0.015, z score = 2.29, significant at the 0.05 level.

TABLE 8.3. *Polarizing Regime Type (PRT) and FDI Net Inflows, Random-Effects GLS*

	World	Oil Exporters	Non-OECD	ARN
PRT	0.116	0.039	0.016	2.573
	(0.039)***	(0.032)	(0.012)	(1.302)**
Market Size	0.015	0.017	0.029	0.035
	(0.004)***	(0.005)***	(0.002)***	(0.006)***
Economic Growth	0.057	0.020	−0.001	0.160
	(0.019)***	(0.008)**	(0.006)	(0.139)
Global FDI	2.053	0.106	−0.008	0.958
	(0.433)***	(0.137)	(0.040)	(0.522)*
Inflation	0.018	0.003	−0.005	4.568
	(0.008)**	(0.001)***	(0.004)	(9.354)
Agriculture	12.868	2.248	2.659	−25.198
	(4.446)***	(1.824)	(0.636)***	(28.930)
Manufacturing	−2.732	−4.677	−5.078	−41.199
	(4.458)	(2.754)*	(1.466)***	(30.385)
Services	0.184	1.739	−0.541	−42.707
	(2.802)	(1.085)	(0.707)	(16.299)***
Trade	0.035	0.021	0.013	0.123
	(0.012)***	(0.006)***	(0.003)***	(0.037)***
Oil Exports	−0.017		−0.008	−0.426
	(0.013)		(0.003)**	(0.167)**
Constant	−8.616	−2.671	−1.081	−4.746
	(2.495)***	(1.083)**	(0.533)**	−14.314
Number of observations	2312	491	1902	39
Number of countries	134	44	111	3
R-squared (overall)	0.49	0.76	0.76	0.88

Random Effects GLS Regression
Robust standard errors in parentheses

* significant at 10%; ** significant at 5%; *** significant at 1%.
Coefficients for the regional variables have been suppressed.

positive, and statistically significant predictor of FDI net inflows. The economic control variables continue to perform similarly as before.

Overall, the results reported provide strong statistical evidence that supports the theoretical arguments of this study. They indicate, to a certain degree, that the theory presented and analyzed throughout this study is generalizable on three dimensions. First, it is generalizable from the

TABLE 8.4. *Polarizing Regime Type (PRT) and FDI Net Inflows, Fixed-Effects GLS*

	World	Oil Exporters	Non-OECD
PRT	0.172	0.107	0.027
	(0.043)***	(0.036)***	(0.012)**
Market Size	0.021	0.024	0.030
	(0.006)***	(0.004)***	(0.002)***
Economic Growth	0.054	0.017	−0.002
	(0.020)***	(0.007)**	(0.006)
Global FDI	2.116	0.147	0.024
	(0.515)***	(0.150)	(0.038)
Inflation	0.011	0.002	−0.006
	(0.007)	(0.001)	(0.005)
Agriculture	15.943	5.242	2.503
	(4.767)***	(2.114)**	(0.857)***
Manufacturing	1.584	−5.742	−6.691
	(6.568)	(2.873)**	(1.490)***
Services	−3.935	0.233	−1.865
	(3.827)	(0.978)	(0.670)***
Trade	0.012	0.015	0.009
	(0.009)	(0.005)***	(0.002)***
Oil Exports	−0.037		−0.012
	(0.012)***		(0.004)***
Constant	−5.699	−2.393	0.234
	(1.814)***	(0.786)***	−0.514
Number of observations	2312	491	1902
Number of countries	134	44	111
R-squared (overall)	0.23	0.15	0.65
Fixed-Effects GLS Regression			
Robust standard errors in parentheses			

*significant at 10%; ** significant at 5%; *** significant at 1%.

three in-depth case studies to all countries in the world. Second, it is generalizable from a specific set of institutional variables to regime type. In other words, the theoretical relationship that I hypothesize between the degree of institutional constraints and competition and FDI levels also holds more generally in the relationship between political regimes and FDI. Third, these findings demonstrate that the theory is not limited to FDI only in the oil sector; it is also generalizable to FDI in all sectors.

The use of both qualitative case study method and quantitative statistical method in this book provides a valuable opportunity to generate hypotheses and test them at the most generalizable levels. The combination of these methods offer both the depth and the scope needed to refine the existing literature on the causal mechanisms between political institutions and the ability to attract FDI.

9

Conclusion

Foreign capital poses major challenges for nation states. In order to receive foreign investments, states need to make certain adjustments in their investment regimes. Not every state with attractive economic endowments, such as significant natural resources, cheap labor, large domestic markets or supporting industries, can successfully attract foreign capital. While these factors are important, foreign investors also look for various legal, fiscal and administrative guarantees and incentives that can secure their property and contract rights throughout the life of their projects. Considering the fierce competition for foreign investment around the world, host governments that need outside financing and expertise cannot overlook these demands from international investors. In order to provide stability, predictability, consistency, and some level of flexibility in their investment environments, governments need to overcome domestic opposition to the terms offered for investors by either excluding or winning over the consent or acquiescence of nonbeneficiaries. As such, domestic politics plays an important role in providing the conditions under which foreign capital is attracted.

Few people would deny that politics matters in the ability of a country to attract FDI. The devil, however, is in the details. What kind of a political arrangement is the most conducive to foreign investors? Which political institutions can better provide for the needs of the investors by shaping the interactions between the opponents and proponents of foreign investment in the economy? What are the trade-offs involved in investing in one political regime as opposed to another? These are the questions that this book set out to find answers for.

The in-depth analysis of three oil producing states, Azerbaijan, Russia, and Norway, as well as the discussion of the Kazakhstan case and the findings from the large-n study all offer a rejoinder to a literature that finds FDI to be compatible with only democracy or only authoritarianism. I argue that given a willingness to open the economy to foreign capital, both of these regimes can be successful in creating an attractive investment environment. Full insulation from potential competitive forces in the state and society gives the decision makers the advantage of flexibility; full accountability to state veto players as well as political parties and interest groups gives them the credibility and stability needed to attract investment.

As the Azerbaijani and Norwegian comparison clearly shows, there are, however, trade-offs involved in investing in an authoritarian regime as opposed to a democracy: investors forgo long-term predictability for short-term high rewards; not all investors can equally benefit from the generosity of the regime; and there is the fear of societal discontent and frustration that can eventually disrupt investment projects. Investors make these short-term and long-term cost-benefit calculations as they search for a country to invest in. The experiences of these four countries and the results of the larger-n statistical analysis suggest that both authoritarian regimes and consolidated democracies have institutional advantages that meet various expectations of foreign investors.

If both regimes are compatible with foreign capital, does it mean that political regimes do not matter? The answer is no; they still matter. The Russian case offers us an opportunity to reclassify regimes and reformulate our hypotheses regarding the relationship between political institutions and FDI. If we move beyond the generic authoritarian versus democratic conceptualization and the readily available numerical indices to analyze political regimes along an institutional dimension that measures the opportunities and constraints facing domestic actors in policymaking, we can capture the political dynamics behind investment policies more systematically. The variation on the degree of executive constraints and political competition gives us a third category of regimes that delineates a different kind of relationship between investors and host governments. The regimes that are less compatible with foreign capital are, in fact, hybrid regimes that have neither high nor low levels of executive constraints and political competition. The lack of full insulation or full accountability creates a condition whereby the state can provide neither enough flexibility to offer generous terms to investors nor enough predictability and stability to guarantee the returns investors expect to get from their investments. Horizontal and vertical accountability need to exist or be absent simultaneously to provide the optimal conditions for foreign capital.

Out of all the possible sectors, this study focuses on foreign investment in the oil sector. According to the conventional wisdom, oil investors do not have any regime preferences; they can work with any regime that provides them some level of stability. Given the capital-intensive nature of exploration and development, and the long lead times in commencing production, generating income and recovering costs, the stability of the investment environment has always been of vital importance to multinational oil corporations. Although it may be true that investors do not openly favor one regime over another, a pattern emerges from the analysis in this book to suggest that oil investments tend, ceteris paribus, to flow to countries with the most advantageous institutional arrangements. The criterion of stability is a function of political institutions. Host governments can provide for that stability by formulating laws that clearly set the investment terms regarding taxation, production ceilings, license requirements, operational safety regulations and dispute resolution mechanisms. Governments are also expected to create a regulatory and administrative framework in which investment laws are implemented and safeguarded. For all these tasks, decision makers have to either exclude or co-opt those that oppose foreign investment. Because the interaction of opponents and proponents of foreign capital takes place in an institutional setting, political regimes matter in the formulation and implementation of investment terms for oil companies.

FDI: Good or Bad?

This book also draws attention to the developmental effects of foreign capital once it is invested. The existing literature generally simplifies these effects as being either good or bad. The three case studies in this book suggest that the direction of the effects, in fact, depend on the political institutions that are in place prior to the flow of foreign capital. The Azeri case demonstrates how an authoritarian regime that has been successful in attracting FDI falls short of setting up an efficient, transparent, noncorrupt, and accountable institutional framework for the use and distribution of foreign capital and the ensuing oil wealth. The lack of executive constraints and political competition has made the Azeri economy more dependent on oil, increased inequality and corruption in society, weakened the government's ability and willingness to introduce reforms and provide for its citizens.

Even though similarly successful in attracting FDI, developmental effects of FDI and oil rents in Norway have been the polar opposite of Azerbaijan's. Norway's democratic institutions have been extremely equitable and professional in distributing the oil riches among the Norwegian people, with even an eye for the future generations. Thanks to the constraints and competition its political regime has provided, Norway has been – for the most part – able to show budgetary restraints and escape the oil curse. In fact, one can easily say that Norway transformed the oil wealth into a blessing for the majority of its citizens and set out a successful example of resource management to be emulated by the rest of the oil-rich states. The comparison between Azerbaijan and Norway challenges the determinism in the rentier state literature that predicts doom for oil-rich states. The differences in the resource management strategies of these two countries demonstrate that political institutions that are in place prior to the flow of foreign capital dramatically shape how investment capital and the ensuing oil wealth are going to be managed later on.

In this book, I also argue that the flow of foreign capital has significant effects on regime type. I challenge the Anglo-American ideological prescriptions, aptly labeled the "Washington Consensus," which assume a direct relation between increased economic openness and democratic transition. According to this line of thinking, the neoliberal policies that increase trade and free mobility of capital bring economic prosperity to countries, and consequently sow the seeds of democracy. The Clintonesque policy of encouraging developing countries to join in global networks of trade and capital has at its base the assumption that financial globalization would not only bring a convergence in macroeconomic policies, but also a convergence toward democratic political systems.

The appearance of the former Soviet republics as new states in the beginning of the 1990s provided a venue to test this neoliberal view. Many in the West initially believed that opening up these formerly planned economies to global market forces would undermine authoritarian regimes and speed democratic transitions. This would not only be the triumph of capitalism over communism, but also democracy over totalitarianism. Almost two decades later, however, the picture is not so encouraging for the advocates of the neoliberal paradigm. As the Azerbaijani case clearly demonstrates, those former Soviet republics that successfully attracted significant amounts of foreign capital, instead of becoming more democratic, reinforced their authoritarian regimes. In Azerbaijan, the cozy alliance between the oil investors and the Aliev family worked mostly to enrich and strengthen the supporters of the regime against its opponents.

Over the years, the regime became even more autocratic: the harassment of opposition, use of intimidation, violations of basic democratic rights and freedoms intensified. The oil rents and the prospect of more provided the incentive and the fuel to exclude the majority of the Azeri people from enjoying the riches of their country. By indirectly enabling the wealth and directly endorsing the authoritarian regime, foreign investors contributed to its persistence and clearly affected the course of political development in Azerbaijan.

Furthermore, I also challenge in this book the dependency theories that emphasize the antidemocratic elements of foreign capital. In Norway, oil investments directly increased the legitimacy of and the satisfaction with the democratic regime. They reinforced the existing regime by also indirectly financing the social programs and thus expanding the welfare system. Oil investments and the ensuing oil revenues also helped create a confident, resourceful, and altruistic Norwegian diplomacy, which over the years elevated a small country like Norway to an important player in the world. The Azerbaijani and Norwegian cases further demonstrate that in both authoritarian regimes and consolidated democracies, foreign investment can have a "reinforcing effect" on the political regime, albeit with opposite results.

Finally, I draw attention to the developmental effects of FDI on hybrid regimes. As the Russian case demonstrates, the hybrid regime that makes it difficult to attract FDI can ironically have the effect of mitigating some of the negative implications of FDI and oil revenues on development. As is widely pointed out, Russia – to a large extent – escaped the economic and institutional malaise that was associated with foreign investment and oil development in the 1990s. However, the competition for FDI in the global economy can force hybrid regimes to make certain institutional changes to be more attractive for foreign investors. In the face of globalizing pressures, that is, the need to attract foreign investment, hybrid regimes are inherently nonviable. They tend to gravitate towards either the authoritarian or democratic regime type. However, the troubling reality is that the urgency to attract foreign investment may leave very few options to the ruling elites. Not being able to make the institutional changes to offer investors the guarantees and incentives that they need means less competitiveness in a world where international investment resources are scarce and states in need of investment are plenty. Especially when faced with serious economic crises, decision makers in hybrid regimes are left with little flexibility and oftentimes are inclined to use exclusionary tactics to overcome opposition rather than include different interests in the decision-making process and engage in institution building. A move towards a more authoritarian regime may be a likely condition for a timely integration into the global economy. Those who are in power may rationalize their authoritarian measures as temporary solutions to overcome economic problems. In other words, they might use the rhetoric that authoritarianism is a necessary step to achieve economic development and democracy in the long run.

Recent evidence from Russia under Putin's leadership shows that this is partly what happened in Russia since the beginning of 2000s. The 1998 economic crisis and the immediate need to reverse the drop in investments forced Putin to make some institutional changes. Even though by all means, there are many other factors shaping the trend towards authoritarianism in Russia today, one can argue that the need for an attractive investment environment was one of the most important justifications for the political change. As demonstrated in Chapter 6, Putin chose to consolidate more power in the state and increasingly deprived certain groups of their rights to oppose and challenge his policies. The state veto players that existed under Yeltsin – de facto and de jure – lost their power to constrain investment policies. Consequently, as evidenced by a dramatic increase in FDI, Putin's authoritarian measures did mean more stability for investors who started to return to the Russian market. Today, the Russian state has enough political and economic clout to set the terms of the relationship with the investors. Foreign investment is sought by the government but is selectively allowed. Thanks to high oil prices and strong economic indicators, the Russian state now has the upper hand.

At first glance, this book's conclusions may seem pessimistic for those who believe in democracy's ability to solve economic problems. After all, I show that both authoritarian regimes and consolidated democracies can be successful in attracting FDI, but that hybrid regimes do not have the institutional attributes to be as competitive in the global economy. However, the comparisons between different resource management models and the discussion of the various trade-offs facing investors provide a more sobering picture of who the clear winner is in the long run. As Olson states "the only societies where individual rights to property and contract are confidently expected to last across generations are the securely democratic societies."[1]

[1] Olson 2000, 42.

References

Ahmedbeili, Samira. 2005. Azerbaijan: Oil Workers Allege Foreign Discrimination. *Institute for War and Peace Reporting* CRS No. 274 (17 February).

Ahrend, Rudiger. 2005. Can Russia Break the Energy Curse? *Eurasian Geography and Economics* 46(8):584–68.

Ahrend, Rudiger, William Tompson. 2006. Realizing the Oil Supply Potential of the CIS: The Impact of Institutions and Policies. *OECD Economics Department Working Paper* No. 484.

——— 2007. Caspian Oil in a Global Context. *Transition Studies Review* 14(1): 163–87.

Akiner, Shirin. 2000. Emerging Political Order in the New Caspian States. In *Crossroads and Conflicts: Security and Foreign Policy in the Caucasus and Central Asia*, eds. Gary K. Bertsch, Cassady Craft, Scott A. Jones, and Michael Beck, 90–129. New York: Routledge.

Aldrich, John H. 1995. *Why Parties? The Origin and Transformation of Political Parties in America*. Chicago, IL: University of Chicago Press.

Alfaro, Laura, Chanda Areendam, Sebnem Kalemli-Ozcan, Selin Sayek. 2003. FDI Spillovers, Financial Markets and Economic Development. *IMF Working Paper* 03/186. International Monetary Fund.

Alieva, Leila. 2006. Azerbaijan's Frustrating Elections. *Journal of Democracy* 17(2):147–60.

Altstadt, Audrey L. 1997. Azerbaijan's Struggle Toward Democracy. In *Conflict, Cleavage, and Change in Central Asia and the Caucasus*, eds. Karen Dawisha and Bruce Parrott, 110–56. Cambridge: Cambridge University Press.

Amirov, Irik. 2000. Simplify PSA Law Substantially- or Investors Will Go. *Oil and Capital* 3:12–14.

Andersen, Robert. 1984. *Fundamentals of the Petroleum Industry*. Norman, Oklohama: University of Oklohama Press.

Andersen, Svein S. 1993. *The Struggle over North Sea Oil and Gas*. Oslo: Scandinavian University Press.

Andersen, Svein S., Maja Arnestad. 1990. The Taming of the Shrewd: Small State Meets Multinational Oil Companies. In *Naïve Newcomer or Shrewd*

Salesman? Norway – A Major Oil and Gas Exporter, eds. Helge Ole Bergesen and Anne Kristin Sydnes, 49–76. Fridtjof Nansen Institute.

Arifoglu, Farid, Shakhin Abbasov. 2000. The Azerbaijani Parliament Hostage to the Executive. *Central Asia and the Caucasus* 6:44–50.

Aron, Leon. 2007. *Russia's Oil Woes*. The American: The Journal of American Enterprise Institute (January/February).

Arrow, Kenneth J. 1951. *Social Choice and Individual Values*. New York: Wiley.

Askari, H. 2003. Caspian Oil Development: The Sooner the Better; a Trade-off Analysis and a Basis for Agreement. *Business Economics* 38(2):43–50.

Aslund, Anders. 2005. Russian Resources: Curse or Rents? *Eurasian Geography and Economics* 46(8):610–17.

Auty, Richard M. 1993. *Sustaining Development in Mineral Economies: The Resource Curse Thesis*. London and New York: Routledge.

2001. The Political Economy of Resource-Driven Growth. *European Economics Review* 45:839–46.

2004. *Patterns of Rent-Extraction and Deployment in Developing Countries: Implications for Governance, Economic Policy and Performance*. Lancaster University, Bailrigg, Lancaster, UK (mimeo).

Auty, Richard M., Indra de Soysa, eds. 2006. *Energy, Wealth, Governance in the Caspian Sea Region*. London: Routledge.

Bagirov, Sabit, Ingilab Akhmedov, Svetlana Tsalik. 2003. State Oil Fund of the Azerbaijan Republic. In *Caspian Oil Windfalls: Who Will Benefit?* ed. Tsalik Svetlana, 89–126. New York: Open Society Institute.

Bahgat, G. 2005. Oil and Terrorism: Central Asia and the Caucasus. *The Journal of Social, Political, and Economic Studies* 30(3):265–83.

Baker IV, James, Natik Mamedov. 1998. Oil and Gas Production Sharing Agreements. *USACC Investment Guide to Azerbaijan*.

Barnes, Andrew. 2006. *Owning Russia: The Struggle Over Factories, Farms and Power*. Ithaca, NY: Cornell University Press.

Barro, Robert J. 1996. Democracy and Growth. *Journal of Economic Growth* 1(1):1–27.

Bates, Robert H. 1983. *Essays on the Political Economy of Rural Africa*. Cambridge: Cambridge University Press.

2001. *Prosperity and Violence: The Political Economy of Development*. New York: Norton.

Bayulgen, Oksan. 2009. Caspian Energy Wealth: Social Impacts and Implications for Regional Stability. In *The Politics of Transition in Central Asia and the Caucasus: Enduring Legacies and Emerging Challenges*, eds. Amanda E. Wooden and Christoph H. Stefes, 163–88. Routledge.

Bennett, Douglas C., Kenneth S. Sharpe. 1983. *Transnational Corporations versus the State: The Political Economy of the Mexican Automobile Industry*. Princeton, NJ: Princeton University Press.

Bennett, Peter D., Robert T. Green. 1972. Political Instability as a Determinant of Direct Foreign Investment in Marketing. *Journal of Marketing Research* 9(May):182–6.

Berrefjord, Ole, Per Heum. 1990. Political Governance of the Petroleum Industry – The Norwegian Case. In *Naïve Newcomer or Shrewd Salesman?*

Norway – A Major Oil and Gas Exporter, eds. Helge Ole Bergesen and Anne Kristin Sydnes, 28–49. Fridtjof Nansen Institute.

Bhagwati, J. 1994. Globalization, Sovereignty and Democracy. In *Democracy's Victory and Crisis: Nobel Symposium*, ed. A. Hadenius, 263–81. Cambridge: Cambridge University Press.

Bindemann, Kirsten. 1999. *Production-Sharing Agreements: An Economic Analysis*. Oxford Institute for Energy Studies. WPM 25(October).

Blinn, Keith W. 1978. Production Sharing Agreements for Petroleum and Minerals. *Private Investor Abroad- Problems and Solutions in International Business in 1978*. Southwestern Legal Foundation, 303–30.

Block, Fred. 1996. *The Vampire State and Other Stories*. New York: New Press.

Blomstrom, M. 1990. *Transnational Corporations and Manufacturing Exports from Developing Countries*. New York: United Nations.

Bollen, Kenneth A. 1980. Issues in the Comparative Measurement of Political Democracy. *American Sociological Review* 45:370–90.

Bollen, Kenneth A., Robert W. Jackman. 1989. Democracy, Stability, and Dichotomies. *American Sociological Review* 54(4):612–21.

Bolukbasi, Suha. 2004. Jockeying for Power in the Caspian Basin: Turkey versus Iran and Russia. In *The Caspian: Politics, Energy and Security*, eds. S. Akiner and A. Aldis, 219–29. New York: Routledge.

Borenzstein E.J., De Gregorio, J.W. Lee. 1998. How Does Foreign Direct Investment Affect Economic Growth? *Journal of International Economics* 45:115–35.

Bouckaert, Peter. 2003. Azerbaijan: A Stolen Election and Oil Stability. *Human Rights Watch* (October 20). Available at http://hrw.org/english/docs/2003/10/20/azerba12934_txt.htm. (Accessed February 27, 2007).

2004. Crushing Dissent: Repression, Violence and Azerbaijan's Elections. *Human Rights Watch*. 16:1(January). Available at http://hrw.org/reports/2004/azerbaijan0104/.

Bradshaw, Michael. 2004. Foreign Investment in the Russian Oil and Gas Industry: Lessons from Sakhalin. In *Proceedings of the 2nd International Conference on Globalisation in Russia's Regions: The Regional Dynamics of Northeast Asia and Russia's Globalisation in the 21st Century*. Seoul, Korea: Hankuk University of Foreign Studies.

Bremmer, I. 1998. Oil Politics: America and the Riches of the Caspian Basin. *World Policy Journal* 15(1):27–36.

Brewer, Thomas. 1991. *Foreign Direct Investment in Developing Countries: Patterns, Policies, and Prospects*. Washington, DC: World Bank, International Economics Department.

1992. An Issue Area Approach to the Analysis of MNE-Government Relations. *Journal of International Business Studies* 23:295–309.

British Petroleum (BP) Global. 2001. Statistical Review of World Energy. Available at http://www.bp.com.

2006. Statistical Review of World Energy. Available at http://www.bp.com.

2007. Statistical Review of World Energy. Available at http://www.bp.com.

Brown, Archie. 2001. Evaluating Russia's Democracy. In *Contemporary Russian Politics*, ed. Archie Brown, 546–68. New York: Oxford University Press.

Buccellato, Tullio, Tomasz Mickiewicz. 2009. Oil and Gas: A Blessing for the Few: Hydrocarbons and Inequality Within Region in Russia. *Europe-Asia Studies* 61(3):385–407.

Buchanan, James M., Robert D. Tollison, Gordon Tullock, eds. 1980. *Toward a Theory of the Rent-Seeking Society.* College Station: Texas A & M University Press.

Buckley, Peter J., Mark Casson. 1976. *The Future of the Multinational Enterpise.* London: Macmillan, UK; and Holmes & Meir, USA.

Business Information Services for the Newly Independent States (BISNIS). *Azerbaijan: Commercial Guide 2000.* Available at http://www.bisnis.doc. gov/bisnis/country/azerbaijan.

Busse, Matthias. 2003. Democracy and FDI. *HWWA Discussion Paper* 220. Hamburg Institute of International Economics.

Busse, Matthias, Carsten Hefeker. 2005. Political Risk, Institutions and Foreign Direct Investment. *HWWA Discussion Paper* 315. Hamburg Institute of International Economics.

Cammack, Paul. 1998. Globalization and the Death of Liberal Democracy. *European Review* 6:249–63.

Canzi, Germana. 1999. One Step Forward, Two Steps Back. *Project Finance* 193:26–7.

Cardoso, E., R. Dornbusch. 1989. Foreign Private Capital Flows. In *Handbook of Development Economics*, eds. Hollis Chenery and T.N. Srinivasan, 2:1387–439. Amsterdam: Elsevier.

Cardoso, Fernando Henrique. 1973. Associated-Dependent Development: Theoretical and Practical Implications. In *Authoritarian Brazil: Origins, Policies, and Future*, ed. Alfred Stepan, 142–78. New Haven, CT: Yale University Press.

Carkovic, M., R. Levine. 2002. Does Foreign Direct Investment Accelerate Economic Growth? *Working Paper Series National Bureau of Economic Research* (NBER) (June).

Carothers, Thomas. 2002. The End of the Transition Paradigm. *Journal of Democracy* 13(2):5–21.

Cattan, Henry. 1967. *The Evolution of Oil Concessions in the Middle East and North Africa.* New York: Dobbs Ferry.

Cavenagh, Andrew. 2006. Putin Blows Out Foreign Oil Companies: What Will the Changed Climate Mean for Future Oil and Gas Investments in Russia and Elsewhere? *Acquisitions Monthly* 262(August):18–21.

Caves, R. 1974. Multinational Firm, Competition and Productivity in Host-Country Markets. *Economica* 41(162):176–93.

Center for Global Development. 2006. *Commitment to Development Index Country Report: Norway.* Available at http://www.cgdev.org.

Central and Eastern Europe (CEE) Bankwatch Network. 2002. Pocketing Caspian Black Gold: Who Are the Real Beneficiaries of Oil Infrastructure Development in Georgia and Azerbaijan? *NGO Study.* (April). Available at http://www.bankwatch.org (Accessed September 13, 2004).

Chaisty, Paul. 2001. Legislative Politics in Russia. In *Contemporary Russian Politics*, ed. Archie Brown, 103–20. New York: Oxford University Press.

2007. The Influence of Sectoral and Regional Economic Interests on Russian Legislative Behavior: The Case of State Duma Voting on Production Sharing Agreements Legislation. *Post-Soviet Affairs* 23(4):302–28.

Chan, Steve, Melanie Mason. 1992. "Foreign Direct Investment and Host Country Conditions: Looking from the Other Side Now." *International Interactions* 17(3):215–32.

Chaudry, Kiren. 1997. *The Price of Wealth: Economies and Institutions in the Middle East.* Ithaca: Cornell University Press.

Chervyakov, Vladimir, Vladimir Berezovskii. 1996. Sectoral Production Capital: Military Industrial Complex and Fuel Complex. In *Post-Soviet Puzzles,* eds. Klaus Segbergs and Stephan De Spiegeleire, chapter 14. Baden: Nomos.

Chivers, C.J. 2005. Energy-rich Azerbaijan Bubbles with Intrigue. *The New York Times,* October 30.

Clague, Christopher Philip Keefer, Stephen Knack, Mancur Olson. 1996. Property and Contract Rights in Autocracies and Democracies. *Journal of Economic Growth* 1(2):243–76.

Cohen, M. 2006. The Effect of Oil Revenues on Transition Economics: The Case of Azerbaijan. *Geopolitics of Energy* 28(6):12–20.

Collander, David, ed. 1984. *Neoclassical Political Economy: An Analysis of Rent-Seeking and DUP Activities.* Cambridge, MA.: Ballinger.

Collier, David, Steven Levitsky. 1997. Democracy with Adjectives: Conceptual Innovation in Comparative Research. *World Politics* 49(April):430–51.

Collier, P., A. Hoeffler. 1998. On Economic Causes of Civil War. *Oxford Economic Papers* 50(14):563–73.

2005. Resource Rents, Governance, and Conflict. *Journal of Conflict Resolution* 49(4):625–33.

Commission of the European Communities. 2005. European Neighborhood Policy, Country Report: Azerbaijan. Available at http://ec.europa.eu/world/enp/documents_En.htm.

Cooper, William H. 2008. *Russia's Economic Performance and Policies and Their Implications for the United States.* CRS Report for Congress. RL34512. Washington, DC: Congressional Research Service.

Corden, M. Wax, J. Peter Neary. 1982. Booming Sector and De-Industrialization in a Small Open Economy. *The Economic Journal* 92(December):825–48.

Cornell, Svante E. 2001. Democratization Falters in Azerbaijan. *Journal of Democracy* 12(2):118–31.

Cornell, Svante E., Fariz Ismailzade. 2005. The Baku-Tblisi-Ceyhan Pipeline: Implications for Azerbaijan. In *The Baku-Tblisi-Ceyhan Pipeline: Oil Window to the West,* eds. S. Frederick Starr and Svante E. Cornell. Uppsala: Uppsala University.

Cox, R.W. 1996. Globalization, Multilateralism, and Democracy. In *Approaches to World Order,* eds. R.W. Cox and T.J. Sinclair, 524–36. New York: Cambridge University Press.

Crenshaw, Edward. 1991. Foreign Investment as a Dependent Variable: Determinants of Foreign Investment and Capital Penetration in Developing Nations, 1967–1978. *Social Forces* 69(5):766–82.

Cummings, Sally N. 2000. *Kazakhstan: Center-Periphery Relations.* Brookings Institution and Royal Institute of International Affairs.

2005. *Kazakhstan: Power and the Elite*. London: IB Taurin.

Dalmazzo, A., G. de Blasio. 2001. Resources and Incentives to Reform: A Model and Some Evidence on Sub-Saharan African Countries. *IMF Working Paper* No.01/86. Available at http://www.imf.org/external/pubs/ft/wp/2001/wp0186.pdf. (Accessed January 29, 2007).

Dam, Kenneth. 1976. *Oil Resources: Who Gets What, How?* Chicago, IL: University of Chicago Press.

Danilova, Maria. 2007. Despite Oil Wealth, Russia Faces Huge Health Care Problems. *International Herald Tribune* (June 28).

De Beer, Shane, Aydine Jebrailov. 1997. Production Sharing Agreements in Russia. *East European Business Law* (November)11:6–8.

De Soysa, Indra. 2000. The Resource Curse: Are Civil Wars Driven by Rapacity of Paucity? In *Greed and Grievance: Economic Agendas in Civil Wars*, eds. Mats Berdal and David Malone. Boulder, CO: Lynne Rienner.

2003. *Foreign Direct Investment, Democracy, and Development: Assessing Contours, Correlates and Concomitants of Globalization*. London: Routledge.

Delacroix, Jacques. 1980. The Distributive State in the World System. *Studies in Comparative International Development* 15:3–21.

Dellecker, Adrian. 2008. Caspian Pipeline Consortium, Bellwether of Russia's Investment Climate? *Russie. Nei. Visions* No. 31. Paris: IFRI Russia/NIS Center. Available at http://www.ifri.org.

Deloitte: World Tax Advisor. 2006. Taxation of Production Sharing Agreements in the CIS. (February). Available at http://www.deloitte.com/dtt/cda/doc/content/dtt_tax_wta_060206.pdf.

Diamond, Larry. 1999. *Developing Democracy: Toward Consolidation*. Baltimore, MD: Johns Hopkins University Press.

2002. Thinking About Hybrid Regimes. *Journal of Democracy* 13(2):21–35.

Dienes, Leslie. 1993. Prospects for Russian Oil in the 1990s: Reserves and Costs. *Post-Soviet Geography* 34(2):79–110.

2004. Observations on the Problematic Potential of Russian Oil and the Complexities of Siberia. *Eurasian Geography and Economics* 45(5):319–45.

Djankov, S., B. Hoekman. 1999. Foreign Investment and Productivity Growth in Czech Enterprises. *World Bank Economic Review* 14:49–64.

Dunning, John H. 1993. *Multinational Enterprises and the Global Economy*. Reading, MA: Addison-Wesley.

Durham, Benson J. 2004. Absorptive Capacity and the Effects of Foreign Direct Investment and Equity Foreign Portfolio Investment on Economic Growth. *European Economic Review* 48(2):285–306.

Dyker, David, ed. 1995. *Investment Opportunities in Russia and the CIS*. The Royal Institute of International Affairs.

Ebel, Robert E. 1997. Geopolitics and Pipelines. *Analysis of Current Events* 9:2.

2003. Projecting the Invasion Impact. *Washington Times*, April 22.

Eckstein, Harry. 1966. *Division and Cohesion in Democracy: A Study of Norway*. Princeton, NJ: Princeton University Press.

Economist Intelligence Unit. 2002. Country Report: Azerbaijan (May) Economist Intelligence Unit, London.

Eifert, Benn, Alan Gelb, Nils Borje Tallroth. 2002. The Political Economy of Fiscal Policy and Economic Management in Oil Exporting Countries. *Policy Research Working Paper 2899*. (August) Washington, DC: World Bank.

Elder, Miriam. 2008. How the State Got a Grip on Energy. *Moscow Times*, March 14.

Elder, Neil, Alastair H. Thomas, David Arter. 1988. *The Consensual Democracies? The Government and Politics of the Scandinavian States*. Oxford: Blackwell Publishers.

Ernst and Young. 1999. *The Investment Climate in Russia*. Ernst and Young (CIS).

Esanov, A., M. Raiser, W. Buiter. 2001. Nature's Blessing or Nature's Curse: the Political Economy of Transition in Resource-Based Economies. *European Bank for Reconstruction and Development (EBRD) Working Paper* No.65. Available at http://www.ebrd.com/pubs/econo/wp0066.pdf.

Eskin, Vadim, John Webb. 1999. Russian Oil Companies in the New Time of Troubles. *CERA Private Report* (January).

European Bank for Reconstruction, and Development. 1998. *Transition Report: Financial Sector in Transition* (November). Available at http://www.ebrd.com/pubs/econo/3542.htm.

Evans, Peter. 1979. *Dependent Development: The Alliance of Multinational, State, and Local Capital in Brazil*. Princeton, NJ: Princeton University Press.

Fallon, G., R. Golov, A. Jones. 2000. Obstacles to Foreign Direct Investment in Russia. *European Business Review* 12(4):187–97.

Feifer, G. 2002. Caspian: Russia, Azerbaijan Sign Agreement on Sea Boundaries. *Radio Free Europe/ Radio Liberty* (RFE/RL) (24 September). Available at http://www.rferl.org/features/2002/09/24092002152937.asp (Accessed September 13, 2004).

Fish, M. Steven. 2001a. Putin's Path. *Journal of Democracy* 12(4):71–78.

2001b. Conclusion: Democracy and Russian Politics. In *Russian Politics*, eds. Zoltan Barany and Robert G. Moser, 215–52. Cambridge: Cambridge University Press.

2005. *Democracy Derailed in Russia: The Failure of Open Politics*. New York: Cambridge University Press.

Foreign Investment Advisory Service (FIAS). 2002. Azerbaijan: Joining the Race for Non-Oil Investment. A Diagnostic Review of the Environment for FDI. (May). Washington, DC: World Bank.

Forsythe, Rosemarie. 1996. *The Politics of Oil in the Caucasus and Central Asia: Prospects for Oil Exploration and Export in the Caspian Basin*. London: International Institute for Strategic Studies.

Fortescue, Stephen. 2006. *Russia's Oil Barons and Metal Magnates: Oligarchs and the State in Transition*. New York: Palgrave Macmillan.

Fossum, John Erik. 1997. *Oil, the State, and Federalism: The Rise and Demise of Petro-Canada as a Statist Impulse*. Toronto: University of Toronto Press.

Fredrik, Engelstad, Trygve Gulbrandsen, Oyvind Osterud. 1999. Elite Compromises in a Stable Democracy: The case of Norway. Paper presented at the Annual Meeting of the American Political Science Association, September 1–5, in Atlanta.

Freedom House. 2003. *Nations in Transit–Azerbaijan*. Available at http://unpan1.un.org/intradoc/groups/public/documents/NISPAcee/UNPAN012372.pdf.

Freizer, Sabine. 2003. Dynasty and Democracy in Azerbaijan: A Warning for Central Asia? *Open Democracy*. (8 December). Available at http://www.opendemocracy.net.

Frieden, J.A., R. Rogowski. 1996. The Impact of the International Economy on National Policies: An Analytical Overview. In *Internationalization and Domestic Politics*, eds. R.O. Keohane and H.V. Milner, 25–47. Cambridge: Cambridge University Press.

Frynas, Jedrzej George. 1998. Political Instability and Business: Focus on Shell in Nigeria. *Third World Quarterly* 19:3:457–78.

Gaddy, C.G. 2004. Perspectives on the Potential of Russian Oil. *Eurasian Geography and Economics* 45:5(July–August).

Galenson, Walter. 1986. *A Welfare State Strikes Back*. University Press of America.

Geddes, Barbara. 1995. Challenging the Conventional Wisdom. In *Economic Reform and Democracy*, eds. Larry Diamond and Marc F. Plattner, 59–73. Baltimore, MD: Johns Hopkins University Press.

Gelb, Alan. 1986. Adjustments to Windfall Gains: A Comparative Analysis of Oil-Exporting Countries. In *Natural Resources and the Macroeconomy*, eds. J. Peter Neary and Sweder Van Wijnbergen, 54–95. Cambridge, MA: MIT Press.

   1988. *Oil Windfalls: Blessing or Curse?* New York: Oxford University Press, for the World Bank.

Gill, Stephen. 1995. Globalization, Market Civilization, and Disciplinary Neoliberalism. *Journal of International Studies* 24:399–423.

Gillis, M., D.H. Perkins, M. Romer, D.R. Snodgrass. 1996. *Economics of Development*. New York: W.W. Norton & Company.

Global Insight. 2006. *Azerbaijan: Current Situation and Highlights*. (27 April). Available at http://www.globalinsight.com. (Accessed January 29, 2007).

Goble, Paul A. 1995. Pipelines and Pipedreams: The Geopolitics of the Transcaucasus. *Caspian Crossroads*, No.1.

Goldberg, Jeffrey. 1998. The Crude Face of Global Capitalism. *The New York Times Magazine*, October 4.

Graham, E.M. 1978. Transatlantic Investment by Multinational Firms: a Rivalistic Phenomenon? *Journal of Post-Keynesian Economics* 1(1):82–99.

Gulbrandsen, Lars H., Arild Moe. 2007. BP in Azerbaijan: A Test Case of the Potential and Limits of the CSR Agenda? *Third World Quarterly* 28(4):813–30.

Guliyev, Farid. 2005. Post-Soviet Azerbaijan: Transition to Sultanistic Semiauthoritarianism? An Attempt at Conceptualization. *Demokratizatsiya*. 13(3):449–62.

Gustafson, Thane. 1991. *Crisis Amidst Plenty: The Politics of Soviet Energy Under Brezhnev and Gorbachev*. Princeton, NJ: Princeton University Press.

   1999. *Capitalism Russian-Style*. Cambridge: Cambridge University Press.

Gyetvay, Mark. 2000. Restructuring, Consolidating Top Solutions for Russia's Major Oil Companies' Woes. *Oil and Gas Journal* 98:11.

Gylfason, Thorvaldur. 2004. Natural Resources and Economic Growth: From Dependence to Diversification. *Center for Economic Policy Research* Discussion Paper No. 4804. Available at http://www.cepr.org.

Haggard, Stephan. 1990. *Pathways from the Periphery: The Politics of Growth in the Newly Industrializing Countries*. Ithaca, NY: Cornell University Press.

Haggard, Stephan, Robert R. Kaufman. 1995. *The Political Economy of Democratic Transitions.* Princeton, NJ: Princeton University Press.

Hanson, Philip. 2005. Observations on the Costs of the Yukos Affair to Russia. *Eurasian Geography and Economics* 46(7):481–94.

2009. The Resistible Rise of State Control in the Russian Oil Industry. *Eurasian Geography and Economics* 50(1):14–27.

Harms, Philipp, Heinrich Ursprung. 2002. Do Civil and Political Repression Really Boost Foreign Direct Investment? *Economic Inquiry* 40(4):651–663.

Heidar, Knut. 2001. *Norway: Elites on Trial.* Boulder, CO: Westview Press.

Heinrich, Andreas, Julia Kusznir, Heiko Pleines. 2002. Foreign Investment and National Interests in the Russian Oil and Gas Industry. *Post-Communist Economies* 14(4):495–507.

Held, David. 1992. Democracy: From City States to a Cosmopolitan Order? *Political Studies* 40.

Helliwell, John. 1994. Empirical Linkages Between Democracy and Economic Growth. *British Journal of Political Science* 24:225–48.

Hellman, J., M. Schankerman. 2000. Intervention, Corruption and Capture: the Nexus Between Enterprises and the State. *EBRD Working Paper* 58. Available at http://www.ebrd.com/pubs/econo/wp0058.pdf. (Accessed March 3, 2004).

Henisz, Witold J. 2000. The Institutional Environment for Multinational Investment. *Journal of Law, Economics and Organization* 16(2):334–64.

Henry, Clement. 1996. *The Mediterranean Debt Crescent: Money and Power in Algeria, Egypt, Morocco, Tunisia, and Turkey.* Gainesville, FL: University of Florida Press.

1998. The Financial Arms of Industrial and Political Activity. Paper presented at International Conference "Role of Business Sector in Economic and Political Change," August 30–September 2, Tunis.

Heradstveit, Daniel. 2000. Elite Perceptions of Ethical Problems Facing the Western Oil Industry in Azerbaijan. *Norwegian Institute of International Affairs (NUPI) Report* 256. Oslo: Norsk Utenrikspolitisk Institutt.

Hermes, Niels, Robert Lensink. 2003. Foreign direct investment, financial development and economic growth. *Journal of Development Studies* 40(1):142–63.

Herzig, Edmund. 1999. *The New Caucasus: Armenia, Azerbaijan, and Georgia.* The Royal Institute of International Affairs.

Heslin, Sheila N. 1998. Key Constraints to Caspian Pipeline Development: Status, Significance, and Outlook. *Unlocking the Assets: Energy and the Future of Central Asia and the Caucasus: Working Papers.* James A. Baker III Institute for Public Policy of Rice University.

Higley, John, G. Lowell Field, Knut Groholt. 1976. *Elite Structure and Ideology: A Theory with Applications to Norway.* New York: Columbia University Press.

Higley, John, Karl Erik Brofoss, Knut Groholt. 1975. Top Civil Servants and the National Budget in Norway. In *The Mandarins of Western Europe: The Political Role of Top Civil Servants*, ed. Mattei Dogan, 252–74. New York and London: Wiley, Halsted Press.

Hines, Jonathan, Dmitri V. Nikiforov. 1999. Russia Improves its PSA Regime: A Thumbnail Analysis. *Journal of Energy and Natural Resources Law* 17:2.

Hirschman, Albert O. 1978. Exit, Voice, and the State. *World Politics* 31(October):90–107.

Hober, Kaj. 1997. The Russian Law on Production Sharing Agreements. *East/ West Executive Guide* (April).

Hoffman, David I. 2000. Azerbaijan: The Politicization of Oil. In *Energy and Conflict in Central Asia and the Caucasus*, eds. Robert Ebel and Rajan Menon, 55–79. Rowman & Littlefield Publishers.

Holsen, John A. 2003. *Macroeconomic Developments and Poverty*. A background paper prepared for Azerbaijan Republic Poverty Assessment. World Bank.

Hoyos, Carole. 2006. Russia's Mixed Message Threatens Oil Investment. *Financial Times*, September 26.

Huger, Katherine. 1976. North Sea Oil Development Policy: A Case Study of the Government- Industry Relationship in Norway and the United Kingdom. *Fletcher Forum* 1(Autumn):49–135.

Hughes, Helen. 1975. Economic Rents, the Distribution of Gains from Mineral Exploitation and Mineral Development Policy. *World Development* 3.

Huntington, Samuel P. 1968. *Political Order in Changing Societies*. New Haven, CT: Yale University Press.

Huskey, Eugene. 2001. Democracy and Institutional Design. In *Contemporary Russian Politics*, ed. Archie Brown, 29–48. New York: Oxford University Press.

Hymer, S.H. 1960. *The International Operations of National Firms: A Study of Direct Foreign Investment*. Cambridge: MIT Press.

International Bank for Reconstruction, and Development (IBRD). 2006. *Country Partnership Strategy FY07–10 for Republic of Azerbaijan*. Report No 37812-AZ. Available at http://siteresources.worldbank.org/ INTAZERBAIJAN/Resources/AzerbaijanCountryPartnershipStrategy.doc (Accessed January 10, 2007).

International Crisis Group. 2008. Azerbaijan: Defense Sector Management and Reform. Policy Briefing No 50 (29 October). Available at http://www. crisisgroup.org (Accessed May 10, 2009).

International Development Association (IDA). 2005. *Program Document for a Proposed Poverty Reduction Support Credit to the Republic of Azerbaijan*. Report No. 31978-AZ. Available at http://www-wds.worldbank.org/external/ default/WDSContentServer/WDSP/IB/2005/06/15/000012009_20050615160 136/Rendered/PDF/31978orev.pdf (Accessed January 10, 2007).

International Energy Agency. 2001. *Energy Policies of IEA Countries: Norway 2001 Review*. Available at http://www.iea.org.

  2003. *World Energy Investment Outlook 2003*. Available at http://www.iea. org.

  2005. *Energy Policies of IEA Countries: Norway 2005 Review*. Available at http://www.iea.org.

International Market Research. 2004. *Country Commercial Guide Norway, Investment Climate Statement*. Available at http://strategis.ic.gc.ca/epic/site/ imr-ri.nsf/en/gr126269e.html.

International Trade Administration. 2001. Oil and Gas Services Update: Norway. *International Market Insight* (June 21).

References253

Jackman, Robert W. 1974. Political Democracy and Social Equality. *American Sociological Review* 39:29–45.

1982. Dependence on Foreign Investment and Economic Growth in the Third World. *World Politics* 34(2):175–96.

Jakobsen, Jo, Indra De Soysa. 2006. Do Foreign Investors Punish Democracy? Theory and Empirics, 1984–2001. *Kyklos* 59(3):383–410.

Janeba, Eckhard. 2002. Attracting FDI in a Politically Risky World. *International Economic Review* 43(4):1127–55.

Jensen, Nathan M. 2003. Democratic Governance and Multinational Corporations: Political Regimes and Inflows of Foreign Direct Investment. *International Organization* 57:587–616.

2006. *Nation-States and the Multinational Corporation.* Princeton, NJ: Princeton University Press.

Jensen, Nathan M., Leonard Wantchekon. 2004. Resource Wealth and Political Regimes in Africa. *Comparative Political Studies* 37(7):816–41.

Jessup, David. 1999. *Dollars and Democracy.* New Economy Information Service. Online. Available at www.newecon.org.

Johnston, Daniel. 1994. *International Petroleum Fiscal Systems and Production Sharing Contracts.* Tulsa, OK: Pennwell Publishing.

Jun, Kwang W., Harinder Singh. 1996. The Determinants of Foreign Direct Investment in Developing Countries. *Transnational Corporations* 5(2):67–105.

Kahn, Jeff. 2001. What is the New Russian Federalism? In *Contemporary Russian Politics*, ed. Archie Brown, 374–84. New York: Oxford University Press.

Kaiser, Mark J., Allan G. Pulsipher. 2007. A Review of the Oil and Gas Sector in Kazakhstan. *Energy Policy* 35:1300–14.

Karl, Terry Lynn. 1990. Dilemmas of Democratization in Latin America. *Comparative Politics* 23(October):1–21.

1997. *The Paradox of Plenty: Oil Booms and Petro-States.* Berkeley, CA: University of California Press.

2007. Oil-Led Development: Social, Political and Economic Consequences. *CDDRL Working Paper.* Stanford University. Available at http://cddrl.stanford.edu/publications/oilled_development_social_political_and_Economic_consequences/.

Katzenstein, Peter J. 1985. *Small States in World Markets: Industrial Policy in Europe.* Ithaca, NY: Cornell University Press.

Kennedy, Craig. 1995. Dream Law or Deal Killer? Russian PSA Legislation. *Cambridge Energy Research Association (CERA) Private Report* (June).

Kindleberger, Charles. 1951. Group Behavior and International Trade. *Journal of Political Economy* 59(February):30–46.

1969. *American Business Abroad.* New Haven, CT: Yale University Press.

Kitchelt, Herbert. 2000. Linkages Between Citizens and Politicians in Democratic Polities. *Comparative Political Studies* 33(6/7):845–79.

Klapp, Merrie Gilbert. 1987. *The Sovereign Entrepreneur: Oil Policies in Advanced and Less Developed Capitalist Countries.* Ithaca, NY: Cornell University Press.

Kobrin, Stephen J. 1979. Political Risk: A Review and Reconsideration. *Journal of International Business Studies* 10:67–80.

1982. *Managing Political Risk Assessment*. Berkeley, CA: University of California Press.

1984. Expropriation as an Attempt to Control Foreign Firms in LDCs: Trends from 1960–1979. *International Studies Quarterly* 28(3):329–48.

Konoplyanik, Andrei A., Nikolai N. Lisovsky. 1992. Russia Aims for Favorable Climate for Joint Ventures. *Oil and Gas Journal* (10 August):19–21.

Kramer, Andrew E. 2008. Awash in Oil Income, Russia Forms Wealth Fund. *The New York Times* (February 1).

Krueger, Anne O. 1974. The Political Economy of Rent-seeking Society. *American Economic Review* 64:291–303.

Kurbanov, E., B. Sanders. 1998. Caspian Sea Oil Riches: A Mixed Blessing. *Occasional Paper in the Center for International Development and Conflict Management Monograph Series*. Available at http://www.geocities.com/CapitolHill/Senate/5521/caspoil.htm (Accessed September 23, 2004).

Kurtz, Marcus. 2004. The Dilemmas of Democracy in the Open Economy. *World Politics* 56(January):262–302.

Landler, Mark. 2007. Norway Keeps Nest Egg from Some U.S. Companies. *The New York Times*, May 4.

Lane, David ed. 1999. *The Political Economy of Russian Oil*. New York: Rowman & Littlefield Publishers.

Larsen, Erling Roed. 2005. Are Rich Countries Immune to the Resource Curse? Evidence from Norway's Management of Its Oil Riches. *Resources Policy* 30:75–86.

Lash, Elizabeth, Elizabeth Remick. 2002. *Azerbaijan and Corruption*. Sommerville: Tufts University. Available at http://www.transparency-az.org.

Latynina, Yulia. 2000. New Investments in Federation Council. *The Moscow Times*, August 2.

Lavelle, Peter. 2005. Analysis: The Kremlin's Majority Share. *UPI- United Press International* (February 11).

Lehmbruch, Gerhard. 1982. Introduction; Neo-corporatism in Comparative Perspective. In *Patterns of Corporatist Policy-Making*, eds. Gerhard Lehmbruch and Phillippe Schmitter, 22–23. London: Sage Publications.

Leif, K. Ervik. 1987. The 1986 Petroleum Tax Regime. *The Offshore Digest* 3.

Leite, Carlos, Jens Weidmann. 1999. Does Mother Nature Corrupt? Natural Resources, Corruption, and Economic Growth. *IMF Working Paper 99/85*. Washington: International Monetary Fund.

Lelyveld, M. 2002. Caspian: A Delicate Balance Prevails. *Johnson's Russia List* (July 17) Available at http://www.cdi.org/russia/johnson/6357-6.cfm (Accessed September 13, 2004).

Levis, Mario. 1979. Does Political Instability in Developing Countries Affect Foreign Investment Flow? *Management International Review* 19(3):59–68.

Levitsky, Steven, Lucan A. Way. 2002. The Rise of Competitive Authoritarianism. *Journal of Democracy* 13:2(2002):51–65.

Levy, Brian, Pablo T. Spiller. 1996. *Regulations, Institutions, and Commitment: Comparative Studies of Telecommunications*. New York: Cambridge University Press.

Li, Quan. 2006. Democracy, Autocracy, and Tax Incentives to Foreign Direct Investors: A Cross-National Analysis. *Journal of Politics* 68(1):62–74.

Li, Quan, Adam Resnick. 2003. Reversal of Fortunes: Democratic Institutions and Foreign Direct Investment Inflows to Developing Countries. *International Organization* 57(1):175–211.

Lieven, Anatol. 2000. Post Communist Sultans on the Caspian. *Eurasianet*. Available at http://www.eurasianet.org/departments/culture/articles/eav110800.shtml.

Lind, T., G.A. Mackay. 1979. *Norwegian Oil Policies*. Montreal: McGill–Queen's University Press.

Lindblom, Charles. 1982. The Market as Prison. *Journal of Democracy* 44(2):324–36.

Linz, Juan J. 2000. *Totalitarian and Authoritarian Regimes*. Boulder, CO: Lynne Rienner.

Linz, Juan J., Alfred Stepan. 1996. *Problems of Democratic Transition and Consolidation: Southern Europe, South America and Eastern Europe*. Baltimore, MD: Johns Hopkins University Press.

Lipset, S.M. 1994. The Social Requisites of Democracy Revisited. *American Sociological Review* 59:2–13.

Listhaug, Ola. 2005. Oil Wealth Dissatisfactions and Political Trust in Norway: A Resource Curse? *West European Politics* 28(4):934–51.

Lobe, Jim. 2003. Washington Trades Human Rights for Oil in Azerbaijan. *OneWorld. Net* (January 23). Available at http://us.oneworld.net/article/view/77470/1/.

Locatelli, Catherine. 2006. The Russian Oil Industry between Public and Private Governance: Obstacles to International Oil Companies' Investment Strategies. *Energy Policy* 34:1075–85.

Loriaux, Michael. 1997. *Capital Ungoverned: Liberalizing Finance in Interventionist States*, eds. Meredith Woo-Cumings, Kent Calder, Sylvia Maxfield, and Sofia Perez. Ithaca, NY: Cornell University Press.

Luong, Pauline Jones, Erika, Weinthal. 2001. Prelude to the Resource Curse: Explaining Energy Development Strategies in the Soviet Successor States and Beyond. *Comparative Political Studies* 34(4):367–99.

Magdoff, Harry. 1978. *Imperialism: From the Colonial Age to the Present*. New York: Monthly Review Press.

Mahdavy, H. 1970. The Patterns and Problems of Economic Development in Rentier States. In *Studies in the Economic History of the Middle East*, ed. M.A. Cook, 37–61. London: Oxford University Press.

Mahon Jr., James E. 1995. *Mobile Capital and Latin American Development*. University Park, PA: The Pennsylvania State University Press.

Mamed-zadeh, Ilham. 2001. Authoritarian Regime in Azerbaijan and its Transformation Potentials. *Central Asia and Caucasus* 3(9):104–14.

Manning, R.A. 2000. The Myth of the Caspian Great Game and the New Persian Gulf. *Brown Journal of World Affairs* 7(2):15–33.

Markusen, James R. 1995. The Boundaries of Multinational Enterprises and the Theory of International Trade. *Journal of Economic Perspectives* 9(2):169–89.

Marshall, Monty G., Keith Jaggers. 2004. Polity IV Data Set. [Computer file; version p4v2004] College Park, MD: Center for International Development and Conflict Management, University of Maryland.

Martin, Hans-Peter, Harald Schumann. 1997. *The Global Trap*. St. Martin's Press.

Maxfield, Slyvia. 1997. *Gatekeepers of Growth: The International Political Economy of Central Banking in Developing Countries*. Princeton, NJ: Princeton University Press.

McFaul, Michael. 2001. *Russia's Unfinished Revolution: Political Change from Gorbachev to Putin*. Ithaca, NY: Cornell University Press.

2002. The Fourth Wave of Democracy and Dictatorship. *World Politics* 54(2):212–44.

Mescherin, Andrei. 2000. Duma prepares Amendments to Complete Work on PSA Legislation. *Russia/Central European Executive Guide* (August 15):10–13.

Mikesell, Raymond F. 1971. Conflict in Foreign Investor-Host Country Relations: A Preliminary Analysis. In *Foreign Investment in the Petroleum and Mineral Industries*, ed. Mikesell, 29–55. Baltimore, MD: Johns Hopkins University Press.

1997. Explaining the Resource Curse, with Special Reference to Mineral-Exporting Countries. *Resources Policy* 23(4):191–99.

Moran, Theodore. 1974. *The Evolution of Concession Agreements in Underdeveloped Countries and the United States National Interest*. Washington, DC: Brookings Institution.

Moser, Robert G. 2001. Executive-Legislative Relations in Russia, 1991–1999. In *Russian Politics*, eds. Zoltan Barany and Robert G. Moser, 64–102. Cambridge: Cambridge University Press.

Muller, E.N. 1988. Democracy, Economic Development, and Income Inequality. *American Sociological Review* 53:50–68.

1995. Economic determinants of democracy. *American Sociological Review* 60:966–82.

Myers, Steven Lee. 2005. Pervasive Corruption in Russia is Just Called Business. *The New York Times* (August 13).

Nanay, Julia. 1998. Azerbaijan's Offshore Oil Consortia. *USACC Investment Guide to Azerbaijan*. Washington, DC: US-Azerbaijan Chamber of Commerce.

Narula, Rajneesh, Brian Portelli. 2004. Foreign Direct Investment and Economic Development: Opportunities and Limitations from a Developing Country Perspective. MERIT Infonomics Research Memorandum Series 2004–2009. Available at http://www.merit.unimass.nl.

Nassibli, Nasib. 1999. Azerbaijan: Oil and Politics in the Country's Future. In *Oil and Geopolitics in the Caspian Sea Region*, eds. Michael Croissant and Bulent Aras, 101–29. Westport, CT.: Praeger Publishers.

Nelsen, Brent F. 1991. *The State Offshore: Petroleum, Politics, and State Intervention on the British and Norwegian Continental Shelves*. New York: Praeger Publishers.

Nelson, David R. 1996. Russia's Production Sharing Law-A Foundation for Progress. *Oil & Gas Journal* 94(5):106–08.

Nichol, Jim. 2008. Azerbaijan's October 2008 Presidential Election's Outcome and Implications. CRS Report for Congress, October 27.

Noreng, Oystein. 1980. *The Oil Industry and Government Strategy in the North Sea*. Boulder, CO: International Research Center for Energy and Economic Development.

1986. Energy Policy and Prospects in Norway. *Annual Reviews* 11:393–415.

North, Douglas C., Barry R. Weingast. 1989. Constitutions and Commitment: The Evolution of Institutions Governing Public Choice in Seventeenth-Century England. *Journal of Economic History* 49(4):803–32.

Norwegian Agency for Development Cooperation (Norad). 2006. Norwegian Oil for Development Initiative: Factsheet. Available at http://www.norad.no/ petroleum.

Norwegian Ministry of Finance. 1973–1974. *Report to the Storting* No.25.

Norwegian Ministry of Petroleum and Energy. 2000–2001. Ownership of Statoil and Future Management of the SDFI. *Storting Proposition* 36.

Norwegian Ministry of Petroleum and Energy and Petroleum Directorate. 2007. Facts: The Norwegian Petroleum Sector 2007. Available at http://www. npd.no.

O'Donnell, Guillermo. 1973. *Modernization and Bureaucratic-Authoritarianism.* Berkeley, CA: Institute for International Studies.

1993. On the State, Democratization and Some Conceptual Problems: A Latin American View with Glances at Some Postcommunist Countries. *World Development* 21(8):1355–69.

1994. Delegative Democracy. *Journal of Democracy* 5(January):55–69.

O'Donnell, Guillermo, Phillippe Schmitter, Laurence Whitehead, eds. 1986. *Transitions from Authoritarian Rule: Prospects for Democracy.* Baltimore, MD: Johns Hopkins University Press.

O'Lear, Shannon. 2007. Azerbaijan's Resource Wealth: Political Legitimacy and Public Opinion. *The Geographical Journal* 173(3):207–23.

O'Neal, John R. 1994. The Affinity of Foreign Investors for Authoritarian Regimes. *Political Research Quarterly* 47(3):565–88.

Obut, Tina. 1999. Roots of Systemic Woes in Russian Oil Sector Traceable to Industry's Evolution. *Oil & Gas Journal* 97(4)(January 25).

Ogan, Sinan. 1993. Baku Petrolleri. *Yeni Forum* 9.

Ogutcu, Mehmet. 2002. Attracting Foreign Direct Investment for Russia's Modernization. Paper presented at the OECD-Russia Investment Roundtable. June 19, St Petersburg, Russia.

Olcott, Martha Brill. 2002. *Kazakhstan: Unfulfilled Promise.* Washington, DC: Carnegie Endowment for International Peace.

2004. Vladimir Putin and the Geopolitics of Oil. *The Energy Dimension in Russian Global Strategy.* Rice University: The Baker Institute Energy Forum. Available at http://www.rice.edu/energy/publications/docs/PEC_ Olcott_10_2004.pdf.

Olenich, Natalya. 2001. Gref's Share: His Ministry Will Be in Charge of PSAs. *Vremya Novostei*, February 7.

Olsen, Johan P. 1983. *Organized Democracy: Political Institutions in a Welfare State: The Case of Norway.* Oslo: Universitetsforlaget.

Olson, Mancur. 1993. Dictatorship, Democracy and Development. *APSR* 87:567–76.

2000. *Power and Prosperity: Outgrowing Communist and Capitalist Dictatorships.* New York: Basic Books.

Oomes, Nienke, Katerina Kalcheva. 2007. Diagnosing Dutch Disease: Does Russia Have the Symptoms? Bank of Finland (BOFIT) Discussion Papers 7.

Organization for Economic Cooperation, and Development (OECD). 2004. *OECD Commends Norway's High Aid Levels, Focus on Fighting Poverty.* Available at http://www.oecd.org.

2007a. *OECD Factbook 2007: Economic, Environmental and Social Statistics.* Available at http://www.oecd.org.

2007b. *Economic Survey of Norway 2007: The Petroleum Sector and Its Impact.* Available at http://www.oecd.org/eco/surveys/norway.

Organization for Security and Cooperation in Europe. 2001. *Parliamentary Elections, 5 November 2000 and 7 January 2001 Final Report.* Office for Democratic Institutions and Human Rights, Republic of Azerbaijan.

Orttung, Robert. 2006. Causes and Consequences of Corruption in Putin's Russia. PONARS Policy Memo No. 430.

Osterud, Oyvind, Per Selle. 2006. Power and Democracy in Norway: The Transformation of Norwegian Politics. *Scandinavian Political Studies* 29(1):25–46.

Ostrowski, Wojciech. 2007. *Regime Maintenance in Post-Soviet Kazakhstan: the Case of the Regime and Oil Industry Relationship (1991–2005).* PhD dissertation. University of St. Andrews, Scotland.

Otto, James M. 1992. A Global Survey of Mineral Company Investment Preferences. In *Mineral Investment Conditions in Selected Countries of the Asia-Pacific Region,* eds. Escap and UNDP. New York: United Nations.

Ottoway, Marina. 2003. *Democracy Challenged: The Rise of Semi-Authoritarianism.* Washington, DC: Carnegie Endowment for International Peace.

Parsons, Robert. 2006. Azerbaijan: Hydrocarbon Boom Sparks Fears of Dutch Disease. *Radio Free Europe/Radio Liberty.* September 20.

Protsyk, Oleh, Andrew Wilson. 2003. Center Politics in Russia and Ukraine: Patronage, Power and Virtuality. *Party Politics* 9(6):703–27.

Przeworski, Adam. 1990. *Democracy and the Market.* New York: Cambridge University Press.

Przeworski, Adam, Fernando Limongi. 1993. Political Regimes and Economic Growth. *Journal of Economic Perspectives* 7:51–71.

Przeworski, Adam, Michael E. Alvarez, Jose Antonio Cheibub, Fernando Limongi. 2000. *Democracy and Development: Political Institutions and Well-Being in the World.* Cambridge: Cambridge University Press.

Pugliaresi, Lucian, Anna C. Hensen. 1996. Improvements in Progress for Russia's New PSA Law. *Oil & Gas Journal* 94(13):56–61.

Randall, Vicky, Lars Svasand. 2002. Party Institutionalization in New Democracies. *Party Politics* 8(1):5–29.

Rasizade, Alec. 2003. Azerbaijan in Transition to the "New Age of Democracy." *Communist and Post-Communist Studies* 36:345–72.

2005. The Great Game of Caspian Energy: Ambitions and Realities. *Journal of Southern Europe and the Balkans* 7(1):1–17.

Resnick, Adam L. 2001. Investors, Turbulence, and Transition: Democratic Transition and Foreign Direct Investment in Nineteen Developing Countries. *International Interactions* 27(4):381–98.

Riker, William H. 1962. *The Theory of Political Coalitions.* New Haven, CT: Yale University Press.

Roberts, John. 1996. *Caspian Pipelines*. London: Royal Institute of International Affairs.

Rodrik, Dani. 1996. Labor Standards in International Trade: Do They Matter and What Do We Do About Them? In *Emerging Agenda for Global Trade: High States for Developing Countries*, eds. Robert Lawrence, Dani Rodrik, and John Whalley, 35–79. Baltimore, MD: Johns Hopkins University Press.

1997. *Has Globalization Gone Too Far?* Washington, DC: Institute for International Economics.

2002. *Feasible Globalizations*. Paper presented at Harvard University, July, in Boston.

Roeder, Philip G. 1994. Varieties of Post-Soviet Authoritarian Regimes. *Post-Soviet Affairs* 10(1):61–101.

Rokkan, Stein. 1966. Norway: Numerical Democracy and Corporate Pluralism. In *Political Oppositions in Western Democracies*, ed. Robert Dahl, 70–115. New Haven, CT: Yale University Press.

Rose, Richard, Neil Munro, Stephen White. 2001. Voting in a Floating Party System: the 1999 Duma Election. *Europe-Asia Studies* 53(3):419–443.

Ross, Michael. 1999. The Political Economy of the Resource Curse. *World Politics* 51(2):297–322.

2001. Does Oil Hinder Democracy. *World Politics* 53(3):325–61.

Rothgeb, John M. 1990. Investment Dependence and Political Conflict in the Third World Countries. *Journal of Peace Research* 27(3):255–72.

1991. The Effects of FDI Upon Political Protest and Violence in Underdeveloped Societies. *The Western Political Quarterly* 44:9–38.

Rubinson, Richard. 1977. Dependence, Government Revenue, and Economic Growth:1955–1970. *Studies in Comparative International Development* 12:3–25.

Rugman, Alan M. 1981. *Inside the Multinationals: The Economics of Internal Markets*. London: Croom Helm.

1985. Multinationals and Global Competitive Strategy. *International Studies of Management and Organization* 15(2):8–18.

Ruseckas, Laurent. 1998. State of the Field Report: Energy and Politics in Central Asia and the Caucasus. *The National Bureau of Asian Research (NBR) Access Asia Review* 2. Available at http://www.nbr.org.

Rutland, Peter. 1997. Lost Opportunities: Energy and Politics in Russia. *National Bureau of Asian Research (NBR) Analysis* 8(5). Available at http://www.nbr.org.

2006. Oil and Politics in Russia. Paper prepared for the American Political Science Association Annual Convention, Philadelphia, PA.

2008. Putin's Economic Record: Is the Oil Boom Sustainable? *Europe-Asia Studies* 60(6):1051–72.

Ryggvik, Helge. 2000. Offshore Safety Regulations in Norway: From Model to System in Erosion. *New Solutions* 10(1–2):67–116.

Sachs, Jeffrey D., Andrew M. Warner. 1999. The Big Push, Natural Resource Booms and Growth. *Journal of Development Economics* 59:43–76.

Sagers, Matthew J. 1993. The Energy Industries in the Former USSR: A Mid-Year Survey. *Post-Soviet Geography* 34(6):341–418.

1994. Observations on Oil and Gas Production in the Timan-Pechora Basin. *International Geology Review* 36(1):33–41.

Saggi, K. 2000. Trade, Foreign Direct Investment and International Technology Transfer: A Survey. *World Bank, Policy Research Working Paper* No. 2349.

Sakwa, Richard. 2001. Parties and Organized Interests. In *Developments in Russian Politics*, eds. Stephen White, Alex Pravda, and Zvi Gitelman, 84–107. Durham: Duke University Press.

Sassen, Saskia. 1996. *Losing Control: Sovereignty in an Age of Globalization*. New York: Columbia University Press.

Schedler, Andreas. 2002. The Menu of Manipulation. *Journal of Democracy* 13(2):36–50.

Schmitter, Phillippe C. 1974. Still the Century of Corporatism. *Review of Politics* 36:85–131.

Schmitter, Phillippe C., Terry Lynn Karl. 1991. What Democracy Is and Is Not. *Journal of Democracy* 2(Summer):75–88.

Schneider, Friedrich, Bruno S. Frey. 1985. Economic and Political Determinants of Foreign Direct Investment. *World Development* 13(2):161–75.

Schroeder, G. 1996. Economic Transformation in the Post-Soviet Republics. In *Economic Transition in Russia and the New States of Eurasia*, ed. B. Kaminski. New York: Sharpe, M.E.

Schumpeter, A. 1950. *Capitalism, Socialism and Democracy*. New York: Harper & Row.

Senecal, Scott C., Elena L. Daly. 1996. Russia. *International Financial Law Review* (April):40–44.

Shafer, Michael. 1994. *Winners and Losers: How Sectors Shape the Developmental Prospects of States*. Ithaca, NY: Cornell University Press.

Sheedy, John F. 1997. Special Tax Regime for Production Sharing Agreements in Russia. *East/West Executive Guide* (August). Concord, MA: World Trade Executive, Inc.

Shepsle, Kenneth A., Barry R. Weingast. 1982. Institutionalizing Majority Rule: A Social Choice Theory with Policy Implications. *American Economic Review* 72(May):367–71.

Shevtsova, Lilia. 2001. Russia's Hybrid Regime. *Journal of Democracy* 12(4):65–70.

Sim, Li-Chen. 2008. *The Rise and Fall of Privatization in the Russian Oil Industry*. New York: Palgrave Macmillan.

Sirowy, L., A. Inkeles. 1990. The Effects of Democracy on Economic Growth and Inequality: A Review. *Studies in Comparative International Development* 25:126–57.

Skelton, James W. 1993. Investing in Russia's Oil and Gas Industry: The Legal and Bureaucratic Obstacles. *Natural Resources and Environment* 26.

1997. Investment at an Impasse: Russia's Production Sharing Agreement Law and the Continuing Barriers to Petroleum Investment in Russia. *Duke Journal of Comparative and International Law* 7:671–89.

Smith, B. 2004. Oil Wealth and Regime Survival in the Developing World, 1960–1999. *American Journal of Political Science* 48(2):232–46.

Smith, David N., Louis T. Wells. 1975. *Negotiating Third World Mineral Agreements: Promises as Prologue.* Cambridge, MA: Ballinger.

Smith, Ernest, John S. Dzienkowski. 1989. A Fifty-Year Perspective on World Petroleum Arrangements. *Texas International Law Journal* 13.

Solnick, Steven. 1999. Russia's Transition: Is Democracy Delayed Democracy Denied? *Social Research* 6(3):789–824.

Stallings, Barbara. 1995. *Global Change, Regional Response: The New International Context of Development.* New York: Cambridge University Press.

Subbotin, Mikhail. 1996. The Law "On Production Sharing Agreements": Hindrances in the Way to Enactment. *The Russian Economic Barometer* 5(3).

2000. The Dangers of Writing Too Much into the Law. *Oil & Capital* 2:14–15.

Synder, Richard. 2006. Does Lootable Wealth Breed Disorder: A Political Economy of Extraction Framework. *Comparative Political Studies* 39: 943–68.

Szymczak, Pat Davis. 1999. Oil Slump Eclipses PSA Triumph. *AMCham Newsletter* (March–April).

Tikhomirov, Vladimir. 1997. Capital Flight from Post-Soviet Russia. *Europe-Asia Studies* 49(4):591–615.

Tompson, William. 2005a. Putting Yukos in Perspective. *Post-Soviet Affairs* 21(2):159–81.

2005b. *A Frozen Venezuela? The Resource Curse and Russian Politics.* OECD. Available at http://eprints.bbk.ac.uk/256/1/Frozen_Venezuela.pdf.

2008. Back to the Future? Thoughts on the Political Economy of Expanding State Ownership in Russia. *The Russia Papers.* Paris: Center for International Studies and Research (CERI).

Transparency International. 2007. *Corruption Perceptions Index.* Available at http://www.transparency.org.

Tsebelis, George. 2002. *Veto Players: How Political Institutions Work.* Princeton, NJ: Princeton University Press.

Ulfelder, Jay. 2007. Natural Resource Wealth and the Survival of Autocracy. *Comparative Political Studies* 40:8(995–1018).

Umurzakov, Kubat. 2003. Investment Climate in Azerbaijan: Country Report. Paper presented at United Nations Economic and Social Commission for Asia and the Pacific, Regional Round Table on Foreign Direct Investment for Central Asia, April 3–4, in Dushanbe, Tajikistan. Available at http://www.unescap.org/tid/mtg/rrtpaper_azer.pdf.

United Nations Conference on Trade, and Development (UNCTAD). 2001. *World Investment Report: Promoting Linkages.* New York: United Nations. Available at http://www.unctad.org.

2002a. *World Investment Report: Transnational Corporations and Export Competitiveness.* New York: United Nations. Available at http://www.unctad.org.

2002b. *Handbook of Statistics.* Available at http://www.unctad.org.

2003. *Foreign Direct Investment in Russia: Is it Taking Off?* Press Release (May 16). Available at http://www.unctad.org.

2005. *World Investment Report: TNCs and the Internationalization of R&D.* New York: United Nations. Available at http://www.unctad.org.

2006. *World Investment Report: FDI from Developing and Transition Economies: Implications for Development.* New York: United Nations. Available at http://www.unctad.org.

2007. *World Investment Report: Transnational Corporations, Extractive Industries and Development.* New York: United Nations. Available at http://www.unctad.org.

United Nations Development Program (UNDP). 2006. *Statistics in the Human Development Report: Beyond Scarcity: Power, poverty and the global water crisis.* Available at http://hdr.undp.org/hdr2006/statistics (Accessed January 15, 2007).

United Nations. 2002. *Human Development Report 2002: Deepening Democracy in a Fragmented World.* Available at http://hdr.undp.org/reports/global/2002/en/.

United States Energy Information Administration (USEIA). 2001a. *Country Analysis Brief: Azerbaijan.* Available at http://www.eia.doe.gov.

2001b. *Country Analysis Brief: Russia.* Available at http://www.eia.doe.gov.

2001c. *Country Analysis Brief: Norway.* Available at http://www.eia.doe.gov.

2002. *Russia: Energy Restructuring* (April). Available at http://www.eia.doe.gov.

2003. *Country Analysis Brief: Caspian Region* (August). Available at http://www.eia.doe.gov.

2006. *Country Analysis Brief: Azerbaijan* (August). Available at http://www.eia.doe.gov.

2007. *Country Analysis Brief: Caspian Sea Region* (January). Available at http://www.eia.doe.gov.

2008. *Country Analysis Brief: Russia.* Available at http://www.eia.doe.gov.

US-Russia Business Council. 2007. *Russian Economic Survey* (May). Available at http://www.usrbc.org/.

Valenzuela, Samuel J. 1992. Democratic Consolidation in Post-Transitional Settings: Notion, Process, and Facilitating Conditions. In *Issues in Democratic Consolidation*, eds. Scott Mainwaring, Guillermo O'Donnell, and J. Samuel Valenzuela, 57–94. Notre Dame: University of Notre Dame Press.

Van de Walle, Nicolas. 1999. Economic Reform in a Democratizing Africa. *Comparative Politics* 32(1):21–41.

Vernon, Raymond. 1966. International Investment and International Trade in the Product-Cycle. *Quarterly Journal of Economics* 80:190–207.

1971. *Sovereignty at Bay: The Multinational Spread of US Enterprises.* New York: Basic Books.

1974. The Location of Economic Activity. In *Economic Analysis and the Multinational Enterprise*, ed. John H. Dunning, 89–114. London: Allen and Unwin.

1980. The Obsolescing Bargain: A Key Factor in Political Risk. In *The International Essay for Business Decision Makers 5*, ed. Mark B. Winchester. Houston: Center for International Business.

Wagstyl, Stefan. 2000. Oil Wealth Offers Many Opportunities. *Financial Times*, November 22.

Wagstyl, Stefan, David Stern. 2000. Oil Strategy Can Change Nation. *Financial Times Survey*, November 22.

Waller, Glenn. 2000. Russia Needs to Establish a Track Record- Waller Demolishes Russian PSA Myths. *Oil & Capital* 3:16-18.

Wantchenkon, Leonard. 1999. Why do Resource Dependent Countries Have Authoritarian Governments? Paper presented at Yale University. (December 12). Available at http://www.yale.edu/leitner/pdf/1999-11.pdf

Watson, James. 1996. Foreign Investment in Russia: The Case of Oil Industry. *Europe-Asia Studies* 48(3):429-55.

Webb, John. 1999a. Election Season in West Siberia: A Signpost for Foreign Investment. *CERA Decision Brief* (September).

1999b. Russia Passes Key PSA Legislation: Too Little, Too Late? *CERA Alert* (February 26).

2000a. Russia's Governors Could Make or Break Industry Reform. *CERA Decision Brief* (July 2000).

2000b. Russia's Novice Legislators Turn to Energy Bills: What's in Store for Investors? *CERA Decision Brief* (March 2000).

2006. Russia's Western-Led PSAs Overcome the Odds: A Second Wave Led by Russian Companies on the Horizon. *CERA Insight* (March 27).

Weber, Max. 1968. Economy and Society. In *An Outline of Interpretative Sociology*, eds. Guenter Roth and Claus Wittich. New York: Bedminster Press.

Weigle, Marcia. 2000. *Russia's Liberal Project: State-Society Relations in the Transition from Communism*. University Park, PA: Pennsylvania State University Press.

Weinthal, Erika, Pauline Jones Luong. 2006. Combating the Resource Curse: An Alternative Solution to Managing Mineral Wealth. *Perspectives on Politics* 4(1):35-53 (March).

Weir, Fred. 2006. Atop Azerbaijan's Oil Boom: Mr. Aliev. *Christian Science Monitor* (November 2). Available at http:// www.csmonitor.com/2006/1102/p06s01-wosc.html (Accessed February 2, 2007).

Weiss, Kathryn Stoner. 2001. The Russian Central State in Crisis. In *Russian Politics*, eds. Zoltan Barany and Robert G. Moser, 103-34. Cambridge: Cambridge University.

Weitzman, M.L. 1993. Capitalism and Democracy: A Summing Up of the Arguments. In *Markets and Democracy: Participation, Accountability and Efficiency*, eds. S. Bowles, H. Gintis, and B. Gustafsson. Cambridge: Cambridge University Press.

Wheelan, Simon. 2003. Azerbaijan Succession is Focus of Oil Conflict. *World Socialist Website* (18 September). Available at http://www.wsws.org.

Williams, Carol J. 2001. So This is Heaven: Norway. *The Los Angeles Times*, November 8.

Winters, Jeffrey. 1996. *Power in Motion: Capital Mobility and the Indonesian State*. Ithaca, NY: Cornell University Press.

World Bank. 2006. *World Development Indicators*. Washington, DC: World Bank.

2008. *The World Bank in Russia: Russian Economic Report* (June). Washington, DC: World Bank.

2009. *World Development Indicators.* Washington, DC: World Bank.

Xu, B. 2000. Multinational Enterprises, Technological Diffusion, and Host Country Productivity Growth. *Journal of Development Economics* 62:477–93.

Yergin, Daniel, Joseph Stanislaw. 1998. *The Commanding Heights: The Battle Between Government and the Market Place That Is Remaking the Modern World.* New York: Simon & Schuster.

Yergin, Daniel. 1991. *The Prize: The Epic Quest for Oil, Money, and Power.* New York: Simon & Schuster.

1998. Historical Overview of Azerbaijani Oil. *USACC Investment Guide to Azerbaijan.* Washington, DC: US-Azerbaijan Chamber of Commerce.

Youngs, Richard. 2004. Democracy and the Multinationals. *Democratization* 11(1):127–147.

Yusifzade, Khoshbakht. 1999. Oil and Gas Industry in Azerbaijan. *USACC Investment Guide to Azerbaijan.* Washington, DC: US-Azerbaijan Chamber of Commerce.

Zhaeikhin, Vladimir. 2000. Putin's Plan Is Formula for Good and Evil. *The Russia Journal* May 29–June 4.

Zhang, K. 2001. Does foreign direct investment promote economic growth? Evidence from East Asia and Latin America. *Contemporary Economic Policy* 19(2):175–85.

Zheng, Yu. 2005. Comparative Institutional Advantage and FDI Patterns in Developing Countries. Paper presented at the annual meeting of the International Studies Association, March 5, in Honolulu, Hawaii.

Index